Praise for *Do Look Now*

Congratulations on your memoir *Do Look Now*. It's very readable and sucked me in immediately, bringing memories flooding back of your home and Dudley's ranch and great parties at 20 Waverley Street Annerley. I think with the smart twin themes of movies and the terrible overlooking of daughters in those days, this book will strike a chord with many.

Dr Hugh Lunn, Brisbane.
Author: Over the Top with Jim, Head Over Heels,
Spies Like Us, Working for Rupert

Your paragraphs describing the accident are short, heartbreaking, perfect. I really like the back and forth in time. This book feels like natural recall and intimate storytelling. The film references throughout are both triggers and anchors, helping you resolve memories.

Deb Polson, Professor, Digital Design, RMIT

Do Look Now captures the social and cultural history of Brisbane in the seventies and eighties better than any other memoir I have read, while the encyclopaedic knowledge of films gives it an unexpected twist from the personal to the universal.

Peter Thompson, London.
Author: The Battle of Brisbane, The Battle for Singapore,
Jack Nicholson: The Life and Times of an Actor on the Edge,
The Quest for Freedom: A Life of Alexander Kerensky,
the Russian Unicorn

Beautiful prose, so cleverly intertwining the cinematic references. To me you capture Gillian Mears' bright prose in *The Mint Lawn* with the elegance and voice of Emily Dickinson.

Dr Margaret McVeigh, Film scholar, Griffith Film School

I love the form you have developed, using films as part of a personal landscape that aids memory, framing context, helping you come to terms with life. This is a contemporary memoir, a compelling account, one that is seeing you journeying into the past, developing hindsight, assisted through cinema.

Sean Maher, Associate Professor, QUT.
Author: Film Noir and Los Angeles – urban history
and the dark imaginary

This is more than a memoir. It is an exciting trip through an exciting life lived in a dangerous reality AND an expanding cinemascape that you dedicated your life to understanding. Frankly, I've never read anything like it. Great yarn. You put your life's work and your philosophy so simply, so directly, so elegantly.

Stephen Stockwell, Professor Emeritus Journalism and
Communication, Griffith University, Gold Coast.
Latest book: The Voyage and the Vision

DO LOOK NOW

A MEMOIR

Helen Yeates

Do Look Now

First published in Australia by Oxlade Salon Press, 2022

ABN: 95139927082

oxladesalonpress@gmail.com

Copyright © Helen Yeates 2022 All Rights Reserved

 A catalogue record for this book is available from the National Library of Australia

ISBN: 978-0-6455017-0-4 (pbk) ISBN: 978-0-6455017-1-1 (ebk)

Written by Helen Yeates © 2022
Cover design by Christopher Cosgrove © 2022

Typesetting and design by Publicious Book Publishing Published in collaboration with Publicious Book Publishing www.publicious.com.au

No part of this book may be reproduced in any form, by photocopying or by any electronic or mechanical means, including information storage or retrieval systems, without permission in writing from both the copyright owner and the publisher of this book.

Memories warm you up from the inside. But they also tear you apart.

Haruki Murakami, *Kafka on the Shore*

Film as dream, film as music. No art passes our conscience
in the way film does, and goes directly to our feelings,
deep down into the dark rooms of our souls.

Ingmar Bergman

CHAPTERS

1.	Wake in Fright	1
2.	Cinema Paradiso	7
3.	Puberty Blues	23
4.	The Getting of Wisdom	36
5.	Love and Other Catastrophes	50
6.	Scenes from a Marriage	59
7.	The Ice Storm	79
8.	Lust, Caution	90
9.	Another Round	103
10.	Almost Famous	113
11.	My Brilliant Career	127
12.	Cocoon	147
13.	The Last Picture Show	162
14.	Stories We Tell	170
	Indexes/References	175
	Credits	183

1.
WAKE IN FRIGHT

In 2016, after dear friend Susie's sixtieth birthday party at the Bronte Surf-lifesavers' Club, old friends and family reconvened in her cosy lounge room. Marge, her flamboyant sister-in-law, proclaimed that she could not see my face properly, calling for bobby pins and other hair accessories, duly delivered. Sweeping my longish hair back behind my ears, she gathered it all up onto the top of my head, complimenting me on how much better I looked.

I felt the exact opposite: semi-naked, embarrassed, even ashamed that everyone would be able to see the jagged old scars on the right side of my face, the imprinted memory of an adult life kept in the shadows, avoiding bright light, hiding the full flush of the disfigurement with concealer makeup and strategically aligned hair cover. I suppose that Marge, an accomplished performing artist, wanted me to perform my untrammelled self, both inside and out.

Decades earlier, I woke in fright, hearing a woman sobbing endlessly, heartbreakingly, in the bed next to mine. I had no idea who she was, or why I was in this public hospital bed, in this busy ward, unable to move. I was dangerously ill, I nearly died in a smash, I remembered nothing. The doctor later called this condition 'mercy amnesia'. Nobody ever calls it that anymore.

When Jimmy's dad's trusty Vauxhall Velox hit the post, at least I didn't catapult into a space of no return, as car accident victims do in Peter Weir's film, *The Cars That Ate Paris,* or in the hyper-crash scenes in George Miller's epic *Mad Max* films. While there was nothing filmic about my personal automobile carnage experience, I should have listened much more carefully, a week earlier, to the fortune teller's prophecies.

Spurred on by several intriguing rumours, my cousin Jan and I decided to book a session with a particular fortune teller, just for fun. Madam X, suitably bedecked in a long, swirling skirt, lacey top and multicoloured silk shawl, practised her mysterious craft in a tiny tea shop cramped into a musty, odd-shaped space, upstairs in the central Brisbane Arcade.

Banned from charging us directly for any psychic service, her fee was included in the inflated price of the tea and cake. She also operated under strict laws not to give her customers upsetting predictions, especially those involving illness or death.

Uncovering nothing at all surprising regarding Jan's future, Madam X spoke of a happy successful life, and an even more predictable grand marriage to a tall, dark, handsome man along with wealth and multiple children. While Jan certainly did not wish for the latter, she felt satisfied that she could handle the rest.

Then Madam X examined my teacup and my hand lines. Firstly, she delivered a few statements about my family, some off-the-wall, some surprisingly accurate. For instance: 'You get on well with your brother. You are missing him at present'. Funnily enough, my brother Peter had just moved south to Melbourne, and I was missing him.

Delving further into my psyche, she slowly shook her head, declaring that a male person, whose name began with J (my then boyfriend, Jimmy?) was, in her colourful words, holding a rose under my nose at the time, and, she warned, he was no good for me. Furthermore, I wouldn't marry him. I would marry someone whose name began with R. Some years later, by a strange coincidence, this turned out to be true, when I married Richard.

Towards the end of this hit-and-miss soothsaying session, Madam X momentarily froze. Trance-like, gently stroking my right cheek with her outstretched hand, she whispered, 'Such beautiful skin, what a terrible shame'. The tension rose another notch when she added, 'Be very careful'.

While she was probably not intending to freak me out, Madam X skated very close to doing so, and, on reflection, to breaking the law. Feeling quite shaken, I pulled back and broke the spell, or whatever it was. At that moment, some people entered, babbling on, distracting her, thanking her for some helpful warning she had given them in the past. Jan and I gathered ourselves, stumbling out into the light of day, trying to laugh it off.

Almost a week after this unsettling encounter, the right side of my face was ripped apart in a car accident, her unnerving prediction regarding the ruination of the soft skin on one-half of my face shockingly fulfilled.

I had, of course, completely ignored her warning that boyfriend J (Jimmy) was unsuitable for me. Proudly displaying my shiny new jacket, I hopped into Jimmy's dad's car that rainy night in early May 1963, relieved that my Friday French class was over. I had just turned eighteen.

At that stage, Jimmy was a fulltime engineering student, while I was determinedly putting myself through a university arts degree by working full-time and studying part-time. That grand plan totally disintegrated after Jimmy, heading along Coronation Drive towards the city, proudly showed me where on the Brisbane River he had rowed that day, representing Queensland in the prestigious Kings Cup. In the act of doing so, he must have become distracted, slamming into a telegraph post by the side of the road, totally writing off his dad's car.

I was sitting up close beside him in the front passenger seat, which, at the time, was spookily known as the suicide seat. Seatbelts were not mandatory car fittings until the late sixties and, for decades prior to the enactment of that particular safety precaution, many a front seat passenger had met an untimely death.

My head smashed into the windscreen, my whole body was flung forward, entangled in the mess. Blood poured out of the major artery on the right side of my face, splattering all over Jimmy, whose head and chest hit the steering wheel. He suffered bruising and mild concussion.

Later, an extraordinary story came to light. Geoff and Coralie Porter, who had studied medicine with my brother-in-law, Lawrie Hawes, happened upon the chaotic scene of the accident that evening. On their way to a Friday night fancy-dress party, decked out in sailor costumes, these two young doctors initially had trouble convincing the ambulance men that they were qualified medical practitioners.

Somehow, the sailor/doctors (who, naturally, did not recognise me at the time) were able to persuade the ambulance people to rush me to Emergency as, in their expert opinion, my injuries were critical. Having mistakenly decided that Jimmy, drenched in my blood, was in a very bad way, the ambos were hurriedly placing him, alone, in the ambulance. They told my heroic rescuers that the plan was to leave me lying quietly near the gutter, with one of them in attendance, while the other made the mad dash to hospital with Jimmy.

Oddly enough, the official police report of the accident mistakenly labelled this as a two-vehicle collision, when it was actually a single vehicle collision into a telegraph pole. I trust that both police and paramedics are much better trained these days. The next morning, I hit the front page of Brisbane's *The Courier-Mail* newspaper, in a small news item, stating that 'Helen Thompson, 18, of Annerley, is dangerously ill in the Royal Brisbane Hospital after a car accident on Coronation Drive'.

My injuries were manifold: broken ankle, ribs, jaw bone; severe facial wounds, massive blood loss, whiplash, brain damage of the right frontal lobe, and pulmonary oedema thrown in for good measure. Lawrie, a hospital registrar at the time, was invited into the emergency operating theatre to observe the proceedings.

It was a great comfort to discover, subsequently, that a close family member had been present at that touch-and-go time – a rare occurrence for any accident victim. With the rain pelting down on a smashed bloodied car, a broken post, dangerously dangling wires into a gurgling gutter, little did we both know that two friends in their fancy sailor suits had miraculously saved my life, with only twenty minutes to spare.

A highly regarded surgical registrar happened to be rostered on duty that evening. Luckily, my facial nerve was not permanently damaged; otherwise, in the long term, the consequences of those bizarrely predicted slashes to my soft facial skin would have been far worse. That same Friday, the sobbing woman in the bed next to mine was accidentally shot in the back by her husband, a farmer. A mother of two children, she would be paralysed for life.

The merciful amnesiac condition I suffered blocked the accident from my damaged brain, for at least the forty-eight hours straddling this life-changing event. Over many years, I gradually regained small, often irrational memory flashes, along with the occasional, purely imaginary blips.

Many years later, in 1997, I sympathised with Lady Diana's bodyguard for not recalling what happened in that historic, fatal accident in Paris. Both Trevor Rees-Jones and I suffered savage facial injuries, and he was also knocked unconscious.[1] As I understood from media reports at the time, as well as from his book, he experienced a similar form of 'anterograde', or good old 'mercy' amnesia. He could

---

1. Trevor Rees-Jones published his memoir in 2005: *The Bodyguard's Story: Diana, the Crash and the Sole Survivor,* Little Brown Book Group.

remember very little, even though he was under excessive pressure to recall the build-up to the accident in that tunnel, the actual event, the horrific aftermath.

Even now, it seems that Rees-Jones and I have regained only partial memory. For years, his credibility was held under the pitiless gaze of the law, the media, the Royal family, and many others. Naturally, I experienced no such high-stakes pressure. No celebrity died in my accident, when I rode in that car with that boy on that riverside road.

I often wonder if some of those jagged, ill-fitting memory shards are other people's memories, unwittingly planted into my brain. Alternatively, perhaps, they could also be mere speculations, conjured-up recovery stories, somehow woven into counter-intuitive comfort blankets, forever tinkering with my brain, forever blotting out the shuddering impact.

A week or so after the smash, the minister from the local Yeronga Christ Church of England loomed out of the fog beside my hospital bed, looking for all the world like the grim figure of Death in Ingmar Bergman's classic film, *The Seventh Seal*. By the skin of my teeth, I had won my own apocalyptic game of chess with mortality. The Reverend Darke, whose name suited both his garb and his modus operandi, chilled me to the bone.

Several years earlier, he had banned my brother Peter and our cousin Geoffrey from attending all church dances, after they defiantly pasted on the drab walls of the church hall some beatnik posters, just to liven things up. For this transgression, Reverend Darke, shaking with fury, deemed them both to be 'devils incarnate'.

Time stood still for me when this same minister of religion leaned over, pronouncing that this 'terrible accident' and my 'dreadful injuries' were 'all part of God's special plan'. I turned away from his cruel, blinkered darkness, forever rejecting both him and his God. Pastoral care, be damned.

That night I asked could I be allowed to see my facial injuries in the mirror. Shocking though they were, I wanted the open-eyed truth, with no further hiding, embroidering or myth-making involved.

I remain haunted, yet, ironically, uplifted by the powerful opening scenes of Krzysztof Kieslowski's remarkable film, *Three Colours: Blue*. Having barely survived a horrendous car accident, the character played by Juliette Binoche wakes up in hospital, understanding neither what has happened, nor what is going on around her. Directed by this grand cinematic master, Juliette captures the identifiable hellish, disoriented feelings of fear, pain, grief, dread, memory, loss.

Speaking of loss, I did not see the driver, Jimmy, for quite a while, although his sister June, embarrassed by her brother's neglect, did visit me. It appeared that he felt guilty, as he had been drinking with his rowing mates at the Regatta Hotel on Coronation Drive, prior to picking me up. Unable to face me or my family, he was, seemingly, too scared to see the extent of my injuries. Whatever it was, these are my remembrances, not his.

A few years ago, in sweeping back my hair, Marge, my friend Susie's vibrant sister-in-law, inadvertently triggered certain dark, taboo memories lurking just beneath the surface. Through that seemingly impenetrable swirl, special films have always shone their bright, beacon lights, illuminating my thinking, granting me another way of looking, a different, more layered remembering.

I never did follow Marge's well-intentioned makeover instructions, baring my face to the world. Despite the 'merciful' amnesia and those erratic memory loops, the chronicle of those foretold scars remains forever embedded in my flesh, my psyche, my sense of self.

***

2.

CINEMA PARADISO

My older sister Jocelyn Thompson was born in Darwin in September, 1939, when Dad was working in an essential service as a weather forecaster with the Commonwealth Government. The Ross and Keith Smith aerodrome (Larrakeyah) where he worked was an army and airforce base in Darwin.

As Jocelyn, the family archivist states, 'We were evacuated following the bombing of Pearl Harbour in December 1941. Mum and I flew back to Brisbane. Dad came later, but before the February bombing of Darwin. On reaching Brisbane we stayed in the crowded Thompson house at Corinda. After that I suspect that Mum, Grandma Browne and I were sent to live in Oakey with Uncle Jack Wright, Grandma's brother. Those were very dark days'.

In 1942, there was another move, even further south. The women of the family headed to Melbourne, where Peter my brother was born in April, 1942.[2] In order to reunite with Dad, they returned to Brisbane when the coast appeared to be clear, and the battleground with the Japanese forces had shifted to the Pacific Islands, especially Papua New Guinea.

Jocelyn further elaborates: 'After Darwin, Dad worked at Archerfield until he was transferred to Rockhampton in 1943. He joined the Royal Australian Air Force, in January, 1943. He was never sent overseas to serve, as his work as a meteorologist was vital to the safety of the aeroplanes. Rockhampton was a strategic city situated on the edge of the Coral Sea'.

The family returned to Brisbane where I was born on 6 March 1945, in a private hospital in the suburb of Sherwood. Around that

---

2. It is claimed by some war historians that the controversial Brisbane Line was drawn then, so that Australia might cede the north of Australia to the Japanese. The decision was reversed, and Australian forces were sent north to Papua New Guinea to fight the enemy there.

time, we had settled in with our mother's mother, Grandma Browne, in Gaba Tepe Street, Moorooka. Post-war, Dad worked for the newly formed Department of Civil Aviation, at Eagle Farm Airport, a job he held until he retired.

Originally from England and Scotland, Dad's parents, the Thompsons, had a large family, comprising four daughters and seven sons, including twin girls. Arthur was the third youngest son. Grandpa Thompson was the Post Master around Queensland, including in Townsville, and finally in Toowoomba. The family lived at the back of the rather grand post offices in such places.

My mother Margaret was the youngest of eleven girls. Her father, Arthur Browne, worked in his cousins' store, Cribb and Foote in Ipswich. Marrying Arthur Browne at eighteen, Mary Wright hailed from our great grandparents' family, Protestants originally from Southern Ireland.

The Wright family owned and developed the coal mines in Tivoli, near Ipswich. Only the surviving sons inherited shares in all the property, including that wealthy mining operation. In the late Nineteenth Century, daughters did not inherit an equitable slice of the family fortune, a profoundly discriminatory custom that would not be tolerated in today's world.

Mary died in 1951. Her husband had died much earlier, when Margaret was only twelve. Up until the age of five, I spent my life being cuddled, and having my every whim tended to by wonderful Grandma Mary, while Margaret looked after the two older kids. Grandma was an expert cuddler.

After her mother's death, Margaret was sad and lonely at home. In order to relieve those feelings, and to build up a deposit on a home of our own, she started work at Thiess Brothers engineering firm as a filing clerk, and later as a secretary.

By then, Jocelyn, Peter and I had settled into Yeronga Primary School, and we became 'latch-key' kids. I had just turned six. As often as he could, Dad, a shift-worker, would pick us up from school, although we did like the alternative, an adventurous walk or bike ride home, across a creek via a steep bush track called the New Road.

Very few children at school, and no one else in our family had working mothers back in the fifties or even in the sixties. Both our parents' working became our new normal. I am very proud of her, standing up to criticism from neighbours and other mean-spirited people, who held the strait-laced, patriarchal idea that 'a woman's place was in the home'. This view was particularly prevalent after the war.

Living in a modest maisonette in Gaba Tepe Street, Moorooka, was pleasant enough in those early years, although we suffered from having some difficult neighbours. The kids next door on one side were rough, anti-social bullies, while the family on the other side had a dog which the father tied up all day. That poor creature used to howl incessantly, driving dad crazy when he tried to sleep after a nightshift. We despaired of this cruel practice. That neighbour wouldn't budge.

By contrast, we thought the people over the road were good neighbours, and I loved the two babies of the son, Mervyn and his young wife, Jackie, while they lived with his widowed mother in that old Queensland house. Little did we realise the escalating abuse that was occurring in that home.

Several years after we moved away, Jackie, deliberately isolated by Mervyn in another suburb, far from her supportive family and friends, killed those two young children to protect them from their violent, drunken father. This was, of course, a dreadful domestic violence tragedy, although the media overplayed the 'bad killer mother' syndrome, largely ignoring what may have driven her, apart from 'mental illness'.

Hearing this neighbourhood horror story a while after we had moved into our new home in Annerley, was gut-wrenching for us all. I could not express it then, but somehow I knew, deep down, in a place where my pre-feminist views were starting to stir, that it was dreadfully unfair to blame Jackie alone for what had happened. The abusive Mervyn was never convicted, and the community spurned the woman driven beyond the limit.

We were lucky to have an abundance of cousins on both sides of our family, whom we saw regularly, enjoying their company at special family events and also on most weekends for lush afternoon teas at someone's place. Several cousins on our father's side grew up with us on Brisbane's southside: David and Diana Suter (for a time), and John, Geoff and Jan Hodsdon. All except Jan were war babies; she was born the year afterwards. At one stage, there was a cousin in just about every grade in the Big School at Yeronga Primary School.

Except when Dad was in a bad mood, unable to get his sleep in the daytime, our growing up in suburban Brisbane in the fifties was a happy experience, with a combination of home, school, sport, reading, play, and lots of relatives. Sport comprised mainly tennis and cricket, as well as table tennis. For recreation, we visited the lavish Oasis Gardens in Sunnybank for a swim and a picnic. We also loved going to the pictures.

The popular Italian film *Cinema Paradiso* explored the coming-of-age of a filmmaker growing up in the late forties and fifties, entranced by movies flickering in the dark. In this film, the boy helped the projectionist at the local cinema, at the same time being part of a squirming horde of young Sicilians, objecting loudly when any romantic, steamy scenes were obviously cut by order of the local clergy.

No such cuts were evident to us back in the fifties. These would have been done more cleanly, more surreptitiously, by order of members of the Australian Censorship Board. Probably these Australians were, in many cases, just as reactionary and puritanical as those Catholic clergy in post-war Sicily.

For much of my life, my passions have been ignited in such darkened places. Recalling the picture theatres I frequented in my childhood, my lifelong love for films was born out of amiable chaos in fifties, sub-tropical suburban Brisbane. Along with a gaggle of cousins, we would head by tram along Ipswich Road for our own form of picture show paradise on most sweltering Saturday afternoons.

We didn't refer to these places of film worship as cinemas. They were picture shows or picture theatres, and we went along to see 'the pictures' on the big screen. Sometimes we would venture further afield, walking or riding our bikes through Yeronga Park, across the trainline to the Ideal Theatre in Yeronga, closer to where our cousins lived. At that stage, the Ideal was owned by the parents of one of my classmates, Lynette.

One year, lucky Lynette held a birthday party inside her very own picture theatre, set up with long trestle tables and chairs, decked out with colourful balloons and streamers. We indulged in the usual party spread, comprising chocolate crackles, birthday sponge cake with cream and strawberries on top, fairy bread (dainty triangular slices of buttered bread sprinkled with multi-coloured hundreds and thousands) along with mountains of liquorice all-sorts, large round peppermints, fantales and jaffas.

We played the traditional party games, such as Pass the Parcel and Musical Chairs. Then her dad projected cartoons onto the big screen, as a unique party treat. Having a sweet singing voice, Lynette, in later life, was our generation's 'Aeroplane Jelly' warbler – 'I like Aeroplane Jelly, Aeroplane Jelly for me'.

Despite this close connection with the Ideal theatre, more frequently I would go, for the regular Saturday matinee, to either the Boomerang, the Annerley or the Odeon picture shows, all conveniently situated along the tramline in our local neighbourhood.

Presenting as a graceful art deco architectural triumph on the outside, the Boomerang theatre revealed, on the inside, an unedifying pandemonium of kids, sometimes with friends, other times accompanied by rather fraught adults. The Saturday afternoon audience scrambled to their seats, stumbling over the wooden legs and sides of the sloping, grey canvas chairs, sometimes landing with a thump on the floor if the canvas was torn. Alternatively, we might head further up to the vinyl covered padded chairs, rather clumsily linked together.

The standard picture theatre design meant that the audience entered from the back and walked down, getting closer to the screen with each step. Unusually for theatres back then, the Boomerang's big screen was at the front, immediately to the right when we first went inside. We walked up the Boomerang aisles, with our backs to the screen. Once seated, we would look comfortably down to the entrance, and to the red velvet curtains, which parted with a flourish as the lights dimmed. This was a rare picture show layout, although the Eldorado Theatre in Indooroopilly had a similar design.

During show time, we youngsters responded loudly and enthusiastically to whatever was happening on the screen, although such antics might be met with much 'shushing' from those wishing to hear all the dialogue. The usual, lolly-fuelled mayhem ruled. Red lolly-coated-chocolate jaffas rolled down the sloping wooden floors, hordes of children munched sticky, jaw-jamming minties, chucking the wrappers on to the floor, slurping liquorice straps and allsorts, blackening tongues, scoring massive sugar hits, aching gums, licking icecreams bought with carefully counted pocket-money, loving the newly created chocolate-covered Peter's icecream-on-a-stick, the sublime Hav-a- Heart, all purchased from rather tackily-dressed temptresses, flaunting trayfuls of sugar highs at interval.

My trusty, regular companion, cousin Jan and I were fangirls, smoothing precious fantale wrappers, tucking these away in our pockets for further study. Fantales, or chocolate covered caramels, often stuck to my teeth, although that didn't bother me. The sweet taste lingered. Annoying cheeky boys behind us would sometimes kick our bottoms, or stick slobbery 'chewy' in our hair. They loved hearing us yelp and scream. We hated the chewing gum marauders, as we knew that later, we would have to endure that 'yukky' gum being cut out of our hair by our mums.

Nevertheless, there were many 'up' sides. Enjoying our newfound independence, Jan and I clambered onto the Salisbury tram going home, hopping off at Chardon's Corner. We counted our leftover pennies, heading straight for the corner fish 'n' chip shop, treating ourselves to potato scallops, brushing greasy fingers on our flowery gathered skirts, skipping down the steep hill to the Thompson dwelling.

Sprawled on my bed in the front room, we avidly shared our new fantale wrapper stories on the movable feast of favourite crushes: Doris Day, Debbie Reynolds, Robert Wagner, Jeff Hunter, Rock Hudson, Tab Hunter. We did not realise that drop-dead gorgeous Rock and Tab were both closeted gays, not even knowing, in any case, what homosexuality actually was.

Occasionally, my sister Jocelyn and I squabbled over who would win the heart of either Rock Hudson or Robert Wagner, whenever he/they happened to swoop down from Hollywood, claiming one or the other of us, in Annerley, Brisbane, Australia. It is strange contemplating such childhood fantasies now, with Rock having died of AIDS, and Robert probably still wondering how Natalie Wood died.

At each and every picture show establishment in our neighbourhood, the program set-up proceeded in much the same order for those popular Saturday matinee screenings. Firstly, everyone stood, rather shambolically, for God Save the Queen, not a Republican thought in our young heads.

Then, a short newsreel blasted onto the screen. Not at all interested in current affairs, we stirred restlessly, waiting for the real entertainment to begin. To our delight, regular cartoons then burst onto the screen: Tom and Jerry, Bugs Bunny, Hekyl and Jekyl, Loony Tunes ('That's all folks!'), Elmer Fudd and Tweetie Pie, Mickey Mouse, Donald Duck, Goofy.

When the inevitable adventure serial followed, Jan and I often found ourselves ducking down, hands over our eyes, peering occasionally, scared by creepy serials such as *The Iron Claw*, made by Columbia in 1941. This weird horror/thriller production screened in Brisbane cinemas well into the fifties – probably a very cheap deal by then.

Luckily, *Batman and Robin* was a less threatening serial, and we enjoyed an early taster of the later classic *Superman* film and television franchise. A huge favourite was *The Phantom*, based on yet another comic book hero. With episodic narratives and cliff-hanger endings, such movie serials hooked us in to return the next Saturday, to follow our particular hero's journey. In those familiar picture show spaces, the serials also functioned as primers for the main event.

Usually, two feature films were shown, the lesser one before interval, the supposedly higher status one, after interval. Our smorgasbord film diet was highly predictable, and, when prodded at and sampled now, the offerings taste rather stale, and not quite so palatable. Many Western movies were dished up, firstly, with all the usual tropes on display. We actually enjoyed the formulaic genre signposts, which, for us, were part of the comforting familiarity of such films.

Stamping on the wooden floor in excitement, we cheered Hopalong Cassidy, Gene Autry, Roy Rogers, Tim Holt and other Caucasian heroes chasing the baddies, always triumphing over shady rustlers, thieves, murderers, con men and, inevitably, the 'Indians'. Good and evil were clearly coded, with very few, if any, shades of grey evident in the mix. Some more nuanced, well-made Western classics occasionally shone, mostly because of especially good levels of directing and acting – for instance *High Noon*, (1952) with Gary Cooper and Grace Kelly, and *Shane* (1953) with Alan Ladd.

However, those quality, more under-stated films were few and far between, and even they tended to recreate the standard colonial myths of the West. Other Westerns featured the cavalry's role in bringing law and order into the expanding settlements, protecting vulnerable settlers migrating into the West on their different forms of transport before train lines, on foot, riding horses, or in covered wagons.

Along with some shady Mexican characters, the main antagonists were the First Nations people, called back then the Red Indians, fighting to protect their lands and heritage, although such important historical facts were rarely fore-grounded and examined. Rather, the Red Indians were often depicted as doomed, once noble savages who must be contained and ultimately wiped out, for white settler progress to inevitably triumph.

Growing up with Saturday matinee fare over many years, I never saw an authentic representation of that bloodbath, the colonial history of the American West. Telling, retelling and over-telling the 'golden age' of American colonising, expansionist myths, such films swam before our bedazzled eyes. We never questioned those supposed truths. While we were witnessing genocide, providing unequivocal entertainment was always the main marketing aim of the film industry.

With the sterling cast of James Stewart, Jeff Chandler and Debra Paget, the film *Broken Arrow* conveyed a rare, sympathetic portrayal of a First Nations character. However, at the same time, the audience knew that this particular 'American Indian' was being played by a white actor, Jeff Chandler. The casting of one Native Canadian Mohawk actor to play the doomed Geronimo in this film was one very small breakthrough.

However, revelling in another seemingly Indian-sympathetic film, *White Feather*, we also knew that the white male and female actors were simply acting as First Nations people, painted 'brownface', robed in costumes, performing rituals designed in culturally ignorant, insensitive ways. Gazing at the screen on those golden Saturdays, we children were oblivious to these darker issues.

War films also commanded our viewing attention on Saturday arvos, feeding our post-war generation's appetite for more excitement and the undimmed, heroic construction of warring masculinity. We had been born during World War Two, or immediately afterwards. It seems that propaganda from our Allies continued throughout the fifties, disguised as thrilling, nostalgic action films for the masses, celebrating victory over and over again.

The best and most relatable, as far as I was concerned, came from Britain. I loved *The Dambusters, The Guns of Navarone, The Bridge on the River Kwai,* and *Reach for the Sky*. They seemed to me to be more understated, and therefore more authentic than the American war films.

Even so, there were some standouts from Hollywood, such as *The Desert Fox, The Desert Rats,* and *To Hell and Back* with Audie

Murphy. Audie Murphy was a celebrated war hero, and the film in which he starred was based on his eponymous best-seller book, recounting his own war story. As a result, he was promoted to yet another fantale crush of ours.

Meanwhile, colonial adventure films featuring a former American Olympic swimming champion, Johnny Weissmuller as Tarzan, king of the African jungle, were also served up from time to time in our weekly film diet. Although they were mostly made earlier, in the thirties and forties, such films were still rolled out for exciting Saturday matinee fare in fifties Brisbane. At the time, brother Peter and I had read all of Edgar Rice Burroughs' Tarzan books, which were, in our eyes, superior to the films.

Even so, I secretly yearned to be Tarzan's beloved Jane, just as I also longed to be the Phantom's love interest, Diana, in those Phantom serials based on a highly popular comic book which we also devoured. I pined for strong, silent men, mysteriously lurking in the jungle, white masculine archetypes who would kidnap, tame, then rescue me from near-death encounters with 'hostile natives' or 'wild animals'.

Such a romanticised, racist scenario is both laughable and disturbing. I wish I could capture, in pure form, my emotional responses when viewing such films and serials for the first time. While at present I enjoy viewing films in different ways, informed reflection and mature re-examination eradicate now the pure, innocent immediacy of those halcyon moving picture days.

Our film highlights and experiences did not end there, of course. Another genre seductively beckoned. Jocelyn, Jan and I found ourselves swept along by a plethora of sugar-coated musical comedies. Peter and our boy cousins were not so impressed by these films. We girls revelled in the colour, the glamour, the improbable fantasies and the spontaneous outbursts of singing and dancing on the big screen.

We did not mind the formulaic, wafer-thin plots, the two-dimensional, stereotyped characterisation, the limited, banal dialogue in such beloved films as *Calamity Jane, Annie Get Your Gun, Brigadoon, Oklahoma, South Pacific, The King and I, Tammy and the Bachelor*, and more. While some of these lively, entertaining spectacles were, arguably, classier than others, invariably they shaped our dreams of romantic love, feeding us impossibly happily-ever-after narratives.

We witnessed the kidnapping of virgins in the highly popular musical comedy *Seven Brides for Seven Brothers,* which we unreservedly adored on first viewing. In this film, romping, randy men held kidnapped women hostage, until the innocent brides succumbed to the brothers' desires.

Yet we lapped it all up, missing the whole creepy subtext, the Stockholm-syndrome allegory, the re-enactment of the Rape of the Sabine Women by the Romans. The eldest brother even mentioned this scene as a heroic event, specifically to spur his younger brothers to abduct the sisters.

Bingeing, well before that practice became a thing, Jan and I enjoyed serial-watching our favourite films over three consecutive weeks, if at all possible. This was a special film-going ritual of ours. We followed *Broken Arrow, White Feather, Annie Get Your Gun, Pillow Talk,* and even the *Seven Brides* film on the Jan-and-Helen geographical viewing trail, from picture show to picture show along the Ipswich Road tram track.

Commencing our own mini-festival on the first Saturday at the Boomerang Theatre, moving along the following Saturday for the second screening at the Annerley Theatre at Annerley Junction, we snuggled finally into the smaller Odeon Theatre at Chardon's Corner near my place, for the third and final Saturday screening. Sorting out our schedules, we were the consummate film 'bingers' at the time, rarely missing a beat, seeing many of our favourites several times over, in quick succession.

Sometimes I skipped the suburban Saturday matinee, and went shopping with Mum into the city centre. As a special treat, post-shopping, we might also go along to either the Regent, the Majestic or the Wintergarden, to view the latest romantic comedy.

Mid-morning, taking a break from our shopping, we often popped into the Carlton Theatrette, downstairs at the old Carlton Hotel in Queen Street, to catch the latest newsreels, screening continuously. People would enter awkwardly in the dark, and then leave as soon as their initial segment popped up again. There was much to-ing and fro-ing, along with interrupted viewing, in that cramped theatrette.

Years later, I treasured the seventies Phil Noyce drama, *Newsfront,* starring Bill Hunter, Bryan Brown, Wendy Hughes and Chris Haywood, all in early, career-defining roles. Recreating the saga of the heroic post-war newsmakers, this Australian film vividly brought back the times my family spent, mainly with Mum, sometimes with Dad, watching the newsreels in downtown Brisbane, until television news became very popular into the sixties.

On one particularly memorable Saturday afternoon at the Regent Theatre, my mother and I were swept away by *An Affair to Remember*, starring dashing Cary Grant and beautiful Deborah Kerr. As the lights came on, we hastily blew our noses, dabbing our eyes with our dainty cotton hankies. Preparing to exit, Mum would usually pop her gloves and hat back on, essential wear for respectable ladies on a Saturday shopping jaunt in town.

However, nodding conspiratorially, we decided this time we would stay in the semi-dark, glued to our seats in the same theatre for the following session. Mum and I fell in love with *An Affair to Remember* all over again, sobbing through the second screening, not arriving home until late afternoon, on a film-induced high, overriding any guilt for having seen the film twice for the price of one admission.

Our normal Saturday tea of lamb chops, chips and peas was delayed that night at the Thompson household. Still feeling the glow, we probably chatted about that film through the meal that night. Usually, the family would sit quietly over dinner, companionably reading our latest books at the dining room table.

Mum, Jocelyn, Peter and I were all avid readers, and loving books was in our genes. Dad made handy book holders to enable us to read comfortably at the table, while he leafed through the newspaper. This was another form of paradise for us. Mum would often prepare dinner while reading. She was an expert at cutting beans and other vegetables, eyes glued to her latest book. I never saw her cut herself with the sharp knife, although she came close at times.

Occasionally on a Friday evening, another captivating story-telling ritual occurred. After a quick early tea, probably savoury mince on toast, cosily dressed in our pyjamas and slippers, we would head off to the new Skyline Drive-In, further south, at Coopers Plains. Muttering quite a few swear words as he wrestled with installing the stubborn soundbox through the front car window, Dad would finally calm down, and we would enjoy a film or two on the large screen under the stars.

Potato crisps and fantales, washed down by Sarsaparilla and Fanta soft drinks were the order of the evening, until we kids could no longer last the distance, dozing off in the back seat of Dad's mushroom-coloured Ford Customline. As we grew older, cousin Jan loved coming with us, spending the whole night at our place. She loved the fact that, for years, our mother Margaret would let all the kids sleep in on the weekend.

Mum would say, 'You never know what the children will encounter in later life. Best to have plenty of sleep now, just in case'. Building up an arsenal of sleep hours during my early teens, I think I have used up those sleep credits, long ago. Our mother was also a softie when it came to letting us stay home from school, in order to have a rest if we were feeling a bit 'off colour', timed often by me and Peter to finish a game of Monopoly, or a book we were reading.

Being the youngest, I was probably the most manipulative stay-at-homer. On those days, occasionally Dad took me out to Eagle Farm airport, to sit and read quietly in a corner of his workplace while he predicted the weather. I loved the way he was a champion chart drawer. Having been severely punished at school as a left-handed child, which was seen then as simply being naughty, Dad had become ambidextrous. He could make his weather charts flow perfectly, continuously, by switching hands half-way through. His colleagues and any pilots waiting for their flight forecast would hang around and applaud Arthur when he demonstrated his effortless, legendary craft.

Films never replaced books for me as a passion in the fifties and sixties, but they came a close second. I read many books by English writers, although, whenever possible, I sought out Australian writers, delving back into my mother's childhood, loving *Seven Little Australians*, by Ethel Turner, which I think I read at least seven times. On the other hand, I saw very few Australian films exploring our own dreams, our special stories and landscapes, gracing those Friday night or Saturday screens.

We did love *The Shiralee*, a heart-warming British film set in Australia, involving a father-daughter relationship, starring the British/Australian actor, Peter Finch. While such local stories were few and far between, this one did not really qualify as being authentically Australian.

More and more, a welcome British film would pop up on screen, at least giving us another cultural perspective. Some contemporary British films certainly stood out, such as *The Doctor in the House*, a delightful film starring the talented matinee idol, Dirk Bogarde, well before he moved on to act in such art-house dramas as *The Servant, Death in Venice, The Night Porter*.

My dear friend Diana Edwards has long enjoyed seeing his films. In later life, she introduced me to Dirk's seven beautifully written memoirs, along with his six novels. The all-encompassing, ripple effect of film love still astounds me.

I recall another delightful British comedy, *The Admirable Crichton*, starring Kenneth More and Diane Cilento. When it was shown at our beloved Boomerang, my school friend Polly Perkins and I rushed along to see it. This was probably Diane's breakthrough film, internationally. We took pride in a local Annerley girl's success, even though we had never actually seen or met her in person.

Nevertheless, we did know the Cilento's grand home on the corner of Ipswich Road and Villa Street, close to both our homes. Hearts were aflutter even more so, when this local girl married handsome actor Sean Connery, from Scotland, who played James Bond many times in that franchise. Sadly, this celebrity marriage, seemingly made in heaven, did not last long enough to sustain our own dreams. He was not such a hero in real life, or so it seems.

Meanwhile, Australian filmmakers were still a long way from revitalising our own home-grown film industry. This industry had slumped since the thirties, even though Australians had produced the first feature film in the world, *The Story of the Kelly Gang*, in 1906. The so-called Second Wave of Australian film burst forth in the seventies, with such films as *Picnic at Hanging Rock* and *Sunday Too far Away*. As captivated youngsters, we did not consciously register such a cultural lack in that fifties and sixties time, even though cracks were starting to appear.

One significant crack in that star-spangled, imported world was the powerful Australian film, *Jedda*, released around 1955 by two well-known Queensland filmmakers, Charles and Elsa Chauvel. This, their last film, was a breakthrough production in several ways, notably having been the first to cast Indigenous Australians, both in the key roles as the doomed lovers, Jedda and Marbuck, and in minor character roles. No culturally insensitive 'blackfaces' appeared in this film.

Jedda was also the first Australian film shot in colour, another groundbreaking achievement for the Chauvels. The rarely seen Australian outback desert landscape, in full colour, made a strong impact on city audiences. Ahead of its time, the film also revealed the tragic failure of harsh Australian assimilation policies and practices.

I was only eleven or twelve when I first saw *Jedda*, at the Boomerang Theatre in Annerley. Not comprehending the cultural and industrial milestones accomplished by the Chauvels, I liked seeing young Jedda, dressed in middleclass white girl clothes, playing the piano. I could relate to her, as I played the piano too.

Her adoptive mother seemed kind, and the disturbing call to go walkabout, the call to country for Jedda, was difficult for me to fathom. However, seared into my film memory is the impact of that beautifully shot desert scenery, in full colour, along with the shock of the disturbing finale on the cliff.

At the time, I had a raw, ill-formed reaction. Because of a gaping hole in my monocultural, colonial education, I possessed very little understanding of Indigenous culture and history. Nothing really matched *Jedda* again, until the works of the powerful Indigenous filmmakers Tracey Moffatt, Ivan Sen, Rachel Perkins, Warwick Thornton and others, appeared on our screens, from the eighties onwards. Such artists often acknowledge the special influence of *Jedda* on their own work.

On the cusp of the sixties, another film world opened up, framing a whole new dimension for my personal dreaming in the dark. I accompanied brother Peter to see our first sub-titled film, *Rififi*, directed by Jules Dessin. Thinking we were both cool and independent, one early evening Peter and I bought our tickets to *Rififi* at the Broadway Theatre box office.

Earlier in our picture-going experiences, we rarely, if ever, had visited the once seedy Broadway Theatre, situated at that first tramline port-of-call heading up Ipswich Road. It had been a forbidden place, catering, as rumour had it, mainly to 'undesirables', such as drunks, and those troublesome juvenile delinquents at the time, the bodgies and widgies.

The year before, Polly and I had encountered a couple of bodgies in a milk bar on Ipswich Road, up near my place. Greasy hair slicked back, these bodgies were dressed in white singlets and worn-out leather jackets. Their widgie partners hung around outside the cafe, guarding the motor bikes, sneering at us from a distance, leaving the face-to-face aggression to the boys.

One of the bodgies menacingly approached us as we stood beside the jukebox, trying not to be rattled, enjoying a hit song we were playing. Wanting to take control and hear a different song, he snarled 'Stop that!', proceeding to stub out his burning cigarette on my hand. The milk bar owner did nothing to help. Polly and I quickly ran outside, past the sneering widgies, down the road to safety. I was scared, sobbing, holding my injured hand.

Entering another supposed hangout of juvenile delinquents and other unspecified undesirables, Peter and I appeared to be going over to the dark side on two counts that evening: seeing our first French film noir on screen, and living a version of it, in reality.

In that year, 1959, Peter turned seventeen, and I was fourteen. He was still in his rebellious Jack Kerouac /James Dean phase – 'Live fast, die young, and be a good-looking corpse'. I had longish hair, owned a bongo drum, wore sunglasses day and night and, as often as I could, dressed in roomy shirts and slacks, projecting the idea of being a beatnik, in style, if not in substance. At the time, my school friends affectionately nicknamed me Helenik.

Luckily for us, the Broadway Theatre owners were making an effort to exhibit the occasional foreign film, hoping to attract a more sophisticated audience. Curious, we ignored any possible risk, heading into that rebranded, low-lit space. They steered us upstairs into the dress circle, another filmland first.

This iconic heist film, *Rififi*, had won strong critical acclaim, along with the Best Director Award at the Cannes Film Festival. We knew very little then about world film festivals, and even less about French cinema. Following the action and keeping up with the subtitles was also a new viewing challenge.

Fortunately, the on-screen burglars in *Rififi* were doers, not talkers, and the dialogue was often sparse and gruff. For us ingenues, the legendary, practically silent heist scene, around thirty tense minutes without dialogue or music, was a relief from the unfamiliar sub-titles and other distractions. Nevertheless, by the time the word FIN came up on the screen, we were captivated by this crime noir thriller – and even more impressed with ourselves for seeing it.

In suburban sub-tropical Brisbane, as we grew older, we would occasionally create our own alternative paradise venues, hanging out with friends in moonlit backyards on rugs and cushions, hired films cranking out from a borrowed projector onto a shaky old screen, a make-do sheet strung up on the back fence or draped over the rotary clothesline. We saw special films such as *Citizen Kane* for the first time, sitting on old kitchen chairs in those dark, makeshift home theatres, peering from ill-lit spidery spaces beneath Brisbane timber houses.

Or, flashing forward to more recent times, in his downstairs Queenslander space decorated with appropriate memorabilia, my mate Mike Witt lovingly curated an intimate Bruce Springsteen concert film bonanza/festival, presented for a decidedly niche audience, all passionate devotees of Bruce, the Boss. For me, *Cinema Paradiso* has taken on many, ever-renewing forms.

***

3.
PUBERTY BLUES

Some of my favourite Australian teen films over the years have been *The Year My Voice Broke, Flirting, The Heartbreak Kid, The Getting of Wisdom* and *Puberty Blues*. While trying to conjure up the fault lines I traced on my rocky teenage way through school, these titles loom large, even though none of these films actually screened in the early sixties. However, in presenting certain dimensions of teenage angst on screen, they trigger memories of my own awkward coming-of-age years, scenarios for a decidedly older version of myself to reflect on.

My friends and I acted out our fantasies, our highs, our lows. We juggled multiple illusions spawned by impossibly romantic storytelling on screen, radio or in books, at the same time regularly encountering reality and disappointment.

One obstacle was definitely sex. In my early teens, I learned a great deal about sexual taboos, even though I didn't know much about sex itself, to put it mildly. Repression stalked from morning to night, in various guises, although my peer group and I managed to work out our own gormless, simplistic rules of sexual behaviour.

My family loosely attended the Church of England. Much to Dad's eldest sister Aunt Ethel's disgust, I wasn't christened until I was ten, and only then because she put my parents under so much pressure that they finally caved in. Baptism and churchgoing turned out to be quite pleasant for me from then on, at least on a social level. And I could choose my own godparents.

In our early teens, Peter and I, along with our cousins Jan and Geoff, and various kids from the neighbourhood, enjoyed the monthly social C of E dances, as well as the Scout dances at a different nearby hall. Jocelyn married young, moving away from Brisbane to Bowen with her husband Lawrie Hawes when she was nineteen, and I was just thirteen. Having met this young graduating doctor at the church, she felt this was another bonus for religion being in our lives.

Both the church and the scout hall venues provided regular flirting and even occasional pashing locations, although frustration was more often the order of the evening. My bestie, Polly Perkins and I practised on each other to better ourselves at kissing the boys we fancied. No doubt the Reverend Darke would have disapproved of such girl-on-girl experimentation, no matter how innocent it was.

Polly and I played spirited catch and kiss games with boys at parties, comparing notes afterwards about our different crushes. As we matured socially, our widening circle of friends had certain rules about how far we would/ could/should go with boys – always causing hilarious after-the-event chat.

These discussions followed a familiar code:
'How far did you go last night?'
'Only two – kissing, a lot, though he wanted four'.

If we had been reckless, and trusted our confidantes, we might report that, in actuality, 'We went to six'.

Very few of us went further than kissing or breast fondling – four was code for caressing outside the bra; six was inside the bra, hand on flesh. The highly taboo number eight was 'downstairs outside', as we called it, while ten was 'downstairs inside', caressing only allowed. I recall that number twelve involved actual penetration with a condom, and fourteen was, in effect, penetration without a condom.

We didn't really know anything about the larger numbers, about actual penetration, or about oral sex. In the early sixties, ironically, the number fourteen stage was seen by white middle-class teenage girls to be the peak of taboo sexual excitement – with no actual reference to mutual pleasure. We didn't have access to informative sex education, nor to that helpful adult sex bible that appeared in the early seventies, *The Joy of Sex: A Gourmet Guide to Love Making*.

The very non-gourmet side of this numerical /sexual juggling act was the ultimate misadventure of 'falling' pregnant, resulting in being shamed and even ostracised. We all knew the backyard abortionist's home along Annerley Road, dreading going past, sneaking a furtive look. In desperation, some girls I knew risked their lives by going there, secretly, illegally, painfully.

My parents lived in ongoing fear of what the neighbours/ other moralising family members might think. Such judgemental attitudes and experiences bestowed on me a fraught, ambivalent relationship towards sexual exploration of any kind. I remember Mum breathing a sigh of relief when, by 1967, all three of her children did not '*have* to get married', the ultimate disgrace.

Polly and I both passed our scholarship exams at the end of primary schooling in 1958. This entitled us to go to the handful of secondary schools available at the time. Yeronga High School did not start until 1960. While Jocelyn went to Salisbury High in the first years of its inception, and had been happy there, things were changing on that front, and Salisbury did not appeal to us anymore.

Protestant church schools were expensive, while Brisbane Girls Grammar School, at that stage in its history, was reasonably priced. The non-denominational aspect of this school situated on Gregory Terrace in Spring Hill appealed to my parents.

The fees around that time were also fairly modest for scholarship holders, at about eighteen pounds a term, fifty-four pounds a year. Mum and Dad calculated that this was manageable, with both of them continuing to work. However, my first year, 1959, was tough for the family, as Peter was finishing Senior next door at the boys' school.

Not everyone had the resources to pay the fees readily. Some dads had to take on two jobs to send their kids to the Grammar schools. My friend Wendie Robinson said they hardly saw their dad except on weekends, as he was always doing double-shifts. Meanwhile, the relative costs were nowhere near as high as they are in the present era, and girls with similar modest means and varying backgrounds were in my class. I loved making new friends from all over Brisbane. And I was at BGGS when I met Jimmy, the boy who drove the car the night I nearly died.

On the short trip from our school in Spring Hill, winding down to the city centre, Polly and I gradually worked out that we could travel on the same bus as our latest love interests. Eyes darting, we only knew most of these crushes from a distance.

Perfect timing was critical. In those cramped buses with strangely phallic electrical hose attachments, Grammar boys pushed and shoved into a heaving testosterone tip up the back, while Grammar girls, invariably, had to pack into the front, trying, against the odds, to remain dainty and feminine on those boiling hot, humid Brisbane afternoons.

This gendered spatial divide rule was strictly imposed, in order to prevent any slippery social/physical/sexual encounters on public transport. No matter how oppressive the weather, we Grammar girls had to wear white cotton singlets under our white blouses, in order to prevent, at all costs, any bare flesh being exposed while straining to hold on to the strap in a crowded bus.

The unspeakable navy-blue-bloomers under our pleated navy skirts were exactly that – unspeakable, reminiscent of those exaggerated ones worn by the naughty girls in *The Belles of St Trinian's*. However, we didn't wear them for laughs; rather, they tended to operate, deliberately, as a dank, itchy kind of chastity belt.

Mum approved of the wearing of a singlet at all times, not for the school's modesty policy reasons, but because, as she said quite often, 'You might catch a chill on your kidneys'. Throughout my childhood, a chill in or on the kidneys appeared to be always lurking, ready to strike.

After wending our way down to the city in those gangly trolley buses, we would sometimes loiter in the city centre, or else head home, south across the Brisbane River on the Salisbury tramline, past the downtrodden areas called South Brisbane and the five-ways at Woollongabba, near the famous Gabba Cricket Ground. The Broadway was the first of four picture theatres we passed on Ipswich Road, on the way home. It was situated close to where the tram turned right on the long journey from the city to the southern suburbs.

We rattled past the Boomerang Theatre on the left, up the hill towards the Annerley Theatre, which stood on the right going home. Opposite that modest wooden theatre – or was it just a School of Arts hall? - lay the street that wound down the hill leading to Junction Park Primary School, which we former Yeronga Primary kids snobbishly called the Junkyard.

From there, Polly and I swayed along the tramlines at a higher speed, past the Annerley Junction shops. The Catholic schools along with the large Catholic church stood on the left of the tramline, where the Micks, as we Prods disparagingly called them, would go to school with the priests and the nuns, a completely mysterious world to me.

Near the top of our parallel streets heading down the hill on the right,

Waverley and Villa Streets, Polly and I came upon the small Odeon Theatre, leading up to the well-patronised landmark, the iconic Chardon's Corner pub, with the stately Cilento home directly across Ipswich Road. Every day, we especially loved passing those picture theatres along the way, checking the upcoming programs on their billboards.

If, instead of alighting at Chardon's Corner, we had continued on that tram journey, we would have clattered alongside Yeronga Park on the right, past the fire station at the entry to School Road, leading up to our old Primary school.

When Ipswich Road split two ways, the tramline followed Beaudesert Road, up another hill, deep into the suburb of Moorooka. We would have glimpsed, on the right, several streets memorialising the Anzacs at Gallipoli, such as Helles Road and Gaba Tepe Street, my family's old stomping ground.

Until the regrettable removal of all Brisbane trams in April, 1969, that tramline finished at the Salisbury terminus along Beaudesert Road, up past Moorooka Primary School, which we derogatorily called 'Moocow'. This modest school was situated on the left, near the matching wooden houses built for returned soldiers and post-war immigrants.

One afternoon, on that homeward-bound Salisbury tram, Polly and I were spotted sitting near the back, with our Girls Grammar hats and gloves resting on our laps. An obsessive old girl, probably a former prefect, was closely following the tram in her car, noting our every transgression. For quite a while, we did not realise she was there.

Waving frantically, she signalled out of her car window, 'Put your hats and gloves back on!' She also appeared to be communicating that we should move to the front of the crowded tram, well away from the supposedly sinister men and sex-starved schoolboys, invariably congregating in the forbidden zone at the back, ready to prey on Grammar girls at any moment.

The front of the tram was packed, as usual, mainly with women, but also with several men who had innocently found a spare seat there. We were supposed to display eternal virtuousness, standing up towards the front, somehow keeping our hats on, despite the crowd and the considerable breeze.

Grouchy Old-Girl-in-the-Car endangered her own life, and possibly the lives of others, insisting that we uphold the Grammar name in public at all times. Long-held school traditions were sacred then, and, seemingly, worth dying for.

Polly and I managed to create our own mini 'rom coms' throughout 1959 and 1960. One series involved meeting my new boyfriend, Jimmy and his mate, Phil, who was Polly's beau at the time, on Friday afternoons after school, acting out our own very tame, urban version of *Puberty Blues*. We played around with some kissing and touching, minus the beach, the surf, the sex, the rampant sexism, the drugs.

Still, we thought we were pretty cool, especially when going up and down in the lifts of the shiny new Prudential Building near the river, looking for quiet, private moments. Jimmy became my boyfriend for about six months in 1960, when I was in Junior and he was in Senior, both attending the respective Grammar Schools, side by side on Gregory Terrace, Spring Hill.

Forging such convenient relationships was the accepted practice of single-sex private school teens, accelerated by close proximity and geographical determinism. Such encounters could spontaneously fire up nearby on Gregory Terrace or around town, as well as at the regular Saturday morning dances, riverside, in the old O'Connor Boathouse.

These cross-school boy/girl relationships could flicker encouragingly for a while, and, suddenly, mortifyingly, crumble into ashes. At the Boathouse one Saturday, I think I caught Jimmy dancing on the rebound, when my savvy friend, Vivienne dumped him. This was not an auspicious beginning for a successful teen romance, in anyone's life-script, although his surname did happen to be Love.

I was tiring of Rod and Paul, two other Grammar crushes at that time. Tall, dark-haired Rod had acquired a motorbike when he turned seventeen, and came to woo me at home with the offer of a spin. I hopped on his bike, immediately burning my bare calf on the hot exhaust pipe. In pain, I rejected his overly busy kisses, one last time.

Paul from down the road was a long-term ping-pong opponent. I gradually tired of the endless table tennis games under my house, followed by his groping, awkward kisses as dusk fell and he had to head home. Jimmy was intelligent, as were both those other boys. He was also a champion rower, a dark, brooding soul who hated his father. Somehow, I found his inner turbulence strangely attractive, deluding myself that I might provide the lightness and joy that he lacked.

Before we left Grammar, Polly and I dared to act in a few transgressive mini-dramas of our own, again nothing on the scale of the *Puberty Blues* story. Although we were instructed that all commercial places were absolutely forbidden, we entered one of the smoky coffee shops popping up in inner Brisbane.

The school rule, repeated often, was that 'no divergence whatsoever was allowed on the journey home'. That edict, naturally, made the newly forbidden, exotic zones even more attractive spaces for us to explore, always with adventurous as well as flirtatious intent.

Challenging the repression matrix took on many forms. Once, for a dare, Polly and I hopped on a New Farm tram. To our gradual discomfort, we discovered that the mostly Italian boys going home on that tramline were very forward, which was fun, for a while. They openly flirted, then, as the journey progressed towards New Farm Park, the boys started rubbing their bodies up against us.

Frotting was definitely not on our agenda. We decided that New Farm was a dodgy no-go place. It seemed safer to hang out in the inner city, and only ever travel on the relatively safe Salisbury tramline. New Farm was a step too far for us, back in sixties Brisbane. Funnily enough, in 2022, I have been living in that once forbidden, frotting suburb since the early nineties.

Another day, we heard on the grapevine that bold Churchie boys were hanging out in De Brazil Café. This place was a den of iniquity in our imaginations, downstairs in Albert Street, right in the heart of the forbidden city. These boys were rumoured to have been generally disruptive, chatting loudly, and even swapping the sugar and salt around to fool serious coffee drinkers.

Liking the sound of those rebellious Churchie boys, we slipped down the narrow stairs to this dimly-lit coffee haunt, one Friday afternoon. Shaking a little, thrilled at our own daring, we sat there, very self-consciously, hoping in vain that some sexy Senior boys from across town would show up and entertain us. Admittedly, we were setting the bar pretty low.

Nevertheless, we were optimistic, although that particular private school boy gang we yearned for, turned out to be a no-show. We later found out they had been suspended from school for their earlier coffee shop antics.

Not long after that failed escapade, Polly and I were, as usual, standing side by side at morning assembly. Consumed by fury, the grim-faced, red-haired headmistress, Mrs MacDonald, named and shamed Dee, a fellow student in our year. Polly and I knew Dee well, from our Yeronga Primary School days.

In my class from the age of five, Dee, a free spirit, always seemed to be having fun on the edge, not caring much about school rules. I recall with horror when, in 1955, at the age of ten, in front of our Grade Five class, she was roughly pulled over the grim headmaster's knees and spanked brutally on her bottom.

Looking back, I realise now that the abominable behaviour of this vicious old man, whom we used to call Stiffy, was a form of child abuse, neither named nor called out then. Too many regular and irregular forms of corporal punishment were enacted at that primary school, and probably at many others.

Cousin David, as well as my brother Peter endured terrifying physical and mental bullying from a dreaded woman teacher, appropriately named Miss Shock. She threw her duster at kids' heads, smacking others viciously with a stick, at the same time humiliating them with a torrent of abuse. Mostly, Miss Shock concentrated on the boys.

As Peter says, 'She used to bash (our older cousin) David Suter's head against the wall. When she kept me in once, I feared I'd get the same treatment'. Luckily Peter was saved that day when an old friend of the family, Dr Malcolm Franklands, who had actually delivered Peter in Frankston, Victoria, came to pick him up, disrupting any further punishment. His firm words, his powerful, sensible presence, calmed things down.

Peter recalls, 'I don't know who got the biggest shock, me or Miss Shock. I hopped in his smart car, not really knowing who he was. I must have looked a real scruff. I never wore shoes and my shorts were usually torn before it became fashionable.' Not long afterwards, Peter was mysteriously transferred to Miss Davies' class, a rather less violent old-timer.

While my Grade Five teacher, Mr Robe, was mild-tempered, I rebelled a little after Dee was publicly slapped. I defiantly, deliberately mis-spelt three of my 'daily words'. I didn't really know how to be very naughty, although I sussed that, if I achieved seven out of ten, or less, I would be sent along to the headmaster's office for punishment. Stiffy was surprised to see me, as I was one of the top kids in the class. Even so, he couldn't resist giving me several smacks around the legs with a ruler. I felt quite proud of myself that day.

No corporal punishment was meted out at Girls Grammar assemblies, although daring Dee suffered a private girls' school form of utter humiliation. That particular morning, she was publicly shamed, stripped of her hatband, tie and badge, and immediately suspended.

Poor Dee sobbed in front of the whole school. She had been sighted hanging out with boys in the city, behaving in 'an unladylike manner', in one of those same wicked downtown coffee places that Polly and I yearned for.

It wasn't clear whether school prefects had sprung her, or yet another rampaging Old Girl had been on the hunt, with Dee's scalp as the prize. Winding up, Mrs Mac declared: 'Any girls who have ever frequented such a place in school uniform, must stay behind after assembly'.

Polly and I quickly looked at each other, then straight ahead, both of us experiencing a momentary rush of guilt regarding our own mildly divergent behaviour in one such taboo place. Thankfully, that moment soon passed. We were both leaving Grammar at the end of that Junior year, and we did not wish to hasten our departure, or to upset our parents. Polly planned to go to art school, while I was heading to boarding school, out-of-town.

Despite such institutionalised measures of suppression and control, we were never nabbed while consorting with our boyfriends that year, 1960. Polly and Phil broke up when she decided to spread her wings. She won the heart of Bob, a handsome, athletic boy from Brisbane Boys' College, sporting that school's signature straw boater hat.

In those days, attractive senior GPS school boys were virtually indistinguishable from one another, except for their sweaty strutting around in differently coloured shirts, once beautifully ironed by their devoted mums. The boys wore rather awkwardly looped ties and crumpled hats of varying material and textures. 'Crumpled hat syndrome' was very much a rogue symbol of honour amongst both the boys and the girls, if one ever dared perform this ritual. Looking too new and pristine was definitely a no-no.

On some Saturday evenings, Jimmy and I would go on dates in his dad's patchy, silvery Vauxhall Velox to the drive-in cinema at Coopers

Plains. At least his 'difficult' father lent him the car from time to time. We would invariably pash through the films, not really paying much attention to whatever we were supposed to be watching.

Over time, we became very skilled in the art of kissing and petting, until our jaws and arms ached. We once sneaked into the Regent Theatre in the city to see Alfred Hitchcock's horror film, *Psycho*. Finding ourselves crashing onto the floor, scared out of our wits at the famous shower scene, there was no quality pashing that particular day.

Not long afterwards, cousin Jan took her sweet revenge on me for describing, in graphic detail, the scary plot of that ground-breaking film. While I was having a shower at home, Jan crept in, roughly pulling back the shower curtain, kitchen knife in hand, totally freaking me out. Thereafter, I always made sure the bathroom door was locked, just in case. And I was careful not to relate any more graphic murder stories to Jan.

Becoming concerned about my drive-in dates with Jimmy, Dad tried to give me his one and only sex talk. This focussed on the issue of young males 'not being able to control themselves'. I kept assuring him nothing bad would ever happen to me. This was of course the classic, galling positioning of females to be alert and responsible at all times, because 'boys will be boys'. My mother's only sex talk had been about girls getting their periods, and what rituals I had to follow.

I was also instructed not to tell Peter or any other boys about female menstruation. I remember being horrified at how many months/years/decades I would have to endure this regular bleeding. For a short while, I even harboured an odd idea in my head, that a woman on her wedding night had to inform her partner about menstruation, as males simply would not have heard about this deep, dark female secret. Adequate, enlightened sex education did not exist, and feature films we saw back then never addressed sexual topics, openly and honestly.

While I was upset to be leaving my Grammar 'gutter gang', (that is, those of us who lunched together in a former gutter) I knew I was definitely not going to miss a couple of staff at that school. The French teacher bullied me for weeks in my final year, ostensibly for not having as neat a French notebook as my German notebook. Once she startled me completely by throwing me out of the class.

I was a high achieving 'A' student in French, but something about me, a 'je ne sais quoi', apparently irritated her beyond measure, after nearly two years of blameless behaviour. My friends were as flummoxed as I was. I guess that, somehow, I didn't fit the goody-goody, classic Grammar mould.

My straightforward demeanour was unlike that of the haughty, 'good' girls in our class. Their behaviour and their uniforms were immaculate, and they always made a show, when, having answered yet another question perfectly, each one would smirk to the others, slide back into her seat, carefully folding the pleats on a perfectly pressed skirt.

Meanwhile, another staff member, the gym teacher-from-hell made me feel I had landed in some kind of authoritarian re-education camp. We were mercilessly drilled and humiliated on slippery old surfaces, fraying ropes, dangerously dangling rings, a rickety gym horse, all acted out in a dusty, mouldy gym, which, to cap it off, gave me acute hay fever.

My trusty brother-in-law, Dr Lawrie, rose to the occasion, kindly writing a note to have me excused from that weekly torture, on valid medical grounds. Gymnastics and I have never been the same since. This was not a good way to instil wellness and a healthy lifestyle into young women of our age.

In the early sixties, another form of darkness was occurring both at Grammar, and more widely in the society. Even though my dear friend, Vivienne, gained high grades in the external Junior examination, her estranged father terminated the fee payment to Grammar and therefore, any further education doors for her were slammed shut from that quarter. Conversely, he continued paying fees for her older brother, supporting him in various ways through medicine as well. Vivienne was just as bright as her brother, perhaps even more so.

I often witnessed such blatant, unjust treatment, purely on the basis of gender, well before I understood feminism and gendered power issues. Misogyny was continually normalised and masked in ways that were deeply, ideologically fraught. In the early sixties, we simply didn't have the words, or the power, to name this masculinist treatment, to call it out, to be enlightened, to resist.

While I was at boarding school, fortunately enabled by my parents to continue my education, Vivienne studied and later worked as a highly respected dental nurse. She also completed an external, part-time university degree in arts, while successfully bringing up three children with her beloved late husband, John. Of course, in the eighties and nineties, her daughter Jane received exactly the same opportunities as her older brothers, David and Richard, all being educated through to Senior, and well beyond.

A similarly discriminatory scenario haunted my cousin Jan. Her dad, my Uncle Jack, despite my parents' and other people's urging to the contrary, insisted on sending her only for the requisite two years' secondary study at the newly opened, local Yeronga State High School. He outrightly refused to pay the Grammar fees: 'Wasted on a girl', he snorted. To many parents, girls' education was seen to be largely a waste of time and money, as it was assumed they did not need a career. They would just get married and have children.

In stark contrast, Jan's brother Geoffrey studied for the full four years at Grammar, later becoming a qualified engineer. Always very bright, just like Vivienne, Jan went on to study for Senior at night as a mature-aged student. Over the years, she gained both an honours and a masters degree, always studying part-time while working full-time, a very hard grind. Ultimately, she became a highly respected Director of Research and Postgraduate Studies at the University of Queensland.

Both Jan and Vivienne pursued their different life paths the tough, largely unacknowledged way, as, in those days, nothing was handed to those talented women, equally, upfront, on the platter of gender privilege. Well into the sixties and beyond, Australian girls still had a long way to go as far as gender equity was concerned, with those from lower-socio-economic groups and Indigenous or multicultural backgrounds being most at risk of not having a fulfilling career and life path.

Dated, privileged white male attitudes die hard, even today. The examples of Jan and Vivienne helped stoke my thinking about the ravages and injustice of gender inequality, even though at that stage I could not clearly articulate such perceptions. It just seemed very unfair.

As the time approached for me to leave Grammar, I knew I would greatly miss the close friends I had made in classes Three B and Four B, especially Helen E. (there was a Helen I., with the same surname), Vivienne, Margaret, Mary and Johanne. Sadly, dear Johanne and Mary died far too young. Meanwhile, the others from that gutter group are currently immersing themselves in artistic pursuits, along with grandmotherly duties. We keep in touch whenever we can, after over sixty years of knowing each other.

Going even further back, I also see some female friends from Yeronga Primary School every six months or so, for a long lunch. It is quite easy to re-engage, to take up those dormant threads again, continuing old conversations and starting new ones, whenever we get together.

A larger mixed group from that same Scholarship year, 1958, have been meeting for a special annual lunch event since about 1988. Polly came along to a couple of these early reunions. Blokes from our class would get up and tell dated, cringeworthy sexist jokes, while one would update us, year in, year out, about his trusty old Holden Kingswood. I enjoyed that ongoing car narrative, although not the sexist repartee.

One year, a person whom Polly and I did not recognise, stood up to announce to everyone that he had loved Nena (Polly) Perkins ever since our fifties school days, baring his broken heart to all. The room went quiet after that unexpected announcement, and some people uncomfortably shifted in their seats, perhaps thinking of their own unfulfilled crushes from our schooldays. Kind Polly later thanked him, and they had a little chat. I don't think he came to any other school reunions after that painful unburdening.

From her first marriage, Polly had two beautiful daughters, one of whom, Jessica, died tragically in a bicycle accident, in her late teens. Polly lives across the border in northern New South Wales, enjoying life, doting on her grand-children, and her daughter Justine Elliot, who is a very bright, hardworking Federal Labor MP. At one stage, when Kevin Rudd was Prime Minister, Justine was the Minister for Ageing. Polly and I were excited about that, as we felt we were moving into the right age bracket, at just the right time.

Back in our *Puberty Blues* days, Jimmy and I floated along for a while until the end of 1960, my final year at Grammar. The future was not looking at all promising. He would soon be studying engineering at University, while I was going to boarding school, out of reach, out of town, out of mind. We acted out a stereotypical, 'GI' ('Geographically Impossible') conclusion to that teen narrative, never realising what was in store for us both, a couple of years into the future.

***

4.
THE GETTING OF WISDOM

My so-called love life more or less ground to a halt when I was tucked away at Mum's family's old school, Ipswich Girls' Grammar, for my last two years of secondary education. It was either that option, or head out west with my parents, and apply for a job in the Commonwealth Bank.

Because his youngest child had reached the school-leaving age, meteorologist Dad had become eligible to be transferred from Eagle Farm airport to work for three years in civil aviation weather forecasting at Cloncurry airport, which, at that stage, was larger than the Mount Isa airport.

Living in Cloncurry, where I knew no-one, was not a welcome life plan for me. For me, the choice of going on to Senior was an easy one to make. Although it was a harder choice for my parents, as would be stretching their tight budget, they decided they might be able to manage the extra school fees, as I was the only child left at home by then. I also flatly refused to continue at Brisbane Girls Grammar as a boarder, despite having a lovely friend, Jenny, who boarded in my year.

At BGGS, boarders were very much in the minority, and the boarding section seemed to me to be rundown, with the occasional rat spotted scurrying around in the smelly kitchen. Of course, their equally gross kin could well have been hanging out in the Ipswich Girls' Grammar kitchen, for all I knew.

Earlier in my childhood, I had devoured Enid Blyton books featuring all girls' boarding schools, loving both the *Mallory Towers*, and *The Naughtiest Girl in the School* series. From a young age, along with many other girls across the English-speaking world, I dreamed of going to such a school. Sometimes when I was naughty, Mum would threaten me with boarding school. I don't think she realised that this 'threat' was, in essence, a promise, as far as I was concerned.

I longed to experience the standard girly adventures, get into scrapes, have delicious midnight feasts, witness the fights between mean girls and fun girls, the encounters with strict or kindly prefects and teachers; in effect, the whole imaginary hurly-burly, hockey-sticks and all, brought to life.

Such novels never strayed into awkward, challenging adolescent issues regarding anxiety, sexuality, and the complex discrimination against girls and women in the wider society, for instance. Nor did they depict the sheer day-to-day sameness and grind. What I discovered did confirm the mean girls/fun girls dichotomy, to an extent, with a few unexpected, simmering subtexts of older/younger girl lesbian crushes.

That outstanding British boarding school film, Lindsay Anderson's *If reveals* shocking, cowardly bullying and repression at an uppercrust boys' school, ending in a chaotic, exhilarating revolution. While systemic horror did not plague us at our provincial boarding school, I had to survive, scholastically, physically, emotionally, while coping, somehow, with the following:

- missing home, family and friends
- keeping my space in the dormitory very tidy (always a strain, as many who know me will attest)
- whisking in and out of three-minute showers, with Matron Lambert banging on the door, when I was a minute over, cawing, 'Helen Thompson! Your three minutes are up! Are you washing your hair?'
- only being allowed to wash my hair on Saturdays, during the day
- sealing letters home to parents, but leaving all other letters unsealed
- eating non-appetising food, most of which comprised overboiled vegetables, an occasional dubious piece of meat, combined with oodles of carbohydrates in one form or another
- observing a catalogue of tedious rules, too many to list…

After some early dithering, given the big move out west, I was a late enrolment, slipping into the school by the skin of my teeth. Two 'fun girls' from Kingaroy High School, Sue Morrison and Cheryl Cardiff, were also starting at IGGS for their final two years of schooling. They had both been booked in for years.

Initially, the three of us found ourselves crushed into a strange little corner room that had once been a linen cupboard, much to the amusement of several scoffing 'mean girls' in our year. I felt guilty, as I was the superfluous person responsible for those cramped quarters. The staff finally found us a larger dormitory to share with a couple of other newbies, and life proceeded more smoothly.

My beloved cousin, Keith Heiner, worked as a dentist in downtown Ipswich. Naturally, it was imperative that I went to his surgery for very regular check-ups. His sister Cecily Mary was his delightful dental nurse. Both were mischievous wags. Keith would quickly check my teeth, while he and Cecily Mary would tell me lots of dirty jokes, at the same time plying me with a bulky feast of chocolates and lollies.

I stuffed those treats down the front of my tunic. Pleasure overcame practicality and health, for both me and my cousins, a familial trait which bound us closely together. Tightening my belt, I walked back up the hill to the school, hands across my chest, fearful this forbidden cargo might spill to the ground, or that a teacher might see me and wonder just how my breasts had expanded so fast.

Another classic ritual would inevitably follow after lights out – the Blytonesque midnight feast with my dorm mates. We ravenously consumed that contraband, much tastier than the lumpy sago or tapioca puddings with dubious canned fruit served up to us in the dining room.

During those two years at boarding school, I indulged in an entirely different delight, taking up piano lessons again. After primary school, I had dropped all music lessons, having played since I was around four years old. Sitting at the piano every day after school in the little music cottage, well away from classroom and boarding house bustle, I enjoyed a treasured escape from school routine.

My new friends SueM and Cheryl also studied the piano. Cheryl was a lovely singer, and I often accompanied her performances. In our final year, I became the official school pianist, equally a pleasure and a pain. I was also made a prefect, probably indicating that, somehow, I fitted into the classic 'Ipswich schoolgirl style', whether I liked it or not. After all, my mother's great-aunt was the first student to go through those imposing school gates on the original opening day, in 1892.

I found the teachers at IGGS to be, on the whole, kindly people, often inspirational in their respective fields. The gentle Dorothy Marsden, the French teacher, and the wildly brilliant Veronica Stark, the Maths and Physics teacher, were the standouts for me, always engaging and encouraging.

Years later, I heard that Vonnie Stark left the school, went to Sydney, got married and, as Dr Veronica James, became a top academic medical researcher and inventor. I wish I had kept in touch with her. Education is supposedly about *The Getting of Wisdom*, fraught though that is. There was still a long way for me to go, wisdom-wise.

Joan 'Benny' Benson, the rough and tumble, cigarette-smoking sports mistress, was a good sport, open and fair. To my great relief, I could relax and enjoy physical education with her, experiencing no more trauma, no more dark-night-of-the-soul gymnasium routines, sucking away my breath and my confidence.

Dad, a champion tennis and golf player, and overall sporting all-rounder, was proud that I represented the school in tennis, as I had done previously at Yeronga Primary School. Obviously, the tennis practice board he built in our backyard was paying some small dividends. I certainly was never in the A teams, but at least I was back on the court.

Compulsory uniform and underwear rules also came under the microscope at my new school. The long, white singlet was mandatory wear in both Grammar schools, even though Ippy Grammar girls wore tunics, not skirts, so there were no bare bellies to worry about. Of course, these white singlets soon became a dull grey colour, thanks to the unsavoury rigours of the mass weekly laundry.

At both all-girls' schools, the repressive nature of our uniforms quelled our individual, stylish desires in many ways, despite an occasional cheeky variation with skirt length, hairstyle, even pretty pink knickers, if you dared. Again, on the practical, caring level, Mum liked the snug cotton singlet, given that chills in the kidneys might creep up on vulnerable girls in those draughty old buildings.

The petite, ageing headmistress, Kit Carter quaveringly decreed, for a time, that all girls had to wear their singlets underneath their bras. Supposedly this was in order to keep us warmer, although there were rumours abroad that bras-rubbing-bare-nipples might cause too much closeted sexual stimulation, and this simply had to stop.

During Kit's alarming spot-checks of the younger boarders, the culprit had to disrobe immediately, placing the virtuous singlet on underneath that tempting bra.

My friends and I in the senior school figured that this misguided woman's peculiar elaboration of the 'singlet riff' was to be resisted at all costs. Fortunately, she never personally checked our underwear. I had never read about such goings-on in those Enid Blyton boarding school fantasies.

As for the boys on offer, a largely gormless bunch of pimply young males would line up in Ipswich at church on Sundays, or at the occasional, forgettable school dance. I had never been interested in immature boys around the same age, and the rare tall handsome one naturally fell for gorgeous Cheryl, with her curly blonde hair and bubbly personality.

After leaving school, Cheryl became a teacher, married John Hughes, and they had a sweet daughter, Dominique. Then Cheryl pursued a new career as a fashion model, subsequently managing successful modelling agencies in Brisbane, London and now in the Cotswolds, where she lives with her second husband, Julian. We are still close after many years, even though, or perhaps because, we have lived very different lives.

Going 'home' to the Queensland outback during the longer holiday breaks was quite an adventure for this city girl, an essential part of that 'getting of wisdom' experience. After flying the long haul from Brisbane to Townsville, via Bowen to visit my sister, Jocelyn, and her husband Lawrie, I would hop on a Fokker Friendship flight, heading off, via Charters Towers, to Cloncurry. Along with a motley bunch of western kids from various boarding schools on the east coast, I inevitably suffered airsickness on that final, rough and bumpy leg.

One boy who was a regular on that torturous flight was Bob Katter. His father was a respected local MP, just as Bob himself is now, writ large. Bob Junior was quite a loudmouth show-off, even then, although I remember that he also vomited most of the way to Cloncurry. That rugged trip was certainly a memorable 'chuckfest', as well as a great leveller.

On some special occasions, I would travel home from Ipswich by train and bus to Annerley, Brisbane, for a boarders' free weekend, catching up with brother Peter, then a cadet journalist at *The Courier-Mail*, the daily morning newspaper, long before it became a Murdoch rag. Turning up in my school uniform, I would change into my civvies, trying in vain to clean the grossly neglected kitchen and bathroom.

Peter shared our parents' simple three-bedroomed house with Dudley, an old schoolmate, who was tall, dark, handsome, athletic – a veritable dreamboat. Naturally, Dudley was surrounded by an abundance of girls from his course at Teachers' College, all vying to be 'the one'.

As Peter recalls, he became Dudley's social secretary, answering the phone to girls asking to speak to Dudley: 'He was a real babe magnet. I remember a knock on the front door after tea one evening in 1961. Four young women, all students at the Teachers' Training College, were standing there. "We've come to see Dudley", one said. I showed them in. They sat in a semi-circle around Dudley's chair and gazed adoringly at him for an hour or so, and then departed'.

Set half-way down a steep hill from Ipswich Road, that plain-speaking fifties wooden home they shared had a low cottage-style front, and a high back, as the land fell away. This meant there was quite a large, cavernous area underneath, containing a laundry, a never-ending workshop, a kind of tool heaven for Dad, and a billiard room, approached from inside via a steep wooden staircase.

On November 17, 1960, before the big move to Cloncurry, I was home alone on 'swat vac', studying for my external exams. Suddenly, the whole house literally shook on its foundations. I felt that either an elephant or a monstrous intruder with huge boots was clattering up our back stairs. Fearing I was in imminent danger, I rushed to lock the internal back door. It turned out that Brisbane was experiencing a rare but momentarily fierce earthquake, magnitude 4.4. Whilst the immediate effect was scary, this was, in the scheme of things, a minor disruption.

Nevertheless, Dad's under-the-house workshop did look as though several mini-earthquakes regularly struck. He was always expanding with extra implements, as well as with a seemingly endless clutter of second hand, broken-down washing machines and motor mowers, with which he constantly tinkered, throwing Mum into quiet despair in the process. Looking at this activity now, through a different lens, I appreciate that he was quite an innovative re-cycler, well before his time. He gifted those repaired machines to various grateful family members.

His beloved billiard table, with its black wooden top, doubled as a ping-pong table as well. Out in the backyard, a flat, grassy area contained a classic rotary clothes hoist, as well as the tennis practice board. Where the grass stopped, a steep, rocky hill with a smattering of weedy-looking plants, rose up quite sharply to Villa Street backyards at the top of our strangely-shaped yard.

When we were young, we used to climb up and play on that rocky knoll, near to where the well-known medical family, the Cilentos, had a grand house above us, on the corner of Ipswich Road and Villa Street. Further down that particular street, which bordered Yeronga Park, Polly and the Perkins family lived, as did other Yeronga schoolmates of ours, Pam and Janet Winship.

Legendary parties were regularly held at our parents' house over those two years of freedom and chaos, before Peter moved on to Melbourne, then to London. It always seemed to be party time at 20 Waverley Street, especially in the late evening, when the journalists would congregate, relieved at having finished the paper ready for delivery the following morning.

Our good friend, Hugh Lunn, wryly immortalised these particular all night shindigs in his second memoir, *Head Over Heels*, published in the early nineties. In some ways, Peter's parties echoed the all-time classic film, *The Party*, starring Peter Sellers.

While brother Peter's guests may not have been part of a glamorous, goofy Hollywood set, many young people-about-town such as journalists, student doctors, nurses, lawyers, teachers, and other hangers-on, would flock to his place. Often it seemed as though these parties never actually ended, a new one forming in a blurry, movable time zone, just as the previous one fizzled out.

Amidst loud music from the gramophone, or cool live jazz and rock 'n' roll played on our piano by Peter's journalist friend, David Bentley[3], the party-goers revelled in the freedom that marked the early sixties. The downstairs billiard table was the popular centre of a smoky place for people to hang out, often playing billiards or snooker, sometimes for profit, other times just for pleasure.

---

3. David Bentley's band Python Lee Jackson had a huge hit in London in 1972 with 'In a Broken Dream', a rock ballad written by David, with Rod Stewart taking time out from the Faces to record the vocals on that and several other Python tracks. Along with sustaining a successful journalism career, David later formed the Dave Bentley Trio, well known around Brisbane and beyond.

Laurie Lawrence, of swimming coaching fame, once sat on that table, singing songs well into the night. The guests were mostly not of the Baby Boomer generation. Rather, many, like Peter and myself, were War Babies, on the cusp of Boomer territory. We heralded in certain aspects of the upcoming sexual and cultural revolutions, life changers for many young Australians. At the same time, the 'revolution' completely missed engaging others in our generation, who tended to stay locked in a more conservative fifties mind-set.

Despite, or, perhaps, because of the frivolity and heavy drinking, three of the major players at those historic parties, the host, Peter Thompson, his friends, Hugh Lunn and Robert Macklin, pursued successful journalism careers across the globe. Between them, they have also published around sixty books. In his writings, Hugh captures a sublime moment, lying on the lounge floor at Peter's place, transfixed, listening to the spell-binding voice of Joan Baez for hours, singing such classics as the 'Mary Hamilton' song.

Hugh was the greatest story-teller we knew. Spellbound, we would listen for hours to the hilarious anecdotes rolling off his tongue, one after the other. Later, of course, he skilfully wove these into his best-selling memoirs, starting with that boyhood classic, *Over the Top with Jim*, set just down Ipswich Road from our place, in that homely, unfashionable suburb of Annerley.

Hugh recalls an all-night 'snogging fest' with Stephanie's cousin, Jacqueline, although I'm not quite sure whether that episode is recorded in any of his books. Lovely Stephanie Bright was a cadet journalist at the Courier, along with Peter, Hugh, Jack Lunn, David Bentley, Robert Macklin, Bill Richards, Cliff Dawson, SallyAnne Atkinson[4] and others. Stephanie later became Peter's wife. Many people fatefully crossed paths in that throbbing little house of pleasure and unpredictability.

Amazingly, the cops only ever turned up once, shutting the party down after a complaint from long-suffering neighbours. Behind their fluttering curtains, the latter probably also spied Hugh's great friend, Ken Fletcher[5] playing endless illegal games of two-up in the front

---

4. SallyAnne Atkinson eventually became the first and only woman Lord Mayor of Brisbane, 1985 – 1991.
5. Ken Fletcher was a champion tennis player, winner of three Wimbledon Mixed Doubles titles with Margaret Court, as well as one Wimbledon title for the Men's Doubles, with John Newcombe.

garden with Robert Macklin. They probably also witnessed the weird spectacle of Peter's good mate, Rob Kenny, heading into the front yard, turning on the hose, pointing it through a front window, and hosing down a rowdy bunch drinking in the kitchen.

Peter vividly remembers that moment: 'Someone then started throwing eggs which splattered against the walls - one hit the wallpaper next to the china cabinet in the lounge. Three very good friends stayed up all night to help me repair the damage. Surprisingly, none of it was visible'. Or so he hoped.

Back in those years, whenever I was on a school break, Jan and I would pile into Hughie Lunn's trusty strawberry-coloured Alpine sports car, and go for a spin, top down, hair flying in the breeze. By some miracle, we fitted into that zappy little car. He and Jan were sweet on each other at the time, and he was also kind to me, the poor deprived sister, living in exile.

I recall the car chugging to a smoky halt on the Story Bridge one day, causing quite a flurry as we spilled out, laughing, finding ourselves in the middle of that iconic bridge. Funnily enough, as I write, I'm not sure now whether this little vignette is just a dream, or whether it actually happened. Either way, it doesn't really matter. As the indomitable Hugh says, 'A milk cart was travelling slowly across the bridge, and I stopped him and bought a bottle of milk. That's how little traffic was around then'.

One weekend, out of the blue, Jimmy rocked up to Peter's party, along with his shambolic, irrepressible mate, Harvey. Coincidentally, I was present, released from the boarding house, enjoying a free weekend at home. No hosing, cops or egg-throwing happened that night, although someone, who later became a well-known doctor around town, mistook the kitchen for the bathroom, with decidedly unpleasant consequences.

Jimmy, Harvey and I, an unlikely trio, ended up together on my parents' old bed. This was actually more innocent than it sounds. We burbled along, had a good laugh, Jimmy and I had a kiss and a cuddle for old times' sake, while Harvey, another great raconteur in our midst, smoked copious 'roll-your-owns', recounting endless, funny stories.

When I returned to school, exhausted and red-eyed late Sunday afternoon, my dorm mates were, as usual, very keen to hear stories about my Brisbane weekend, my unconventional older brother, and all the shenanigans. The more epic and outrageous those tales were, the better for my eager audience.

Once my final Senior exams and boarding schooldays were over, I settled into living in that rather battered and bruised family home on Waverley Street. The last place I wanted to live was in the outback with my dear parents, who were still stuck in Cloncurry, both working. Peter's journalism career was on the move, as was he. As the youngest A-grade journalist in Australia at the time, he was on a roll.

That year, 1963, I shared the house with my sister, Jocelyn, her doctor husband, Lawrie, their three-year-old child, Margaret, and newly born twin girls, Diane and Elizabeth. They had newly arrived in Brisbane after a stint for Lawrie as the doctor at the Bowen Hospital in Northern Queensland. As they filled that family home with very different, adorably cuddly bodies and sounds, I imagined that this neglected house shifted a little on its uneven high stumps, creaking the occasional sighs of relief.

In an attempt to be independent, I started work at the local Annerley Municipal library, while studying both a part-time Arts Degree, and a Library certificate. I drifted towards Jimmy Love again. Several of our old friendship circles still intersected, and we both were keen to restart whatever had been going on between us.

Despite his dark side regarding escalating tensions with his widowed father, and despite hints and warnings about an even darker side from my cousin Geoffrey, who had been at school and university with him, I was still attracted to Jimmy. Having him around was pleasant, especially as, after two years holed up at boarding school in another town, I knew very few eligible young men.

Jimmy was kindly and respectful towards me, and I never saw the crude, heavy drinking side that Geoffrey related. Jimmy offered to pick me up every Friday after my university classes. We established a pleasant, easygoing routine which suited us both. The chemistry was reignited, there was a little flirting, lots of snogging, the occasional date. On the first Friday in May, I ignored the fortune teller's prediction and drove along Coronation Drive with Jimmy, not realising he had had one drink too many.

Nearly five months after that calamitous car accident, having avoided me for that traumatic post-smash time, Jimmy reappeared. Things became complicated, on a number of levels. We had a few clumsy dates, which

I kept secret from my parents, both of whom had returned from the outback. They were angry with Jimmy, on a number of levels. Eventually I persuaded them to let me see him again. And then, in the midst of these confused emotions, Jimmy asked me to marry him.

Totally unprepared, I was far too young, and also in no fit state to deal with the thought, let alone the reality, of a lifetime partnership. His guilt weighed heavily on me, as well as on himself, entangled with my deep-seated fear that, because my appearance had been badly affected in the smash, no one would ever want to marry me.

I still had some romantic feelings for him, built up in my mind in the dark of night, post-accident. Absurd though it sounds, I imagined we were inextricably bound by fate because of the accident, while at the same time, I was, in fact, drowning. In the cold light of day, I realised that Jimmy was not my knight-in-shining armour, and not just because Madam X had thus decreed, in that weird, pre-accident fore-telling. After a little while wrestling with all these mixed emotions, I refused any further commitment to him.

About the same time, Peter's former housemate, Cuddly Dudley, as I privately called him, dropped by, bestowing on me his precious, personal copy of a Nina Simone LP record I had always loved, her early classic, *Nina Simone at Town Hall*. Heart pounding, I would lie on the floor, wailing along with Jan to such soulful songs as *Wild is the Wind*, dreaming of cuddling Dudley, I suppose.

Jan and I repeatedly played Nina's records, along with the early albums of Joan Baez and Bob Dylan. Their songs had a visceral, uplifting power. Jan's mum, sweet Auntie Stella, expressed concern as we crooned, always a little off-key, to such Nina laments as *Trouble in Mind*, one version of which goes, 'I wanna lay my head on some lonesome railroad track …and let the 2.19 train ease my trouble in mind…'. No wonder Stella worried about our wellbeing.

In 1964, while I was still in slow recovery mode, post-accident, post-Jimmy, Dudley invited me to visit his family property, miles away, near Goondiwindi in Western Queensland. Years before, at the age of about ten, I had avidly consumed Mary Grant Bruce's books set in the outback, lapping up *A Little Bush Maid* and *Nora of Billabong* in particular. Identifying with plucky Nora, I harboured fantasies about being a jillaroo, riding horses, and living a life of love and adventure out West.

Once physically on such a property, my childhood dreams were dented, if not shattered. While the family members were very warm and welcoming to me, I found myself setting off on a wild kangaroo shoot with Dudley, his brother Max, and some very blokey jackeroos.

This was their usual routine, the exact opposite of romantic, and, in retrospect, freakishly parallel to the graphic, bloody kangaroo hunt scene featuring an out-of-control Jack Thompson, in that iconic Australian film *Wake in Fright*. It would appear that this seventies film contains ongoing resonances for me, imaginatively, literally.

Jan, along with old friends from Brisbane and Ipswich, especially Polly, Vivienne, Helen E, Margaret, Sue M and Cheryl, were kind and generous, keeping me company during my long convalescence, from May 1963 through to early 1965. Meanwhile, Jan and I were thrilled to be given free tickets by one of Peter's kind old mates from *The Courier-Mail*, to the Beatles' live concert at Festival Hall. I think it was most probably Hugh Lunn who passed these on to us.

On that historic night, 29 June 1964, wishing to be super cool and sophisticated sitting in the Festival Hall area upstairs, above the fray, Jan grew more and more painfully embarrassed by my over-excitement at seeing the Four with their mop-tops and cheeky grins, especially John Lennon. For me, uninhibited primal screaming was just what the doctor ordered.

Occasionally that same year, we were lucky enough to borrow Jan's oldest brother, John's car. With Jan confidently at the wheel, we would take off, looking forward to a beach adventure, staying in a cheap motel in Surfers Paradise, usually right on the busy Pacific Highway.

We dashed to the beach in our togs (the Queensland word for bathing suits), lying on our beach towels, literally frying in the sun, our exposed white Anglo skin covered in a highly suspect concoction called Hawaiian Oil. We yearned for fashionably tanned bodies. No one ever mentioned skin cancer.

When we were little kids, Jan and I had bonded while sitting in the dark at her place, out the back on the dunny, screeching at the possible red back spiders, shivering at my scary stories, wiping our bums on carefully-trimmed newspaper. Later we squealed in delight, playing Murder in the Dark with our cousins.

Together we sobbed when Dad made us carry bricks for one of his endless projects, or when our brothers murdered our dolls, leaving them hanging by the neck on the clothes line under the house, bloodied with tomato sauce knife wounds, with real knives sticking out of them.

As we grew older, we would sit side by side, enraptured by those pictures flickering on the big screen at the Boomerang Picture Theatre. On holidays away, we mucked around together on Currumbin Beach, sometimes daring to peek at the lifesavers in the shower from a secret vantage point on Elephant Rock.

In our late teens, after a day on the beach at Surfers Paradise, with not a naked lifesaver in sight, we popped on our colourful 'mini' sun frocks, our bodies bathed, overly pink, peeling, shiny from the sun/humidity overdose. Hanging out, under age, in the Skyline Lounge bar in the Chevron Hotel, we shared our first 'orgasms' together – in the form of a barely drinkable cocktail called a Pink Elephant Orgasm.

Going to such drinking, dancing, smooching venues did present quite a downside for me. Falling over themselves to be with Jan, a veritable bloke magnet, young males would often recoil from me, rudely, bluntly saying 'Shit, what happened to you?' or 'Bloody hell! Did you run into a bus?'

At such times, I felt marked in the same way as the characters in such films as *Scarface*, and *A Woman's Face* are branded as repulsive and even downright evil. In the latter film, Joan Crawford plays a woman with a disfigured face: one side is beautiful, the other, grotesque. Even after plastic surgery, whenever the once damaged side of her face dominates her personality, she becomes an evil criminal.

I started to feel that I, too, was cursed forever. Criminality was not on my mind; just a pervasive feeling of being damaged, unworthy. Around July, 1964, amidst various social misadventures, I was relieved to meet John, a shy, nice-looking young man, who seemed neither to care about my facial scars, nor deem me to be in any way transgressive or unattractive.

However, as it turned out, he was yet another tortured soul with complex father issues. First Jimmy, then John; I seemed to be enacting some kind of futile rescuer pattern in my relationships. Not long after I started seeing John, he had to leave Brisbane, heading north to escape his bullying dad, a well-known, colourful Brisbane businessman at the time.

My health declined, I lost weight, suffering a kind of breakdown. Probably I had an undiagnosed form of post-traumatic stress disorder from the accident. Such a condition did not really 'exist', medically, at that time. It wasn't until after the Vietnam War, well into the seventies, that PTSD was named and acknowledged, although it was a difficult condition to diagnose and treat.

My doctors prescribed both uppers and downers, all freely available at that time: for instance, Ritalin as an upper and Pentabarb as a downer. I consumed strong barbiturates, such as Pethadene for pain. And I took Nembutal to put me to sleep. Looking at that cocktail now, I wonder how I ever survived.

On a brighter note, I was no longer singing from that defunct Jimmy songbook anymore. He disappeared into the ether. Many years later, I heard that my ex-sister-in-law's sister-in-law had run off with him. As usual, small-town Brisbane spared no-one. By then, I gather he had given up engineering, and was training bored housewives and others to fly planes.

Peter used to enjoy drinking with Jimmy's mate, Harvey Williams (of my parents' bedroom fame), meeting up occasionally in bars with him and Des Park, a dapper fellow party-goer. Des later married Kiri Te Kanawa. Sadly, no one seems to know what happened to Harvey, who was a true original.

In early 1965, I decided to challenge the specialist's bleak prognosis that, as my brain was irrevocably damaged, I would never be able to study again. Helped by some superficial facial surgery and a potent fistful of drugs, I commenced a fulltime Arts degree at the University of Queensland, spurred on by the seemingly flimsy hope that both my body and my brain could somehow function together in that fresh environment.

On 10 March 1965, Australia's Vietnam War commitment was escalating. The first birthday 'call up' lottery conscripted young nineteen-year-old men into the army. They weren't even old enough to vote. I headed out to the university campus at St. Lucia where the anti-war, pro-civil rights protest movements were on the rise. I had just turned twenty.

***

5.
LOVE AND OTHER CATASTROPHES

Back and forth to the university along that ill-fated riverside drive, I resisted both the threat and the lure of the sturdy, new telegraph post, calling to me, like a siren. Trying instead to focus on whatever the future may hold, I reclaimed my studies, along with my mind, within the imposing sandstone buildings of the University of Queensland.

It is difficult to find any Australian feature film concerned about the highs and lows of studying at university, apart from Emma-Kate Croghan's charming *Love and Other Catastrophes,* which tells a story of Melbourne share houses, university study and politics, self-discovery, sexuality, and even film studies, for good measure. It's been a long time between drinks on that filmmaking score.

Throughout my time at two single-sex secondary schools, I did not venture much outside the standard gendered box. As a girl who excelled in the arts rather than in the sciences, I was socialised into considering teaching or librarianship as the most suitable career paths open to me. No one ever suggested politics, the foreign service, or law, for instance; not that these options represented welcoming pathways for women in the sixties.

On my return to study, I tried to imagine a different career, separate from the stereotypical ones. I had nothing to lose. As I was on a Commonwealth Scholarship Grant for students who performed well in the Senior examination, I did not have to pay any university fees as a fulltime student.

However, given the ominous brain damage cloud hanging over me, I was still unsure as to whether I could even manage studying again. Trying to be optimistic, I thought I'd start by combining French with political science, in order to see if those subjects might head me towards a career as a diplomat in the foreign service, about which, admittedly, I knew very little.

In any case, such a possibility sounded more intriguing than law or teaching. Journalism was another possible pathway, although I didn't really wish to follow in my brother's footsteps. That career was largely a man's world, with women often only writing puff pieces on the social pages. I also knew, deep down, that I would always be compared to Peter, which was probably not good for either of us.

My dear, departed friend, Leith McNaught, sat beside me in our political science tutorial class, run by Ralph Summy, an American with a Harvard background, who had fought against the far-right politics of the McCarthy era, and the excessive nuclear militarism of Cold War America. Leith was a determined leftie, even though, or perhaps because, her parents had made great sacrifices to send her to the posh girls' school, Clayfield College, all the way across Brisbane from their working-class home in Moorooka.

She had a brilliant mind, and went on to specialise in the classics. Despite being very ill with a chronic kidney disease, she fulfilled her dream of living in Greece for a few years after graduating. Sadly, she died there in 1970, in her late twenties, just before my then husband Richard and I were about to visit her in Athens.

Before all this happened, back in early 1963, Leith and I worked together, briefly, at the Annerley Library. I am grateful to her for encouraging me to head back with her to the University, two years' late. We had both been delayed by medical dramas.

I enrolled in English, French, ancient history and Australian political science, while Leith took ancient history and Australian political science with me, along with her specialties, Latin and Greek. Film and media studies subjects did not even exist within the university's arts offerings in those days. I never even thought about pursuing a life in film academia, my ultimate career path, until well into the eighties.

For quite a sizeable chunk of time, 'Pol Sci' was concerned with the dramatic ALP/DLP split in the fifties, given that the Professor had written a rather dry book on that topic. The subject livened up with the lecture series on British politics by a lecturer from England, Philip Richardson, whose nickname, in some quarters, was 'Filthy Phil'. Leith and I were spellbound by him and his stirring lectures on radical Marxism, along with many political topics and perspectives that blew our minds.

We made sure we arrived early each week at the large lecture theatre, B 9, in the Main Building, so that we could sit up close to the podium. Latecomers had to find a place on the floor in those crowded rooms – the post-war baby boomer generation was arriving in force, and the old facilities were cracking at the seams. And no one wanted to miss Filthy Phil's entertaining lectures.

Outspoken and passionate, he sparked a palpable taste for revolution, along with a jaunty sexual frisson. With an impeccable upper-class English accent, this declared Marxist in a crumpled suit stirred our imaginations, our longing for understanding and change.

We were stimulated by his wordly embodiment of a class-based incongruity, reflected in his upper-class background, juxtaposed against his cutting ideological analysis of the British Westminster system, the repressive class structures, and the grinding scourge of capitalism. He performed his self-proclaimed radical role with a certain panache.

Over coffee one day, Leith and I discovered that pretty, long-haired Nikki from my English tutorial was having a wild affair with Filthy Phil. She fuelled our fantasies with tales of their sexual exploits, which often involved threesomes with another of his girlfriends.

As he usually looked dishevelled, overtired, even unwashed in class, Phil certainly lived up to his reputation. Somebody once suggested that his teeth had an odd greenish tinge, but I never got up close enough to him to check that particular detail. In any case, he was grunge personified, well before grunge became a thing. Those were heady times, and we relished inspiring, non-conformist academics. The more controversial, the better.

Our political science tutorial class, run by Ralph Summy [6] featured a swag of males who dominated proceedings, confidently arguing politics, history, ideology.[7] As first year progressed, I found myself in awe of those bright, vocal male students in that tutorial. They all shone in that discursive firmament, arguing political points confidently, effortlessly,

---

6. Ralph Summy was a dedicated civil liberties and anti-nuclear activist. He started the radical journal 'Social Alternatives', and was a world leader in peace and non-violence studies, working at UQ, and later at the University of Hawaii. We became close mates and comrades from the late seventies, until his sad death in 2018. His lovely wife Hilary mourns him, as do his children and grandchildren, and all who knew him.
7. Andrew Olle, Angus Innes, Drew Hutton, Brian Toohey were among the brightest and most vocal students in that Political Science class. Andrew and Brian became successful journalists; Angus, a barrister, led the State Liberal Party; Drew became a successful academic in history and education, a strong political activist and a leader of the Greens. I don't recall any outspoken young women in our class.

signalling their respective future successes in teaching, journalism, law, politics, academia and broadcasting.

While our tutor Ralph was open-minded, he also presented as quite intimidating, at first. On the one hand, we were excited by all the competing arguments, and, on the other, quite overwhelmed. Although Leith and I did all the reading and came to class well prepared, we rarely felt confident enough to express our own views. In the mid-sixties, it was still a man's world, no matter how liberal and open the discussion.

As I wasn't achieving very high marks in political science, I started to realise that a career path in politics or as a diplomat was probably not for me. In any case, even if I did succeed in obtaining a public service career in foreign affairs, I would have to resign if and when I became a married woman. This was decreed in order for misogynist normalcy to be restored, for the idealised nuclear family to thrive. Talented women had to make way for a male, who was deemed more suitable merely by virtue of his gender. At the time, such was the patriarchal logic, having nothing to do with merit, and everything to do with gender inequity and discrimination.

I began to realise that such blatant limitations regarding female equality of opportunity in the workplace were, self-evidently, worth fighting against. More and more, feminist ideas were beginning to frame my way of seeing the world and my own rather precarious future in it. Radical changes were needed in attitudes, values and legislation, at all levels of society. The personal was definitively political.

Nevertheless, I did see some light shining here and there along this tricky higher education tunnel. I relished the non-conformist academics, the more controversial, the more mind-expanding, the better, as far as I was concerned. I was striving to hold on, dealing with the repercussions of that severe head injury. I worked hard, slowly rising to the challenge, in fits and starts. For me, nothing rated as highly as the healing power of a brilliant lecture or a stimulating tutorial.

Critiques of political ideologies and establishment structures held me riveted, opening up a whole new way of thinking. Filthy Phil and Ralph were great influencers, as were other outspoken, committed radicals on campus, such as feisty Dan O'Neill, one of my lecturers in English, and the eloquent political philosopher, Peter Wertheim.

My conservative, middleclass values, underpinned by a rich seam of private school education, were being challenged and gradually ripped apart, largely through my University encounters, both in the political science class, and in the stirring public debates on campus.

I read widely, wrestling with many social justice issues I had formerly taken for granted. Most members of my family were quite conservative. Often hot current affairs and anti-war debates were both exhausted and exhausting at family gatherings. We could never agree on the basic assumptions from which to even begin an argument about the Vietnam war escalation, or about gender equality, both inflammatory issues at the time.

Giving me little credit for my intelligence, and my independent pursuit of enlightenment, people in my family simply mouthed what the reactionary media was saying on student protests, claiming that I had been 'brainwashed by those dreadful radicals on campus'. The usual blinkered assertions followed, putting a lid on any possibility of a productive, more nuanced discussion.

For years, they tried to bait me, especially around issues of feminism and women's rights, as did several of my friends' husbands in later life, brandishing their own patriarchal swords, sometimes supposedly in jest, but mostly with underlying, serious intent of cutting me to the quick. Ultimately all this became quite tiresome, although the educator in me still tried to rise to the occasion, hoping for a breakthrough, a move from stubborn denial to enlightened understanding.

As my first year progressed, I longed for a completely different form of stimulation. I needed to restore not only my mind, but my stalled social life as well. Unpacking my nearly two years of convalescence, I can see now, retrospectively, that I was a kind of *Girl, Interrupted*, recovering from trauma, stumbling around, often messing things up. Of course, I was never incarcerated in a psychiatric hospital as was the Winona Ryder character in that film, although the title itself has strong resonances for me. Films may captivate me from many different angles.

Whatever the consequences, I wanted to have some fun, and, clearly, old school virginity was a definite block to successfully fulfilling such an enterprise. The sexual revolution was unstoppable. As my facial scarring had faded a little, I no longer seemed to frighten people so much.

One of my new university friends, Maria O'Reilly, was much more sexually advanced than I was. I noticed that many girls from the Catholic schools, in particular, seemed to be busily shedding their inhibitions as soon as they arrived at university. Looking forward to orchestrating the virginity scoop of the year, Maria made it her mission to introduce me to a former lover of hers at an upcoming party.

Feeling that I looked rather fetching in my short navy-and-lime-green cotton frock, I was introduced to my blind date, bright-eyed Tim. Doing a double take, I stepped back, not because I found him repulsive; rather, the whole experience suddenly shifted onto a more disturbing level, at least from my point of view. Tim had a vivid, purple birthmark covering one side of his face.

At that moment, it dawned on me that, consciously or unconsciously, Maria was setting us both up, in the insensitive, tone-deaf hope that our shared disfigurements, rather than anything else, might make us compatible lovers.

At least, that was how I interpreted it. On another level, Tim and I had become two unwilling protagonists, stumbling through our lines in Maria's own clunkily directed scene from her version of *Clueless*, based on Jane Austen's novel, *Emma*. This timeless narrative resonates strongly now on a number of levels, given the pushiness of the central, misguided busy-body, whose match-making machinations fail, in the novel, in its many adaptations, and in our doomed 'real life' version. This was also *Love and Other Catastrophes*, writ large.

At roughly the same time, I was improvising off-script, as I had my eye on dashing Brian Wilbury from my English and ancient history classes. He was a journalist, trying to catch up on some uni study, full-time. Like me, he was also a mature-age student, a comforting fact, as so many of my peers were at least two years' younger than we were. Blond-haired Brian had a swashbuckling air about him, which I found appealing.

Despite Maria's efforts to steer me in Tim's direction, Brian and I started hanging out, on and off campus, half way through our first year. We would meet in and out of class, and during the week, we would say a fond farewell in the city centre, where we usually parted ways, heading off to our respective homes to study.

In the early evening, as I waited alone at dusk for the southbound tram on the corner of George and Queen Streets, a woman would sometimes come up very close beside me, and say: 'Move on, why don't ya? This is my corner!' I would promptly move to another tram stop, not wanting to cause any trouble.

In certain parts of Brisbane's inner city, just across the Brisbane River in South Brisbane, and in Fortitude Valley to the north, the nightlife could be very edgy. For decades, the police turned a blind eye to prostitution, graft, illegal gambling, drug-dealing and many other activities, especially as the criminal class paid them for such a service.

Week in, week out, often in the very early mornings, Dad would drive through Fortitude Valley after plotting meteorological patterns and predictions for pilots and their planes at Brisbane airport. He would pronounce on his arrival home that he had seen many scandalous sights, and that I should never, ever go to the Valley after dark. Such a warning certainly made the Valley sound very enticing, and naturally I tucked away this intriguing information for a later time.

I was living with my parents again in our fifties home, that old wild party house, in hilly Annerley. When I suffered a mysterious bout of measles for a few weeks during term time, Brian came to visit me in quarantine, hopping into my bed, holding me close, cheering me up. There was no such thing as social distancing in 1965. And both my parents were often out in the daytime.

At the end of our first year, fed up with fulltime study, Brian decided to resume work on a newspaper, this time far away in the Northern Territory. We had become lovers, and on the night he left, we embraced tearfully, with our corny signature song, The Seekers' hit *The Carnival is Over*, playing mournfully in the background. We corresponded intermittently and I enjoyed his warm, witty letters.

When I progressed into my second year, I was happy, yet nervous, to be invited to enrol in English honours. In the mid-sixties, the masculinist literary canon was followed religiously in English literature studies. This meant that we barely studied any acclaimed female writers, except for George Eliot and Jane Austen, who were considered part of the revered canon, although, at best, quite marginal figures. The Bronte sisters tended to be relegated to the final years of secondary English education.

Exciting, positive female role models in the flesh were also not easy to find. However, I vividly recall one particular woman lecturer in the English Department, Felicity Currie, who imprinted on me, in 1966, the need to be my own person. Felicity had moved from England, to Brisbane with her husband Malcolm, who was my esteemed French tutor and lecturer. Liberated in thought, manner, appearance, Felicity's stringy shoulder-length blond-brown hair, daring short skirts, and funky boots made quite an impact.

She taught rich units seemingly remote from the burning, 'trendy' issues of the day. Even so, I loved going on a deep dive into her subjects, embracing the literature of Anglo-Saxon English, Old Norse and Old Icelandic. Her feminist affect also sat very well with me, as my narrow world was expanding. And I excelled in her subjects.

As best I could on a tight budget, I started wearing slightly more stylish clothes, with Felicity as my role model. I played down my blue velvet pantsuit and tried other combinations. By then, women students and staff alike were openly defying the old-fashioned patriarchal regulations, shedding the rigid, repressive dress codes, for starters. That pantsuit had been bought under the new university rules that women could, finally, be allowed to wear long pants on campus, as long as they wore matching tops, with no deviation.

At least the pantsuit revolution heralded in a welcome change from the usual, stale 'feminine' look, of formal skirts, long-sleeved blouses, modest dresses, jackets, stockings. This shift symbolised a celebration of individual expression by women, not always approved by conservative women academics. Some of them could be more conservative, even more sexist than their male colleagues.

My friend Jeanne Scott loved wearing her liberating hot pink pantsuit, while another friend, Robyn Hargreaves, ever stylish in her pantsuit, was berated by an intolerant woman professor, harking back to the good old days: 'Whatever is the world coming to?' she snarled at Robyn, as if it was all her fault that women were becoming more liberated in thought, deed, and fashion.

Second Wave feminism was starting to have an impact on that university campus, after too many years of enforced modesty and moralism. Women were breaking away on many levels, although in the mid-sixties there was still a long way to go. I was learning that feminism was always about the nature of power, its lack, its imbalance.

In second year English literature, I surprised myself, and everyone else in that highly competitive, male-dominated honours class, by coming equal first with another quiet young woman, Margaret. Poetry was one of my passions. As my prize, I chose the complete works of the Irish poet, W. B. Yeats. In retrospect, it would seem as though I was overly influenced by the plethora of famous male writers I was studying. In my defence, I barely knew the names and works of female poets, nor did I know much about Australian writers, living or dead.

That legendary academic inspirer, Phil Richardson, eventually disappeared back to the 'Home Country'. About a decade ago, I heard, via several relatively reliable Brisbane grapevines, that he had transformed himself into quite a disgruntled Conservative. If this were true, I felt quite shocked and disillusioned.

One theory circulating was that he reverted to his class origins in order to inherit the family fortune, although no one could confirm what the real reason was. One can only speculate. In any case, it would seem, anecdotally, that the old Marxist spark had been extinguished.

My friend, Stephen Stockwell, now a retired professor, vividly recalls: 'I had my one and only epic encounter with Phil in a 1973 Modern Political Ideologies class. I was captivated by Phil's erudition and deep research in that mind-blowing guest lecture on the Kronstadt uprising, the Makhnovite revolt in the Ukraine and other left-wing opposition to the Bolsheviks after the 1917 Russian Revolution'.

This brief experience was pivotal in helping change Stephen's life path and philosophical orientation. For many of us, Phil ignited an enduring fire in our hearts, minds and bellies, despite what changes in later life may have occurred regarding his own world view.

Towards the end of my second year, after having been incommunicado for quite a while, Brian unexpectedly swooped back into Brisbane, from the even deeper north. Apart from working as a reporter in Darwin, he had done a stint down a mine near Tennant Creek. Communicating from there had been difficult, apparently.

Before we had a proper chance to speak, Brian blurted out a proposal, proclaiming: 'You're cleverer than I am, Helen, but I still want to marry you' – a rather strange way to frame a declaration of undying love. His timing was also impossible, as I was about to become engaged to someone else whom I had met during that monumental year of 1966. Gathering myself together, I gently explained to Brian my current relationship with Richard Yeates.

***

Helen 11 months, 1946

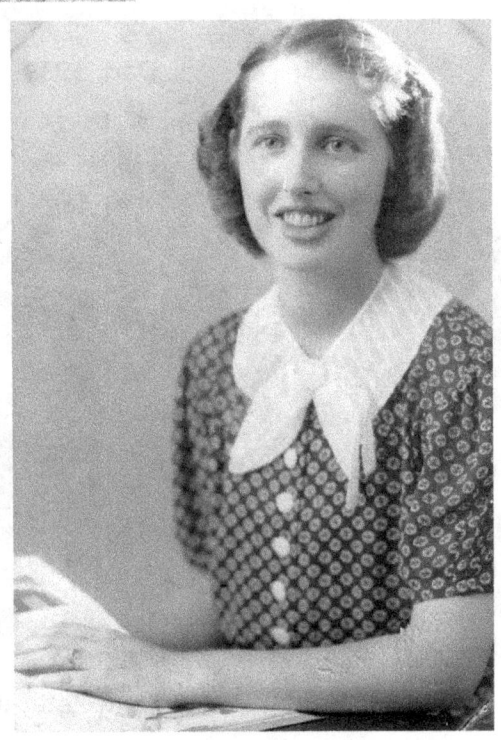

Mum, 1939

Dad, 1939

Helen, Jocelyn and Peter in Moorooka

Helen and Polly at the Exhibition, 1958

Boomerang Theatre, Annerley

Helen's first day at Grammar, 1959

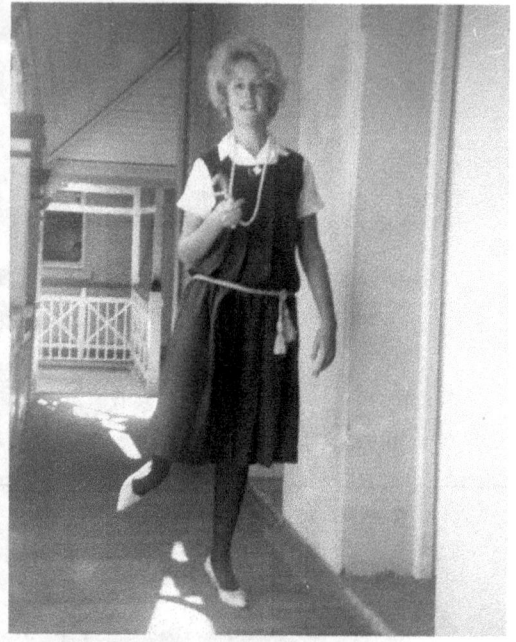

Cheryl dressing up at IGGS, 1962

The gutter gang, BGGS, 1960

Helen and Dudley,
Annerley, 1962

Helen (19) and Jan (18),
Gold Coast, Easter 1964

Helen's 21st birthday

Easter Bride, March, 1967

Helen and the bridesmaids, Jan and Pauline

Helen with English class, St Peters, 1969

Helen in Venice, 1970

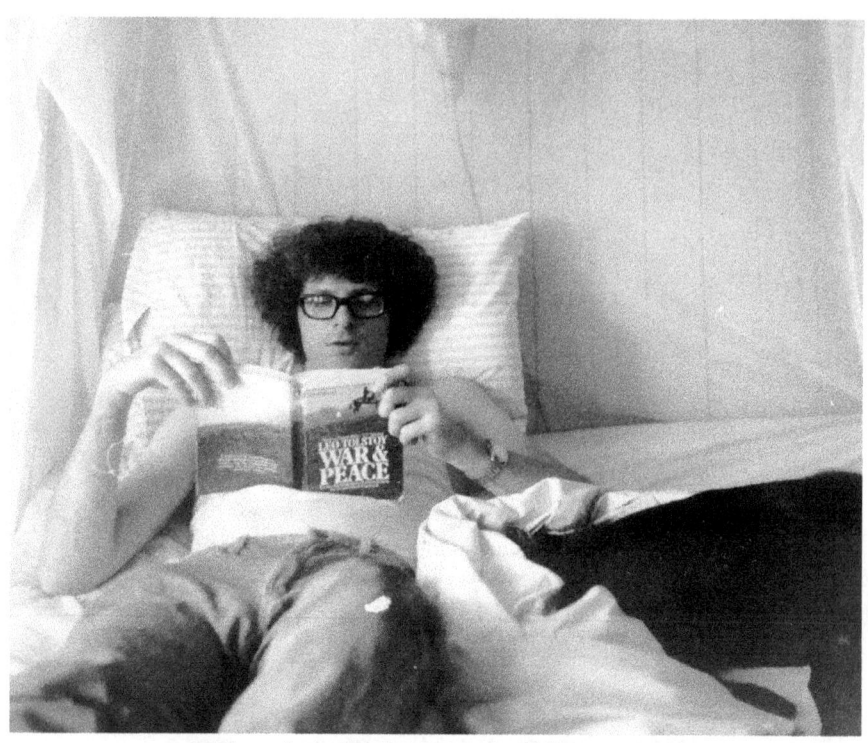
Richard and Oliver on holidays, 1974

Charlie and Chloe on the bed

My nieces Diane, Margaret, Elizabeth, Jennifer (front), early 70s

Directing The Importance of Being Earnest at IGGS, 1972

Richard becoming a vege gardener, 1976

Ron holidaying in Byron, 1978

Pierre and Janetta, Sydney, early 80s

Stephanie and Peter, London, Christmas 1981

With old school friends - Helen E., Vivienne with baby Jane and Margaret, early 80s

Cossack Peter and Savannah Susan, early 80s

Helen and Jenny Wren, early 90s

Dennis and Gerry, 1983

Brian Williams (QFC), Helen & Dan Petrie (Hollywood filmmaker), 1985

Richard Lowenstein, 1985

Fridge in Rainworth home, 1987

Helen in a boob tube, Rainworth party, 1984

Helen and Susie, Rainworth, 80s

Ann and Pam, ATOM conference, 1988

Graham and Helen, Brisbane, 1989

Ian in Bloomsbury, London, 1993

6.
SCENES FROM A MARRIAGE

While Brian was living far away during my second year, Richard Yeates and his friend Roger Stuart turned up in the university refectory, seeking to join a group of dedicated, activist students who regularly discussed, over coffee, the significant issues of the day, spurred on by the latest media reports and the radical on-campus speeches.

I met each week with group members such as Leith, Sam, Nick, Chris and others, discussing the latest political dramas, both state and federal, and planning the best kind of strategic action to help bring about progressive social and political change. Youth culture was on the move, rebelling against repressive ideas and controls, and we were seriously committed. [8]

Richard, this attractive, cheery, curly-haired newcomer to that protest discussion group, was majoring in history and politics, later adding Russian language into the mix. Over the following weeks and then months, we met many times, with Richard telling me that he had grown up in the country town of Boonah, where his recently deceased father had been the local doctor.

Following in his older brothers' footsteps, Richard was sent as a boarder at the Church of England Boys' School, 'Churchie'. He had hated being there, unlike his brothers, Bruce and David, who thrived, going on to study medicine.

---

8. This ferment was embodied in the burgeoning protest movement at UQ, regarding, for instance, the Vietnam War and the vicious repression in Queensland under the National Party governments of Frank Nicklin (1957 – 1968), and the notorious Dr. Sir Johannes Bjelke-Petersen, later, from 1968 to 1987. This Party governed via an outrageous gerrymander, which, if it had not been so serious in its consequences, would have been laughable. Their track record on civil rights was appalling, and continued to be so, over many dark years for those of us who didn't head south and abandon Queensland as a lost cause.

After school, Richard worked in a bank for a while. Then he won an Ansett Airlines scholarship in a bid to become a pilot. Sadly, his eyesight deteriorated, and his flying dreams turned to dust. Hence, four years out of school, as yet another mature-age student, he headed to St. Lucia to study in an entirely new field. Thanks to a mutual passion for civil disobedience and coffee, our paths crossed. The sexual attraction was intense, and unstoppable.

Luckily for us, political protest and the sexual revolution co-existed. After nearly six unruly, passionate months, juggling our studies and trying to see each other often, Richard and I decided that, crazy as it may seem, marriage was the only possible solution to our mutual desire to be full-on loving partners. Living separately was no longer a viable option, and neither his widowed mother, Charlotte, nor my parents, Arthur and Margaret, approved our desire to 'live in sin' together.

His old school friend, Roger was the only admirably advanced person we knew who was cool enough to live then with a female partner in unmarried bliss. We were not able to embrace a similar kind of freedom. As full-time students, we relied heavily on our respective families' generous support.

Loving Bob Dylan, we believed that the 'the times' definitely were 'a-changin' in our favour, on so many levels. However, we also knew that certain family considerations had to be respected. At the very end of 1966, we became formally engaged, a couple of weeks after I refused Brian's ill-timed, shambolic proposal.

I proudly wore the delicate diamond ring I'd inherited from dear Auntie Ida, one of Mum's ten older sisters. We planned to marry at Easter the following year, when we would both still be full-time students. The main reason we pushed for an early wedding was that our love and passion for each other was irrepressible.

I tried to explain our relationship to Arthur, my dad, describing us as a modern Romeo and Juliet. As an honours student of English literature, I should have realised that tragic analogy was entirely inappropriate. Nevertheless, dramatic secrets thrived and risks were taken. We were constantly in danger of being sprung making love in my bedroom at home. Attempting to be intimate in Richard's sister Diana's very small Beetle VW was even more hazard-ridden. For starters, Richard was over six feet tall and his long legs protruded through the window.

To earn some cash, Richard spent the long break in January and early February, 1967, working on a smelly leaky trawler, harvesting prawns, a gruelling experience, but all in a good cause. I did some high school student tutoring, quite successfully. I also applied to be a cleaner at a local motel. The owner of that motel took one look at me and said a resounding 'No', for which I am eternally grateful.

Slaving away at the notorious Golden Circle Pineapple Factory in Northgate was also not an option for me. Many poor university students nearly broke their backs and their spirits, working there through the breaks. I simply did not have the stamina. Overall, choices were then very limited for uni students in the casual employment world.

Our nuptials were booked to take place at the grand St John's Cathedral on Easter Saturday, 1967, in my third year, and Richard's second year. While neither Richard nor I followed the Anglican faith any longer, we figured we might as well have all the ceremonial trimmings of a cathedral wedding, including the organ's soaring riffs and the angelic tones of the choir boys, singing Bach's haunting piece, *Jesu, Joy of Man's Desiring*.

Richard had served his time as a boarder at the Anglican Church Grammar School, while I had earned my stripes in my early teens, playing the organ for Evensong at the Yeronga Anglican Church, with the minister standing far too close behind me while I practised.

The bridesmaids, my cousin Jan Hodsdon, and Richard's sister Pauline Yeates, looked splendid in dusky, midnight blue, while the best man Roger Stuart and the groomsman Brian Harris spruced up very nicely. I was just twenty-two, and Richard was twenty-four years old. Based on a photograph I'd cut out of a fashion magazine, my supposedly nouveau chic wedding dress turned into a shattered dream, a veritable nightmare.

The dressmaker I employed to make this French-inspired garment had a nervous breakdown in the week leading up to Easter and simply could not finish the gown on time. She said she 'might be able to finish it next week', which was, of course, a week too late. Shedding many a tear in disbelief, I picked up this unfinished debacle late on Easter Thursday.

My mother Margaret and I panicked, as neither of us could sew to save our lives. A friend helped, and some rather clumsy tacking stitches somehow kept the whole back seam and other pieces together. Fortunately, the uneven back of the dress was disguised by my veil which stretched in a small train behind me. Miraculously, this seemingly cursed dress did not fall apart on the day.

Richard and I spent a complimentary night in the honeymoon suite at Lennon's Hotel in the city after a pleasant little reception there. On Easter Sunday, we moved into our small one-bedroomed flat at the back of a converted old wooden Queenslander house, perched on top of a leafy hill in Toowong, conveniently close to the university.

On that Easter wedding weekend, the centre-spread of the Women's pages in the *Sunday Mail* newspaper declared that I had been the Most Modern Bride of the day, with a lavish photograph of a windswept me, alighting from a sleek limo near the Cathedral steps. In the annual Easter Bride competition, I was awarded second prize of $30, a very handy sum for newlyweds with barely a cent between them.

Rumour had it that I was probably ineligible to win because my brother had once worked for that newspaper. Nevertheless, it seemed that the sub-editor decided that the photograph of me in that bespoke modern dress, should feature quite prominently, along with a picture of the more traditionally-garbed winner. And no one in the media or at the wedding noticed that my gown was in danger of falling to pieces.

After putting our wedding presents to good use, we enjoyed developing our own little domestic rituals. Noticing that we would set the table at night for our breakfast the following day, Roger once teased us, saying: 'Why don't you have breakfast now and save yourselves time in the morning?' It was almost as though Richard and I were playing house, discovering our own ways of being co-habiting adults.

One early problem was that I was suffering from that common bridal affliction, honeymoon cystitis, not exactly an auspicious start to a marriage supposedly made in heaven. Furthermore, in the middle of the third night, things turned seriously unpleasant, when we woke up to find ourselves drenched in a foul-smelling liquid.

Hearing thumping and scratching noises overhead, we realised there was a lodger in the ceiling: a wild possum, in the very act of pissing on us. Frantically washing ourselves and changing the sheets and pillow cases, we arranged a couple of umbrellas to shield us from any further desecration. There was no point in moving the bed – the possum had a free run of the entire ceiling.

In those first few weeks of spending whole nights together, I also discovered that Richard had vivid nightmares, and sometimes sleep-walked. I had been told about his sleep-walking antics as a child, but I certainly did not expect both those and the nightmares to recur so regularly, and, in the latter case, with so much ferocity.

Occasionally I would wake in fright, with Richard crying out, eyes vacant, practically strangling me, his hands firmly around my neck. Somehow, I managed to wake him, and escape, just in time. It seemed that the nightmares arose out of his fears of being conscripted for the Vietnam War, and in those dreams, he was fighting an unseen enemy. He probably needed some kind of calming therapy, but that wasn't readily available in those days.

Cystitis, a shambolic wedding dress, a pissing possum, and nearly being strangled in my sleep; these were not the most promising omens for a life of marital bliss. Despite such signs, we nurtured a common dream to be free of the conventional 'ties that bind'. Not wishing to ossify as a standard suburban nuclear family, we saw ourselves as very much in the moment, on a number of levels.

For instance, we applauded the Zero Population Growth recommendation to plan for only two children to replace ourselves on earth. This movement had strong links to environmentalism and feminism. Over the years, we tried to reverse the trend set by two of Richard's siblings who reproduced six children each. Being in harmony together on the political front, we also adopted other radical causes, remaining committed to the ongoing action for civil liberties in Queensland, the anti-apartheid movement and the peace/anti-war movement.

While we would join in the protests, we were never centre-stage. I was concerned about being bashed, manhandled and arrested. When the police viciously attacked the marchers, we would mingle with the watching crowd on the side, for safety's sake. In my defence, I was still not at all physically robust, and Richard was looking after my welfare. Admiring the brave souls who defied the violent police, ending up in a cell, we supported them with donations towards their copious fines.

Towards the end of the first year of our marriage, a disruptive, upsetting situation occurred in the English honours cocoon at the university, where I was in the throes of completing my third honours year. The glowing Felicity Currie and her husband Malcolm abruptly headed back to England, never to return.

Malcolm had embodied another breath of fresh air at the university, teaching me French language and literature for my first two years. Thanks to his kind encouragement, I could read seventeenth century French texts in the original, without having to translate. While losing him on campus reverberated quite profoundly for me, my cherished high hopes of continuing a close academic relationship with Felicity, by being supervised by her in my fourth year of English honours, were totally dashed. I was inconsolable.

Felicity and a male student engaged, for a time, in a steamy affair, which we all knew about. They were caught 'in flagrante' by Malcolm, who came home early from one of his night classes. I cannot help but blame that swaggering student for helping to bring about such calamity and personal loss, along with academic disruption for many students, myself amongst them.

She had been a unique gift. I regret that I never contacted her and Malcolm years later at the University of Warwick, where they worked for a time. I always hesitated, thinking they might not want to be reminded of their ill-fated time in Brisbane.

I finished my undergraduate arts degree at the end of 1967. Because I was already a married woman, I found that, in 1968, I was ineligible for a scholarship to study a Diploma of Education in Queensland. This was the first tangible discrimination on the basis of gender that I had personally encountered in my life. On the other hand, I was grateful to be awarded a University of Queensland honours scholarship, which, sadly, I had to turn down. While this small stipend may have helped sustain me, to an extent, it certainly was not sufficient for the two of us to live on.

Not only was Felicity Currie no longer teaching at UQ, but also our financial circumstances meant that I urgently needed to seek a fulltime job in a private school, where teacher training was not, at that stage, a compulsory requirement. Teachers' wages had only just become equal for males and females in Queensland, and I remember thinking how unjust the laws had been until then, as the work load was so obviously equivalent.

I was appointed as an English and ancient history teacher at St. Peter's Lutheran College, commencing in late January, 1968. As the first non-Lutheran staff-member at this very religious private school, I broke with tradition on a number of levels. I did not always see eye to eye with some of the entrenched, chauvinistic male staff, who disapproved of the cut of my jib — that is, my left-wing political views, the way I looked and dressed, my atheism.

I was also directed not to teach the early section of the ancient history syllabus, concerning Neanderthal/Neolithic man, as that era was too problematic from a fundamental religious perspective. Up until then, I had never known that ancient history itself could be so controversial.

Thankfully, the principal, Bill Lowe, backed me over my two years working there, as much as he could. Calling me into his office one day, he awkwardly explained that parents of the boys in my Senior English class complained that my skirts were 'far too distracting for their sons', especially for those seated in the front row. Their results in English were slipping.

I replied that the boys were making up excuses for their laziness. Because of their over-involvement in sport (many of them were in the top football teams) they were often tired and ill-prepared in class, resulting in poor concentration and low marks. I further ventured that I was possibly setting a higher standard than their previous teacher had. Finally, to cap it all off, I pointed out that, as I could not sew at all, I was unable to take those offending hems down. He accepted my explanation, and nothing further was ever said on that topic.

In my second year at the school, certain people also frowned on my growing support for the students' wishes to organise dances, and for their demands to have much better meals served in the boarding school dining room. St Peter's was a strong boarding school then, with many of the students coming from Papua New Guinea and other outlying Lutheran Missions, well away from Brisbane. I knew only too well how hard distance and alienation could be for a boarder. And the food there was unspeakably bad.

In 1969, the Supreme Court case concerning my damages claim against Jimmy's dad's insurance company drew to a close. Another lovable cousin, Graham 'Diddley' Heiner, was my solicitor, although I forget who the barrister was. That same afternoon, the front-page headline in the Brisbane Telegraph newspaper blared: BRILLIANT TEACHER WITH BRAIN DAMAGE. I was named and, I felt, shamed.

My facial scarring was described in gruesome detail, as well as my long-term, permanent brain injury, proven in the court, despite the dismissive argument from the lawyers for the insurance company, particularly in relation to my high marks at university. I was anxious that, after reading this sensationalised news story, some St Peter's parents might complain to Mr Lowe about their precious girls and boys being taught by such an afflicted person.

Not a word was ever spoken. This eerie silence meant only one of two things: that all staff and parents were very considerate, or that no one connected with that conservative school would ever risk being seen buying that shabby afternoon tabloid. In any case, I was planning to leave at the end of that year.

While it was sad saying farewell to my students and some of my colleagues, I was pleased to be heading overseas, thanks, in large part, to the generous insurance money settlement I had received for my pain and suffering. Like many Australians, before and since, we dreamt of travelling to the UK and Europe for a significant rite-of-passage adventure. Back then, Anglo-Saxon Australians still saw Britain as the mother country.

The night before we sailed out of Sydney Harbour on the *Fairsky* cruise liner, we took my parents to see the musical *Hair*, an eye-opener for all, especially when the semi-naked, mischievous performer, Reg Livermore, leapt off the stage to sit on my lap while he serenaded everyone. Although they enjoyed themselves, Margaret and Arthur were quite overwhelmed. Richard and I felt happily in tune with this psychedelic, anti-war, anti-establishment show, an exhilarating kickstart to our delayed honeymoon.

As a result of the Six-Day War with Israel, Egypt had closed the Suez Canal. On New Year's Day 1970 the *Fairsky* streamed through the Sydney Heads en route to Britain, the long way round. This one-class, Italian-styled, turbine steamship was charted to go via Tahiti, then to Panama City, through the Panama Canal, across the Atlantic Ocean to Lisbon, and from there to Southampton, England. We planned to disembark in Lisbon, head overland by train to Madrid, and on to Paris, enjoying time in each city on the way, before arriving at our ultimate destination, London.

Nearly five weeks at sea was not the uplifting experience we had anticipated. To our great discomfort, we were stuck for every meal at the same dining table with two boring middle-aged sisters from the Midlands.

It was fortunate that polite conversation soon dried up because one sister actually spat out bits of her food whenever she spoke. For us, this random misfortune represented a deeply unlucky draw.

No matter how much we pleaded with the dining staff, we were not allowed to move timeslots or change the seating arrangement for the whole trip. To make matters worse, the food was very ordinary, as was the grindingly shallow, poorly organised entertainment. On the other hand, the immensity of the ocean renewed my respect for our ancestors who had travelled from Ireland, England, Scotland and Wales to the Australian shores in the nineteenth century. We were literally going 'over seas'.

In Papeete, Tahiti, our longed-for first stop, we nearly crossed the road to our deaths. Still on shaky sea legs, Richard and I momentarily forgot that the traffic there drove on the right-hand side. After that near miss, we hired a little plane and flew to scenic Moorea, or Magical Island, for an escapist lunch, restoring some romance to this, our delayed honeymoon.

Once in Europe, on dry land, our time in quaint Lisbon was very welcome. However, we weren't experienced tourists and, on our first night out, we forgot the name and location of the hotel we were staying in. The taxi driver gradually worked out which hotel, after much embarrassing driving around in circles.

The next evening, we went to a traditional Fado folk restaurant, where we enjoyed sampling ethnic food, local wine, live music and dancing. Most of the other customers at that café were male. Richard and I danced to the music, smiling and enjoying ourselves, while others clapped. The night took an unexpected turn when some of the men asked me to dance. This was fun, for a while.

However, the pressure became too intense, and everything started to turn ugly when I refused yet another stranger's advances, his excessive touching, and being passed from male to male. We were out of our cultural depth, and the atmosphere had changed from welcoming to threatening. We signalled to the waiter that we wanted to leave.

Later we discovered that a woman seen with a man in certain situations after dark, was usually deemed to be a prostitute, and therefore fair game. No respectable woman would ever be out carousing at night. Luckily, we remembered the name and address of our hotel that particular evening.

Another disconcerting custom for us gormless Australians was that Portuguese people regularly, randomly, spat in public on the cobblestoned pavements. One vivid recollection I can never unsee, is of a well-dressed middle-aged woman walking in front of us, suddenly clearing her throat very loudly, then emitting a large globule of phlegm onto the footpath in front of her. She walked on calmly, as if nothing had happened.

While we had read up on Portugal and Lisbon in the standard travel books, we realised that we needed to be more sophisticated, more knowledgeable of the culture and history, much better prepared. Before we moved on, we did enjoy driving to the coast, experiencing how beautiful the mountain villages and coastal towns were. And we liked drinking one of our favourites, the Mateus Rose wine, in its country of origin.

Madrid, our next stop in Europe, was all about exploring the art treasures within the Prado, as well as the delicious yet unaccustomed Spanish cuisine. Following in Ernest Hemingway's path, we turned up to a bullfight outside Madrid, where we encountered the violence, the cruelty, the sweat, the strutting masculinity on display, along with the thunderous shouting and stamping of the crowd.

We thought we would be better prepared for such a cultural spectacle in the flesh, having read books, and seen bullfights portrayed in films. But we were still just tourists, wet behind the ears, deeply affected by the cruel machismo on display.

By contrast, beautiful Paris was an enchanting mecca, seemingly created for us. We felt more urbane there, more in control, at least in our imaginations. From the first breathtaking moment when we arrived on a chilly winter's day, I experienced a kind of catharsis. I felt that my dreams had come true, and I was home at last.

Later that year, I experienced the same transformative coming home feeling in Delphi, Greece. Most probably I was being overly romantic regarding places I felt I already knew so well from my years of studying French and ancient history. I gather other travellers might similarly discover that same gut/spiritual feeling, when they imagine they have found their lost soul 'home', wherever that may be.

Regrettably, my everyday French vocabulary was limited, very disillusioning when it came to imagining a viable life in Paris. While at school and university, I could read French newspapers and literature comfortably. However, the oral, idiomatic side of the language defeated me. Sadly, I could never realise my goal of having vibrant, life-changing conversations with French writers and philosophers at cafés such as Les Deux Magots or the Café de Flore on the Left Bank of the Seine.

Arriving in cloudy London in late February, it was great to catch up with some old friends, Kathy Stuart, Roger's younger sister, and Helen McNeil, sister of another of Richard's boarding school mates, Rodney. Regrettably, Peter and Stephanie, my brother and sister-in-law had just moved from London back to Melbourne for a while, and our paths did not cross.

We rented a tiny flat with dubious plumbing above a shabby Indian restaurant, not far from the posh Belgravia end of Sloane Square, Chelsea. We didn't really mind the aroma of Indian spices wafting into our living space, and we often treated the place as our own dining room. The King's Road, the epicentre of Swinging London, was on our doorstep. This was the Age of Aquarius and we believed the promises: peace would guide the planets and love would steer the stars.

Our grand plan was that we would travel as much as we could and, if we found jobs we liked, we might stay longer than a year. There was one warning signal: salaries in England were pitifully low compared to those in Australia in the early seventies. On the work front, things started to go downhill very quickly, and not just because of the wages. Richard loathed the job he landed in an international bank, where he was directed to manage the offshore accounts of such exclusive clients as the Vatican.

Many of these clients had massive amounts of money stashed away in tax havens such as Panama City. On our way across the seas we had witnessed, first-hand, the appalling poverty and rotting slums in that city, noting, with churning stomachs, the stark divide between the elite, super wealthy and the oppressed, desolate masses.

When we asked the taxi driver showing us around that city, 'Who actually lives in those luxury homes overlooking the water?' he replied, 'Thieves!' That said it all. Very soon, it became impossible for Richard to stay in that job, supporting the obscenely rich from behind that complicit desk.

My own search for employment also failed, even more dismally. Jill Henry, a Queensland teacher we knew, was appointed to a very poorly resourced area in East London, where at least one staff member a week was seriously hurt in a knife attack. Many Australian teachers were sent to the East End or other challenging London districts, straight off the boat, so to speak.

On day one, Jill's Aussie accent and her Queensland vocabulary caused an unholy riot, when she said to a huge class of restless fourteen-year-olds: 'Please open your *ports* and take out your *pads*'. Such an instruction did not translate at all well in the East End. If she had said, 'Please open your *school bags* and take out your *workbooks*', she might have kept them in check, but the damage was done. The class fell about laughing and hooting uncontrollably. To them, ports meant something else entirely to them, in the boating sphere, while the only pads they knew were sanitary ones.

Whatever happened, I had no desire to experience similar humiliation. Instead, I tried to earn some money as a 'temp' office clerk, managing only one full day's paid work. I was summarily dismissed for being far too slow, even though it seemed that I had been quite thorough. That was certainly not my dream career path, it would seem.

For the next six months we drove around Europe and the UK in our dark green Morris Minor, Millie, staying at camping sites, or the occasional bed and breakfast establishment, especially in the UK. The most unnerving part of the trip occurred in Greece. Our dear friend from uni days, Leith, died just before we arrived. Furthermore, having seen the radical film, *Z*, we understood some of the background history of the Junta which controlled Greece with an iron fist.

Our eyes were opened even more by the day-to-day reality of the absolute power of the Junta. The cradle of democracy was indeed no longer free. With our long hair and casual, hippy-style clothing, we attracted the attention of the authorities, but our presence was tolerated. We were tourists and the regime needed foreign currency.

We travelled extensively through France, Italy, Greece, the former Yugoslavia, Switzerland, Germany, Denmark, England, Scotland and Wales. Back in London, we found a new home in Kensington. We lived and breathed London's theatre, film, art galleries, pubs, restaurants, people-watching, shopping – the whole cultural package from the King's Road to Carnaby Street. I also bought some gorgeous outfits at Barbara Hulanicki's Biba store in Kensington Church Street.

Our second apartment in Marloes Road, Kensington, was more upmarket than the first one. Just before midday on the eighteenth of September, we peered out of the front windows after hearing frantic sirens and seeing an ambulance screech into the emergency entrance of St Mary Abbot's Hospital a few doors down the road.

Jimi Hendrix had been rushed from the Samarkand Hotel in Notting Hill, but he had stopped breathing and was declared dead at 12.45 pm. The official version was that he died choking on his own vomit after an overdose of barbiturates, although there are many theories still circulating around the actual cause and the controversial circumstances of his death. At twenty-seven, he was the same age as Richard, and just two years older than I was.[9]

Life became more tenuous after that. And more precious. On this extended holiday, I had tried to go cold turkey on my own prescription drug addiction, with some degree of success. Hooked on certain tablets prescribed for headaches, mood swings and insomnia ever since the car accident back in 1963, I was suffering negative consequences in relation to my ongoing health. Our relationship was also impacted by my desperate need to sleep, and I wanted to put that right.

Wishing to settle into a more normal, anti-dependant lifestyle, I managed to relinquish quite a strong cocktail of drugs, including the sleeping pills Mogadon and Nembutal. Both of these drugs were readily available then, while now they are used with great caution, if at all. For some, Nembutal forms part of a euthanasia cocktail – a sobering thought, given how many I was taking. Sometimes, however, I wish I still had some stored away in a closeted stash, just in case…

We travelled home to Australia by air, via Paris, New Delhi and Singapore. Our final visit (our third) to Paris was tinged with nostalgia. Richard and I idealised the writer/philosophers, Jean-Paul Sartre and Simone de Beauvoir. For many years, they lived in separate rooms in the same Left Bank hotel in Paris, meeting daily at Les Deux Magots with an entourage of friends and writers including Albert Camus, robustly discussing philosophy and the burning issues of the day. They were

---

9. The so-called '27 Club' comprises famous musicians who tragically met their untimely deaths at age 27: Jim Morrison, Janis Joplin, Brian Jones, Jimi Hendrix, Kurt Cobain and Amy Whitehouse. A grim series of coincidences…

actively, passionately bound together, but never lived domestically in a conventional, monogamous way.

Over the years, I read most of Simone's books as well as many of Jean-Paul's existentialist works. I especially admired her autobiographies, and the ground-breaking book *The Second Sex*, empathising with her early feminist version of male-female relations under patriarchy. The imbalance of gender and sexual power on so many societal levels resulted in inequities that hurt most women, including herself, personally and professionally. However, despite a great deal of hurt, she did stay with Sartre, leaving another lover to be with him at the end of his life in 1980. They were a hard act to follow.

In late 1970, we returned to Brisbane. The following year, drawing on more of my accident money, we purchased a pleasant home on a quiet cul-de-sac in a leafy suburb. Of course, nowhere in this city could match the cosmopolitan lifestyle, the hotels, the restaurants, of the Left Bank or the Marais. While I embraced many aspects of the sexual revolution, I still resisted the idea of living separately but together, à la Sartre and Beauvoir.

The pressure mounted. I did not wish to indulge in an open relationship with multiple partners. I loved Richard and that was enough. Fidelity, love and trust still meant everything to me, old-fashioned though that view may have been, according to some alternative views at the time.

After Richard and I had travelled freely for most of 1970, I was pleased to be appointed, on our return, as a teacher of English and French at my old boarding school, Ipswich Girls' Grammar, thanks to the encouragement of Thalia Kennedy and Dorothy Marsden, two of my teaching heroes and mentors.

Along with Alison Goleby, Joan Benson and Deirdre Brown, these women seemed almost immortal, like characters from the film, *The Prime of Miss Jean Brodie*. Or perhaps they needed a different film, to be made purely about them. We always imagined that their lovers had died in the Second World War, a fate that many single women suffered in both world wars.

Travelling up and down to Ipswich each day had its disadvantages, although it could be fun, share-driving with friends such as Lilias Rush and Richard's sister, Pauline Smith. Happily, Pauline worked there as the librarian, and on many a late afternoon, we went 'play shopping' at the shiny new Indooroopilly Shopping Town on our way home.

In 1972, Richard and I had found our black puppy, Oliver, at the RSPCA, going there with Pauline, who adopted her own puppy, Spot, on the same day. We employed one of my former students, Tony, from St Peter's College, to come and 'dogsit' the two puppies together, while we were out at work.

A couple of years later, we rushed Oliver to the Vet, as he had a nasty tick bite, very hard to remove. The vet asked us, casually, if we would like to adopt twin ginger kittens. We were captivated by the way the vet's dog, a huge German Shepherd, was licking and caring for these tiny balls of fur. Falling for the vet's spin, we took them both home a few weeks later.

Oliver was not at all impressed. We had foolishly hoped he would cherish them, just as that vet's dog had. Instead, many a territorial skirmish broke out between him and the cats, until a kind of uneasy truce was eventually called. Today I guess these three pets would be called our fur babies, substituting for real babies. They were our family.

In Ipswich, I enjoyed teaching English throughout the school, and French in the lower school with the easy-going Lorraine Mansfield and Dorothy Marsden. Bright-eyed Janetta Hargreaves and Susie Scott were in my Junior class when I first arrived. For the next two years, I taught Janetta through to Senior, and she and that arts-strand class were a joy to teach. For the last two years, Susie was in the science/maths strand.

Those were heady times of educational change and student activism. The external Senior exam had also been disbanded by then in Queensland, with internal assessment brought in, a more enlightened system. After much discussion, in 1973, the school management agreed to abandon the old hierarchical prefect system, and bring in a democratically elected school council system. I admired and encouraged the girls' independent decisions, as they made changes to the way students actively took on responsibilities, wrestling with decisions within the school.

During the time I taught at IGGS, I was juggling teaching out-of-town, studying a Bachelor of Education Studies degree at night at the University of Queensland, enjoying my leisure time with friends and family, and, at the same time, being deeply committed to married life.

By the end of 1974, I left IGGS, taking timeout in 1975 to complete my education degree fulltime, and indulge myself by taking a fine arts unit as well.

Run by the legendary Nancy Underhill, that Fine Arts in the Renaissance subject was a total gift. I was in heaven, discovering that I had a hitherto unknown aptitude for art history, and a strong visual sense that had never been nurtured before. It was the latter in particular that helped me find, a decade later, both my eye and my voice in the burgeoning world of film and media studies.

Richard and I had a deal that we would give each other time out, usually a year without working, to follow our dreams, our career aspirations, whatever. This was my turn. We had both shared the time off work, travelling, in 1970. Richard's second individual stint (his first had been in 1968) came in 1976, when he enrolled fulltime in a Graduate Diploma in Librarianship, while I began teaching at the University of Queensland in the Education Faculty.

He had been employed at the state library since our return from overseas, a job he liked, and he had ambitions to be a well-qualified research librarian. This was a career opportunity, much more promising than the job he had endured as a public servant, back in 1969. As an employee in the Federal Department of Social Services, he was instructed to work hard to find people receiving overpayments in their pensions or unemployment benefits. Anybody who did discover an overpayment would be called out and applauded, which was quite sickening. Of course, this is reminiscent of more recent persecution horror stories under Scott Morrison, with the Robodebt scandal.

Even though giving each other time off from working was a deep, abiding commitment, the pressure for a more open marriage became an escalating source of contention between us. I did not wish to indulge in an open relationship with multiple partners. Love, along with old-fashioned fidelity and trust still meant everything to me in my relationship with him. Liberation had certain boundaries, as far as I was concerned.

Someone we knew summed up the way the sexual revolution, combined with Second Wave Feminism, was changing his sex life for the better. He claimed, 'When I tell them I'm a feminist, I can have sex with many more women'. Mouthing some version of feminism became a seduction tool, and little else, although he probably believed, in theory at least, that women should be shaking off the shackles of right-wing patriarchy, as well as hopping freely into bed.

For me, the personal was indeed political, and feminism was about equality for women from all backgrounds, gaining power over their individual lives, fighting repression, along with female consciousness-raising on many levels. This did not include left-wing men simply scoring more fucks.

I disliked the way men on the left, including Richard, still manipulated women to do their bidding, particularly, but not solely, in both the domestic sphere and the sexual sphere. Sexual liberation and women's liberation were parallel, irresistible developments, often triggering unease and even chaos in heterosexual relationships. There was a lot of sex, too many drugs, too much rock 'n' roll.

Richard's increasingly reckless drug use (mainly dope) fuelled the 'modus operandi' he used to charm other women into bed, while at the same time tearing me apart. He may well have used the 'I am a feminist' line, as well. The central, most corrosive lie he told, to anyone who would listen, was: 'Everything's okay. Helen and I have an open marriage', while his parallel spin to me, 'I will always love you, you are my soulmate, the centre of my universe', kept hooking me back in.

I was a *Fool for Love*, echoing the title of Sam Shepard's play, and then the film of the same name, in which he played the lead character. The symbolic conflagration at the end of the film when the motel burns down, seems an apt parallel for the way my own love life was heading.

I think Richard may have believed that statement of love and commitment when he mouthed those words, until the burden of lies and mystery lovers became too great. He would allow me certain, edited snippets of the truth, telling me cruelly, intimately, about some of the women he played around with, who, supposedly, meant nothing to him: 'Yes, she came here when you were out. She liked your shoes'. If I objected, cried, or threatened to leave, he would take the high ground, claiming to be more liberated than I was, and even a 'better feminist'. The latter charge rendered me speechless.

'What hooks you into a loving relationship is often the very thing that ultimately destroys that relationship'. I had once read this rather corny mantra, or words to that effect, probably in either *Cleo* or *Cosmopolitan* magazine, both popular women's magazines in the seventies. Neverthelesss, this rang true for me, increasingly so, over the years of our marriage.

When I fell in love with Richard, I had been totally charmed by his cheeky spontaneity, his youthful, good-looking 'Peter Pan' glow, his sexy ways, his radical politics, his endearing stutter. Gradually, over the years, some of these attractive qualities lost their polish, becoming problematic, at least from my point of view, while he most probably felt the same about me.

The Ingmar Bergman film *Scenes from a Marriage* was released in Australia around 1974, at a pivotal point in our marriage. This highly charged Swedish film, laced with intense, frank dialogue, seemed painfully real, and all too pertinent. The viewing experience knocked both of us sideways. We identified too closely, too uncomfortably with the male and female protagonists. Their frank dialogue about intimacy, infidelity and marital breakdown was excruciatingly authentic, resonating with us both on many levels.

It is said that this film, along with the original television mini-series of the same name, triggered a sharp rise in divorces in Sweden, with a similarly potent ripple effect in other countries, including our own. Probably, at that juncture, after seven years, we should have split up before inflicting any more layers of hurt on each other. However, teetering on the brink as it was, our marriage somehow survived several more years, and, regrettably, many more dramatic scenes, before it completely unravelled.

A different kind of scene from our own marriage happened in late 1975, when we gathered in our dimly lit dining room, on the sort of business that could have ended in long prison sentences. Richard and John Tomlinson, our fiery, bearded friend, were hatching a plan to assassinate the front bench of the newly formed Fraser/Anthony Coalition government in Canberra. Preposterous as it seems now, it seemed perfectly rational then. Social justice demanded the death of the traitors who had stolen our liberty; it was practically our democratic right.

The longed-for election of Gough Whitlam to the Prime Minister's Lodge, three years earlier, had filled us with hope. Queensland might have been stuck in a time warp under the oppressive Bjelke-Petersen regime but the new Labor Federal Government in Canberra promised liberation in many areas of our lives.

They gave us a cornucopia of gifts: opened up free university and further education, ended conscription, completed the final withdrawal from the dirty war in Vietnam, Cambodia and Laos, introduced cheap contraceptive pills, provided an exciting boost in arts funding and took steps towards equal pay and equal status for women.

On 11 November, 1975, I was on campus in the refectory when the shocking news roared out on a loud speaker: 'Whitlam has been dismissed'. These words struck me like a slap in the face. I froze. It did not seem possible that such a crime could have been committed against the people of Australia. Outside, students moved haphazardly around the campus, sobbing or shouting in disbelief.

Shades of the 1969 film *Z*, the Costa-Gavras political thriller about the Colonels' military coup in Greece, haunted me. The title *Z* was a protest in itself; it meant 'He lives', referring to Grigor Lambrakis, the inspirational politician killed in 1963, an event which ultimately sparked the catastrophic takeover.

Whitlam was still alive but for how much longer? If the Governor-General, Sir John Kerr, the Queen's representative, in collusion with the Opposition, could sack the Prime Minister and his democratically elected government, then anything seemed possible. In common with many other Australians, Richard and John, and their willing partners and accomplices, Claire and myself, did not recognise the new Fraser government.

> 'Extreme retaliatory action is called for', someone said.
> 'Nothing short of a bloody revolution will do.'
> 'Yes, it's entirely necessary', everyone agreed, 'and completely justified.'
> 'Pass the Glenfiddich.'

Over the ensuing weeks the 'killer plan' kept stalling. We had no weapons and knew no terrorists. On those heightened, conspiratorial evenings we consumed much curry, or roast lamb and three veges, the Glenfiddich flowed, then the cheaper whisky brands, along with Richard's not-so-secret specialty, the sharing of multiple joints.

Claire and I participated in the plotting over the in-vogue Lindeman's Ben Ean Moselle, the mildly sparkling Barossa Pearl, or the more exotic

Portuguese Mateus Rosé. We didn't need to smoke the dope to get high; inhaling the vapour cloud hanging over the dining table was potent enough.

After several weeks of fervent plotting, enthusiasm began to flicker and fizzle like a wax-laden candle in its much-used Mateus bottle. Managing the means, the logistics, the aftermath went from an absolute necessity to a definite maybe. It ended when John and Claire moved to Darwin.

At the end of my gap year, 1975, I was offered two tutoring jobs in education at the University of Queensland. As I preferred face-to-face teaching, I rejected the one in external studies. My life was moving in a more academic direction, which pleased me.

***

7.
THE ICE STORM

Enjoying my liberating role in tertiary education, I began teaching the feminist education electives I designed, along with broader cultural studies offerings. I was a tutor in the post-graduate Diploma of Education, at the University of Queensland in the Education Faculty, along with great colleagues including Jill Borthwick, Michael Macklin, Ron Wilkes, and my special mentors, Ted D'Urso and Eric Bowker.

Initially, I shared an office with Bruce, a high school teacher on a year's sabbatical at the university. Year in, year out, he and others would come to the university in order to engage in further tertiary study, as well as to assist with the teacher training process in their particular curriculum strand, which, in Bruce's case, was science.

A sociable bloke, Bruce put pressure on Richard and me to attend the 'key' coupledom orgies he and his wife, Joy, held, once a month. He pitched that it was all open, clean fun, with no hurtful consequences. Swinging was in vogue in the seventies. However, while Richard and I were often invited by Bruce and others to participate in such parties, where swapping keys meant exchanging partners, we felt we were much too sophisticated for such parlour games.

Brisbane was still a large country town until well into the eighties. Few degrees of separation seemed to exist between the people we knew or met. In the largely WASP, educated, heterosexual, middle-class bubble in which we operated, everyone seemed to know each other's business.

People were branded by where and how they fitted into certain social hierarchies, including which family they belonged to, where they lived, whom they had gone out with/married/divorced, and, all too importantly, which secondary school they had attended. In our town, there was literally nowhere to hide. This quite possibly made the act of swinging almost incestuous.

Although produced in the late-nineties, Ang Lee's brilliant film

The Ice Storm remains one of the most insightful representations of the devastating outcomes of privileged, careless sexual experimentation amongst middle-class American communities in the seventies. On the other hand, the landmark late-sixties film, *Bob & Carol & Ted & Alice* was a smug, sanitised Hollywood version of first world sexual liberation and experimentation. This film has not stood the test of time.

Despite what my colleague Bruce said, complex multi-layered narratives did play themselves out, often calamitously, pointing to the authenticity of *The Ice Storm* over the shallow *Bob & Carol & Ted & Alice*. Jo, a friend, left her home, her husband and her children to be with a male neighbour, Sam, after several steamy, wife-swapping parties in a sprawling, wealthy suburb, where this free-range sexual activity appeared to be particularly prevalent. In a seemingly fair and happy exchange, Sam's wife paired up with Jo's husband for a while.

However, this re-partnering playfulness eventually splintered into serious heartache and bitter recriminations, beneath that supposedly cool, trendy surface. Meanwhile, Jo was unfairly damned as a heartless mother for leaving her children and following her heart. Within one turbulent year, Jo and Sam had partnered, splitting up when he left her for someone else. Jo never fully recovered from her distress and the burden of shame, while Sam, who had also left his children, simply did not suffer the same vicious gossip and condemnation.

Anne Summers' feminist book *Damned Whores and God's Police*, published in 1975, was very timely. She charted the historical injustice of women being labelled as perfect mothers, the pillars of society, monitoring the behaviour of the opposite stereotype of bad girls, dismissed as 'damned whores'. This gendered, hypocritical double standard has been writ large in Australian cultural history.

Summers also argued that women need to find their own untrammelled way in the world, against the retrograde forces of misogynistic judgementalism by both women and men. It is galling to think that these 'harmless party games' were mostly labelled 'wife-swapping', as though the wife herself was simply a chattel of questionable value to be traded. Despite Second Wave feminism and the sexual revolution of the sixties and seventies, the forces of patriarchy still ruled, and sexist double standards have remained palpably alive and well to this day.

I recall another story that captured the mood of the seventies, along with all its contradictions. Seriously straight, rather dour George engaged in the burgeoning sexual revolution in an unusual way. Enrolled in a post-graduate degree, his special topic focused on the nature of the female orgasm. This empirical research involved the use of surveys, coupled with intimate questionnaires, complemented by his forensically 'testing' the orgasms of multiple female students – literally, a trifecta of methodologies.

All students in the psychology faculty had to be the subjects of some form of research, in order to pass that degree. My friend Savannah Susan[10] was a reluctant subject of this particular research project, pulling out immediately after George turned up to her home, unannounced, supposedly for some deep discussion and, possibly, some field research. Looking back, she says, 'I just found the whole thing very creepy'.

George's marriage to Jackie lasted barely a year after he began this 'orgasm project'. I knew Jackie around the traps, via an old school friend, and sympathised with her. He had changed quite dramatically from the quiet man she had married. The research escalated, especially when young women would turn up at their home, to engage in his significant field work, all in the name of self-discovery, and gaining university marks.

One day, Jackie came home early and found him in bed with one of his participants. Their marriage abruptly ended. Even in seemingly backward Brisbane, swinging was happening in quite unusual ways, in this case, driven by a male with his own spin and for his own purposes, in the name of academic research. Patriarchy was continually, cleverly evolving, even on that supposedly liberated front.

Although Richard and I may have resisted going to spouse-swapping parties out in the 'burbs, I decided to take on a lover, very much encouraged by Richard, who swore, over and over, that I was still, and always would be, at the heart and soul of our love-life. Ron Wilkes, a colleague I worked with at the University of Queensland, was living, 'separately under the same roof' with his wife and four children.

Under constant pressure, the institution of marriage itself was shifting, becoming more elastic, breaking, tearing apart, with people redefining their commitment boundaries, sometimes in inventive ways, often in shattering ways. By and large, sexualities were still binary then, at least

---

10. I called Susan 'Savannah Burgundy' in my blog. She liked a glass of good Burgundy and Savannah sounded exotic. This nickname has stuck.

on the surface, although those traditional markers, heterosexuality and homosexuality, also were blurring.

Attracted to each other, Ron and I had long, serious conversations about life, love, marriage, eventually starting a love affair. I found him to be a nice man, sexy and caring. This liaison lasted a while, both before and after my separation from Richard. Pleased and even excited by what was happening, Richard was, however, gaining too much power, given that I was totally open with him, which, for me, was part of the contract.

Knowledge, after all, is power. At times, we three experimented with a ménage à trois, our new arrangement being an open secret within our close friendship circle. My dear Janetta sent me letters whenever she was away, signing off with love to all three of us. I saw Ron every day at work, and we would spend Friday nights together. He stuck by me, although, in a way, he was also seduced by Richard's charmful manipulation.

Certain films do treat the 'threesome theme' quite deliciously. For instance, the classic French film *Jules et Jim*, and the Mexican film, *Y tu mama tambien* (And Your Mother Too). The American film, *Henry and June*, based on an autobiographical novel by Anais Nin, is also quite subtle and erotic. Over the years, such films have helped to ground me, giving me another way of looking at what was going on back then, so close to home.

We were attempting to fulfill our increasingly blighted interpretation of living the Jean-Paul Sartre and Simone de Beauvoir dream, in which we would openly experiment with lovers, but remain bound together, forever. I continually pushed for more openness and honesty, while Richard operated shadowy, mind-bending scenarios. For him, these were more taboo, more risky, more exciting, I suppose. Inevitably, everything came unstuck, in a chaotic overload of duplicity, drugs, pain and passion.

Whatever Richard was up to in his parallel, private world was still largely a mystery, at least to me, and our friends regrettably became caught up in that sticky, murky web, plunging me into a toxic world of self-doubt, reminiscent of the 1944 film *Gaslight,* starring Charles Boyer and Ingrid Bergman.

This film noir production captured the malevolent impact such manipulation from a loved one can have on the heart and mind. 'Gaslighting' itself has become a word commonly used to describe a shadowy, insidious form of cruel, coercive power involving relationship trickery and abuse.

In some countries, including Scotland, such coercion is now considered illegal. Even though I had a sharp analytical mind, I was trapped in a blurry, alternative psychic and emotional maze. Under the illusion that I still had significant agency, inadvertently, inevitably, I was losing it.

While my perception of what was happening was consistently denied and reframed, Richard's drug-taking increased, making me wonder, 'Who is this person I'm speaking to, and living with? What drugs is he even taking now?' At the same time, I was struggling with my own addictions: to him, to love, clinging to my shattering dreams, to a non-viable future. We still made love, frantically, wildly, as if there was no tomorrow.

Nothing made sense anymore. No longer did we partake in the recreational enjoyment of regular, affable evenings in the past, with close friends such as Susie and Janetta, coming over for a joint and a joint. I would happily cook a tasty roast joint of lamb, while, amidst much hilarity, he would roll and share the other kind of joint – a veritable joint fest.

In 1975, while complications were escalating between Richard and me, Susie and Janetta were sorting out their uni student lives, teaming up with Susie's sister, Jeanne, of hot pink pantsuit fame. Jeanne had just returned from two years in San Francisco, after her first marriage broke down while on a trip in South America. She returned to Brisbane for a tutoring position in occupational therapy at the university.

These three women rented a welcoming old Queenslander, situated at 57 Swann Road, Taringa. We all admired Jeanne, who brought with her the very latest feminist news from San Francisco, where she had lived in a thriving women's collective. We avidly read the book *Our Bodies, Our Selves* from the Boston Collective, and Jeanne passed on tips regarding the use of a speculum to check out our vaginas, given that most women had never seen theirs, or anyone else's, in all their glory. At that time, Germaine Greer's *The Female Eunuch* was also one of our feminist bibles. Her lightning-rod work influenced us for years.

When I think of 57 Swann Road, I recall with great fondness the warm energy in that place. These young women would hold regular evening soirees, essentially a party where all guests were invited to participate through performance. Once Richard and I carefully rehearsed the Marianne Faithfull song, *As Tears Go By*, with him singing along to my piano accompaniment. He had a good singing voice.

However, that night we were overwhelmed by the marvellous Susie on her flute, lovely choral singing, and by the semi-professional musicians there, such as Prue Gibbs, and her band, The Silver Studs. We decided we were too amateur to proceed. At another soiree event, Janetta and I, dressed appropriately in costume, performed a reading from *Damned Whores and God's Police*. I played the straightlaced God's Police character, Janetta the sexy damned whore. This feminist performance piece was warmly received.

In some ways, their lifestyle mirrored that of the young, single protagonists in that Australian film about the highs and lows of university life, *Love and Other Catastrophes*. Richard and I were envious of the share-house experiences at 57 Swann Road. There we witnessed a freedom and openness, a close-knit, loving community life that we had never experienced. We were, it seemed, born too soon, or, perhaps, had coupled too early. We also discovered the meaning and practice of the delicious word 'alfresco' over those two years of visiting Swann Road.

Chatting and laughing on a Sunday morning, we would sit around the kitchen table, high above the sloping backyard and the rest of Taringa and Indooroopilly, enjoying our own version of a shared alfresco brunch, comprising home-made muffins, granola and lots of fruit and vegetables.

In order to study her music more deeply, Susie went to Sydney, in mid-1976. Susie's farewell soiree was a triumph. We hung out with the young aspiring architect, Gavin Patterson, the glowing musician Prue and her wonderful brother Harry Gibbs, the poet and landscape gardener, Odo Strewe and many others, all interesting, creative people.

Janetta stayed on in the house for another six months or so, renting out the spare bedroom to cheery Peter Baillie, who later became a quality boat builder and furniture maker. Jeanne and her partner Nicholas Pounder also moved to Sydney early in 1977, and Janetta followed them by the March of that year. Nicholas was totally into books, setting himself up as a well-respected bookseller and collector of precious first editions, and other rare books. The halcyon days at Number 57 were suddenly over, although that distinctive vibe was creatively re-forming in Sydney and beyond.

Closer to home, much of the fun from that golden window of time screeched to a halt, especially when Richard secretly allowed a drug-dealer friend to store drugs under our house, because the police were seriously pursuing him. I was called a party-pooper, and worse, when I insisted that this illegal cache be removed.

In those tough times, being caught having a visitor come to the house with just one marijuana cigarette on his or her person, could mean a five-year jail sentence for the householder, with a heavier sentence for the user. This covert storage caper on our premises was worse, as far as penalties went.

Wishing to pursue a career in academia, I longed for us both to abandon the draining, divisive aspects of our lifestyle, to cease destructive, shape-shifting behaviour, to regain trust in each other. On the other hand, more and more, Richard dreamed of dropping out of the mainstream, starting a hippy farming lifestyle, growing fruit and marijuana in the Sunshine Coast hinterland. Our very own ice storm was gathering momentum, unstoppable in its ferocity.

After ten years together, that storm finally hit. Richard became increasingly involved with Libbie, an anorexic, waif-like creature, a poisoned hippy fairy, from my point of view. They had met while studying fulltime for the Graduate Diploma in Librarianship. By early 1977, Richard was back working as a well-qualified research librarian at the State Library of Queensland.

In our personal lives, for months, he 'covered up the truth with lies' as in Dylan's epic song, *Idiot Wind*, about couples brutally splitting up. Night after night, Richard played *Blood on the Tracks* incessantly, the album that song featured on, nearly driving me mad. While I now recognise this album as Dylan's best, I still find it painful to listen to.

Swearing that he and Libbie were just good friends, Richard declared that I was a nasty, cold person, not wishing to befriend or look after her. I was strong, she was fragile. Apparently, she needed him, much more than I did. He especially admired her because she had lived close to the edge, having suffered a near-death, drug-induced coma in a Moroccan gutter.

It appeared that my own near-death, gutter-side experience in the car crash, years before, no longer had sufficient seductive cachet, despite the financial security the Supreme Court injury compensation case had brought us for years. I simply could not compete anymore. On Anzac Day 1977, I flew to Sydney to spend a few days escaping from the messy marital breakup, hanging out with sanity-restoring Janetta, Susie, and Jeanne, the old '57 Swann Road' crew.

Horrified by the escalating hurt caused by Richard's behaviour, close friends stood by me. Some wavered, caught up by his spin, his lack of boundaries. Probably, at the end, he didn't know anymore what was real, and what was not. Several people in our close circle were inevitably lost to me. Everyone seemed to have an opinion or a reaction regarding our breakup.

My parents grieved, as they had always welcomed and loved him as a dear son, and my nieces Margaret, Elizabeth, Diane and Jenny cried when they lost their Uncle Richard, whom they adored. On his side, I was sad to lose contact with his nieces and nephews, along with other family members, especially his dear mother, Charlotte. Concerning his younger sister, Pauline Smith, we pledged to remain friends, no matter what the fallout was. Thankfully, this precious closeness has continued to this day.

One not-so-close family member, ever judgemental and insensitive, declared: 'If only you and Richard had settled down with a couple of kids, you would still be together'. In her eyes, my apparently wilful childlessness, along with caring too much about my career, had paved a slippery, feminist (that is, negative) path to an inevitable marital breakdown.

Of course, as the divorce rate was relentlessly escalating, many people, including her, were probably panicking. Was it a virus? Could they catch it? As my dear mother said, 'No one should ever comment on another person's private life. For all she knows, Richard and you might have been trying to have a baby for years, and were heartbroken'.

While my biological clock had been ticking, the right time had never presented itself. In any case, instinctively, I knew that I would be left holding that mythical baby, and I certainly had no desire to be a single mother. I had just turned thirty-three.

Regarding my career choice / personal life balance, my time at the University of Queensland coincided, at least for the first few years, with the maelstrom of my drawn-out marriage break-down. No baby was ever going to fix that, even though at one stage, with everything slipping off the rails, Richard suddenly had a bad idea that we might enter into parenthood.

Ongoing personal distress and positive career progression did not sit well together. However, I did have some small work triumphs: I designed and taught the first elective units on feminism in that faculty, and I co-edited a cultural studies reader with two close colleagues, Michael Macklin and Carol Mohle. Along with a vibrant research team, I delved into the issue of women returning to study, thanks to Gough Whitlam's earlier reforms.

In the seventies, feminism was flourishing on campus in other disciplines such as sociology and literature. Attending national conferences in Australian Women in Education and Women in Labour was very significant for my growth as a feminist. Finding like-minded women and sharing ideas was crucial, even though I did feel intimidated at times by some of the powerhouse feminists.

I discovered there are many feminisms, and that feminism is not a monolith beset by decrees. At times, I am still quite affected by divisions over issues such as pornography, the LGBTIQA+ debates, as well as cultural, racial, socio-economic issues. Yet this energy has kept me engaged, and 'feminisms' are in an exciting state of flux. I do not embrace the lazy, slippery use of the term post-feminist. The struggle is not over.

In 1979, a Sydney newspaper twisted my words in a well-received, feminist paper I presented at an education conference. My research was based on many one-on-one interviews, relating to the personal complexities and triumphs for mature women returning to study in higher education at the University of Queensland. The reactionary headlines blared: *Women Studying Destroys Marriages*, completely misrepresenting the point of my paper.

This was the first time I had experienced my careful feminist research being distorted and even mocked by the hard-nosed, masculinist media. Similarly, in the nineties, my work on sporting masculinities and toxic male violence, both on and off the field in Rugby League football, was slammed by shock jocks, and even by some women radio announcers. By then, I was more capable and ready for such appalling undercutting and diminishing.

Regrettably, back in the late seventies, I had become too distracted by the personal tsunami in my private life, to complete my masters degree on women returning to study. My two supervisors also caused me sone angst and confusion, given that they disagreed vehemently regarding the methodology I was to use in my research.

Meanwhile, I was still involved with Ron, right up to when he went on study leave in 1979, the year before the completion of my university contract. Looking back on that turbulent time, Pedro Almodovar's witty film from the late eighties, *Women on the Verge of a Nervous Breakdown* now gives me some reflective relief from Bergman's unremitting *Scenes from a Marriage*. Bringing absurdity and high comedy to a painful breakup situation, Almodovar has an inimitable way of focussing on women, coaxing humour out of outlandish relationship circumstances, while simultaneously hitting close to the bone.

Being on the verge of my own mini-breakdown, I remained in the Rainworth house, thereby becoming the custodian of those twin ginger cats, Charlie and Chloe, and of Oliver, our black bitzer dog. From late April, 1977, I found it hard to control Oliver, in particular. Over the years, Richard had been the main carer of the dog, while I was the cat person. I received hefty fines and ultimately a last chance letter from the council, threatening that my dog would be impounded and even destroyed, if he ever escaped onto the streets again.

While never proven, it was rumoured in the neighbourhood that Oliver would leap over the fence, hopping onto the local bus with his best mate, a golden Labrador. They would enjoy an occasional free ride together into the city. The two dogs had even been spotted getting off the Rainworth bus on George Street, near the department store, McDonnell and East.

Whatever was actually happening, Oliver's antics were simply too much for me. I handed over custody to his role model, Richard, who, in turn, quickly passed him on to his mother, Charlotte, in their old home town, Boonah. Oliver then scampered off to live happily-ever-after with the local fireman at the Boonah fire station.

Chloe and Charlie, excessively indulged, saw out their final days at my Rainworth abode. Grumpy old Charlie, however, did have the unfortunate habit of energetically biting the heels of any gentleman callers. In an odd way, he seemed to be getting a kind of belated revenge on Richard, while giving other blokes a stern, advance warning.

Many years later, around 2012, the old newspaper wedding article and photograph from Easter, 1967, spookily popped up on public view again, gracing one section of the famous Brisbane fashion designer Gwen Gillam's retrospective exhibition at the Queensland Museum. There I was, behind some glass, still tagged as the 'most modern bride of the day'. Gwen's elegantly designed, more traditional gown had won the Easter Bride $100 first prize, back on that fateful Easter Saturday in 1967.

In this glittering tribute exhibition, the winning bride's photograph was displayed in that same newspaper spread, her actual dress adorning a mannequin. Having retired by then, and feeling my age, I somehow knew, deep in my bones, that the museum archive basement was a fitting burial place for my long-extinct marriage. I trust that the rapidly fading newspaper photograph of me in that bothersome wedding dress never sees the light of day again.

***

8.
LUST, CAUTION

During one of those epic soirees held in the house at 57 Swann Road, I met Peter Gall, whom I call Pierre, one of Janetta's firm friends. He was gay, very amusing, majoring in French and German at the university.

When our friends moved south to Sydney, I would often see Pierre out at the university, where I was working. We became good friends, and in the late seventies, Pierre and I travelled together through France, on a group tour of the Four Corners of France, organised through the French Department at the University of Queensland, along with the Alliance Francaise.

As a handy, inexpensive way to travel to romantic France for Christmas, this trip was a great way for me to be out of the country for the 'silly season', always a painful time following a separation. No individual bookings and planning were involved, and I could just go with the flow, and maybe even find romance in Paris, the city of light.

The dark, evocatively titled film, *Lust, Caution*, directed by Ang Lee concerns a female honey pot trying to entrap and kill a traitor, during the Second World War in China. The sex scenes between her and this tainted, irresistible married man are creatively shot, erotically charged and very confronting. Nothing quite so dangerous happened in any of my own lust, caution tales, set in wildly different contexts. Nevertheless, I find this film's title and mood very provocative, on a number of levels, when applied to my life post-marriage.

A special treat on this French trip was hanging out with Angie, one of Peter's smart university friends. We three experienced some rather unusual adventures, separate from the larger travel group. For instance, we went skiing with Jacques, the Mayor of Nice, who took an instant shine to Angie. Trying to impress her with his slick black Mercedes, and even slicker black hair, he insisted on taking Angie and us, her friends, up to the ski fields one chilly December day.

Being from sub-tropical Brisbane, none of us had ever skied before. Despite our insistence that we were absolute novices, he laughed, shaking his head in disbelief, while speeding up to a high-risk slope on the steep snow-covered mountains behind the coastal city of Nice. Suffice to say, we definitely did not learn to ski that day, trying but failing even to remain upright.

A classic alpha male show-off on the ski fields, our host Jacques was also a reckless driver on the hazardous winding road up and down those mountains. Hanging on for dear life in the back seat, Pierre and I clutched each other, whispering our fond goodbyes, while Angie screamed the whole way back to Nice. With too much lust, and caution thrown to the wind, Jacques over-reached. Needless to say, things did not end well between them.

At twenty-two years old, Angie could speak French and Greek fluently, while Pierre could speak French, German and Dutch. People from those countries would often find it difficult to tell that this gifted young man from the working-class Brisbane suburb, Oxley, was not one of them.

A Dutch person we met in France became increasingly annoyed and frustrated with Peter's perfect Dutch, unconvinced by Peter's true story that he was not actually Dutch, that he came from Australia, and had taught himself this fourth language while studying French and German at university. Pierre could also speak Spanish, Italian and Japanese well, along with several Scandinavian languages, although not quite as impeccably as his main three, or four, when English was counted in the mix. Both Angie and Pierre became great language teachers.

After a dreary, poorly organised Christmas day in Geneva, our tour group yearned for a much classier, more exciting New Years' Eve. Still trying to deal with my recent separation, I figured that celebrating the New Year in Paris would definitely be a restorative tonic, blowing away the cobwebs of 1977, welcoming in a totally fresh year, 1978.

As it transpired, unforeseen excitement erupted on the streets of that fair city, and the anticipated fun and release on New Year's Eve turned, instead, to fear. At one stage, our breakaway group found ourselves hiding at a Greek restaurant around midnight on the Left Bank, while chaos reigned outside.

This drama erupted on the cusp of 'Dix Ans Apres'/'Ten Years After', commemorating the fiercely fought 1968 cultural revolutions that had swept France, Italy, Germany, Prague and other Western countries.

Building up to that New Year's Eve, we had seen the *Dix Ans Apres et Quoi?/Ten Years After, So What?* graffiti and signs posted all around the inner city. Knowing a fair smattering of French history, we understood that this was a call to the disenchanted radical community to protest on the streets at midnight, heralding in a new year, a new decade, in the hope of stirring memories of 1968, and thereby, perhaps, a follow-up revolution in 1978.

Demanding the fulfilment of broken promises and the need for positive, lasting change, the organisers were understandably frustrated, questioning what had actually been achieved in those ten years since the 1968 turmoil, demanding urgent industrial and educational reforms.[11]

That afternoon, we visited the Rodin Museum, fairly close to our hotel. On the way there and back, we observed, firsthand, the sinister spectacle of many buses apparently lying in wait. Fully geared-up riot police sat very still in those threatening vehicles, fully prepared to strike later that night in strategic parts of inner Paris.

While we were sympathetic towards the upcoming protest, we also wanted to enjoy our first New Year's Eve in Paris. We played down the chilling images of those police squads-in-waiting, naively imagining that, as foreign tourists, we would be untouchable. At the same time, we also felt a frisson of excitement regarding the upcoming demonstration, knowing that, historically, the French have always been passionate protestors.

Around 11.30 pm, the situation became increasingly heated. Protesters marched along, waving banners, chanting slogans. Some people charged randomly along the streets, causing havoc, smashing shop windows. Or maybe they were a bunch of anarchists, or even right-wingers, with their own agendas, trying to disrupt or malign the protesters. At the same time,

---

11. Despite the rhetoric of French politicians and top bureaucrats, little progress had been made, particularly with regard to the education system and other pressing social justice reforms affecting youth, workers, and the left generally.

nervous restaurant owners were hastily ordering increasingly fearful patrons out onto the streets.

As long as we could, our group, including Angie, Peter and myself, stayed glued to a table near the front of the restaurant, in the vain hope that we might be allowed to sit there safely, sheltering from the mounting fracas on the footpath outside. A gaggle of drunken men, spying the women in our group through the window, suddenly lurched into the restaurant, demanding New Year's Eve tongue kisses and embraces, an unwanted overload of lusty testosterone on offer.

Despite our resistance to their increasingly unwelcome advances, we were ordered by the restaurant management to leave. We were even blamed for triggering a different kind of fray, not at all connected with that of the radical protesters. Just as the riot police started attacking the nearby throng with batons and tear gas, that restaurant manager summarily herded us outside. Stumbling into the lusty path of the drunken maulers, we also found ourselves too close to the protesters and to the riot police.

Resourceful Angie spied a possible sanctuary, a Greek restaurant situated down a side street. We rushed inside, even though the staff were frantically starting to close. Being very beautiful and speaking fluent Greek, Angie charmed the maître d' into letting us shelter there for a while, although time and their patience were fast running out. Much to our distress, we discovered that all public transport systems had been shut down early because of the civil disobedience crisis.

Fortunately for us, one of the waiters was very much taken with Angie. Brave, switched-on girl that she was, Angie flirted with him, trying to persuade him to lead us safely back to our hotel, quite a distance away. She left the idea of any possible reward dangling, although, to our great relief, there was sufficient charm, along with a hint of lust, to hook him in.

Dodging and diving, somehow sticking together, we followed the hordes of protesters as the formidable riot police advanced in grim formation. Choking and spluttering on the tear gas, we somehow managed to escape the indiscriminate baton attacks. Totally disoriented, we were guided back to our hotel, exhausted, very relieved. As any good Greek girl would, Angie warmly expressed her gratitude, claimed sorrowfully that she was very tired, and bade a firm au revoir to the crestfallen waiter.

I started to wonder whether the disrupted Parisian New Year celebrations might signal an unpredictable, torrid decade ahead for me, my own form of 'et Quoi?'/'So what?' At least some comfort emerged from it all. After our trip, Pierre and I bonded even further, happily sharing my house for nearly two years, before he moved to Sydney to continue working as a French and German teacher at an elite boys' school, Knox Grammar.

In late 1978, my lover, Ron, was granted a year's sabbatical in Canada. Although we hung on, vowing to stay involved with each other and always to tell each other the truth, letters criss-crossed out of synch, and communication channels ultimately broke down.

We split up while he was away. He had been kindly, a good lover, and I had had warm feelings for him, although I never loved him as deeply, crazily as I loved Richard. Ron had also been a loyal academic colleague, helping to keep me afloat in my job tutoring trainee secondary teachers in the Diploma of Education, despite my personal life being in turmoil.

On a lighter note, he earned a big tick by coming with me and Janetta to Bob Dylan concerts, night after night, in 1978. He later married, then rather quickly divorced, my ex-sister-in-law's sister, while my old boyfriend, Jimmy, ran off with my ex-sister-in-law's sister-in-law. Nothing more needs to be said, except that at all times, caution should be observed in my home town, with its barely three degrees of separation. Both Jimmy and Ron have sadly passed away in the intervening years.

I 'played the field' for some time in 1979 and into the eighties, my own personal version of Dix Ans Apres, et Quoi?. Playing the field is a curious, incautious expression in itself, originally taken from British horseracing, where it meant, simply, to bet on every horse except the favourite – a rather strange definition. Pierre and I had a great time taking chances, playing our own versions of some field or other, at times pretending to vie for the same person on the dance floor or at a party.

At one such party, I was wearing my navy blue, strapless, bra-less 'boob tube', in vogue at the time, with a matching cotton floral skirt. For a while I became the centre of attention out on the verandah, when a few males came up close and personal for a little chat and a flirt. They were fascinated by the visible fact that I shaved neither under my arms, nor on my legs. Nor was I wearing a bra. I was asked, 'Are you *actually* a feminist?' meaning, I suppose, 'Why aren't you an ultra-feminine, passive, non-threatening woman?' To them, I was from another planet.

I explained how I didn't want to comply with patriarchal myths that pushed misogynist ideals of a hairless, infantilised female body. I also pointed out that many women around the world, for example, the French and the Italians, did not shave under their arms, this being considered very sexy in those cultures. And I did not burn bras – that was another media myth. I chose to wear them or not, whenever I liked.

Suddenly, their wives started circling, I shifted from being the most popular woman in the room, to somewhat of a hairy pariah. Later I wondered why the God's Police did not invite me to their next dinner party in respectable coupledom-land. It was well known that, for starters, a newly single woman threatened to make the sacred table seating uneven.

Of course, this woman with the hairy armpits, undoubtedly one of the 'damned whores', might also seduce one of the husbands around the table. Anne Summers' cultural history views on particular kinds of tribalism and the polarisation of Australian gender relations rings true, both then and even today.

By contrast, ironically, a newly single man, hairy or smooth all over, was usually very welcome at those early eighties dinner-parties-from-hell. The hostess always seemed to have a needy single girlfriend, ready and primed for a dinner party match made in heaven. However, had I still been married, with an attractive husband in tow, the God's Police might have approvingly opened those bourgeois doors for both of us.

The popular American film *An Unmarried Woman* was released in 1978, coincidentally in the year of my official divorce. This film about a betrayed, upper middleclass woman, played by Jill Clayburgh, whose husband leaves her for a younger woman, rang all sorts of bells, given its perfect zeitgeist timing for me. For instance, she finds herself quite isolated socially, being snubbed within some of her former circles. Coupledom can be its own smug, exclusionary fiefdom.

Sadly, I didn't have an affair with handsome actor, Alan Bates. He played a conveniently unattached artist in this film, although she was still cautious about commitment, which rang true, at least. And I liked the way she would not take her husband back when his relationship with the younger woman broke up. Nevertheless, even such a sympathetic film about uncoupling was still pushing a classic romantic line about coupling being the ideal way to live. I would have liked to see a more postmodern representation of the joys to be found living as a single, independent woman. Possibly that outcome would have been too progressive for 1978.

Each morning, Pierre and I would ask each other, in appropriately quavering voices, 'Are you still alive dear?' Once we heard a sweet elderly couple say on ABC Radio National that they always checked with each other in this manner, every day. We decided this was a comforting ritual for us to follow. A further ritual consisted in keeping my deteriorating French language skills alive. Speaking in French together for at least one day a week, Pierre was the best possible companion on that front.

At other times, solely for our own entertainment, we would spend a Saturday afternoon at home, performing play-readings, with Janetta often joining us. Our favourite play was Edward Albee's *Who's Afraid of Virginia Woolf?* which we would read and perform with great gusto in the lounge room, swapping parts and genders along the way.

One escalating downside was that Pierre's extravagant shopping sprees triggered his bank manager to call me, requesting that, as a supposedly responsible person, I grab some scissors and proceed to cut up all his credit cards. The bank's plan was that Pierre would be shocked into realising he had to stop falling into the never-never, the credit card trap of excessive debt.

They had already begun garnisheeing his salary at Brisbane Grammar School, where he taught, a mortifying practice of involuntary debt-gathering. Arguing with this pompous bank manager, I blamed credit companies, banks, advertisers, consumerism, in effect, the whole capitalist system, for Pierre's spiralling, crippling debt.

Reluctantly, however, I gave in, performing the dramatic slashing ritual, while we both wept. Predictably, that bank and others kept on tempting him with multiple new credit card offers, showing that the profit motive is totally bereft of conscience or ethics.

Meanwhile, that old first-year university crush, Brian, and I found each other again, catching up in Sydney one weekend. Things didn't work out too well between us, yet again. It transpired that he had been working with the American forces in Vietnam during the war as a foreign correspondent, and quite quickly, we discovered that our political views were polar opposites.

Never mix sex, religion or politics is always a good code to live by, although, regrettably, I have had a few slippages on that score over the years. After a day and night together in our increasingly suffocating hotel room, I felt that Brian might be some kind of secret agent. He was asking bizarre, searching questions about my own political views, as well as about those of some Sydney friends and acquaintances.

Apart from regularly protesting on the streets, these young people also had a nude *Das Kapital* reading group, held every Sunday in their share house in Surry Hills. He was much too interested in such goings-on, and certainly not because he longed to join that dedicated Karl Marx cohort. I had to divorce him too, in a manner of speaking, all desire withering in an instant. I have since heard on the grapevine that he suffered a heart attack and died, far too young.

I was still working at the University of Queensland while I was living with Pierre. In the seventies and eighties, the well-loved University of Queensland Staff Club, now long gone, was a special kind of cultural microcosm, which, at times, morphed into quite a steamy sexual playground for consenting adults.

Going to the club regularly for a casual lunch, I would sometimes follow up with late afternoon/early evening drinks, if I were free. For a more private meal, people would meet upstairs at the more sedate, upmarket restaurant, with great views of the grounds and the river beyond. Various friends such as tall, beautiful Jill, from the education faculty where I worked, would accompany me down the hill to the staff club.

I would also arrange to meet up with cousin Jan, who was working in the architecture faculty, close to the club. Ralph Summy from political science, my former tutor, lover, then friend for life would also hang out with me there. Both licking our wounds after our respective marital breakups, Ralph and I had re-connected after a party thrown by some mutual colleagues in the late seventies.

After yet another sociable encounter at the club, one night I found myself at an evening dinner party thrown by a friendly laidback colleague, Doug Ogilvie, in Paddington. Doug's partner, Janey, sat gloriously on the floor, naked apart from a shawl resting casually around her shoulders. I found it hard to avoid looking at her pretty boobs, her glorious tuft of pubic hair, and her vagina, which seemed to be winking directly at me.

A little disconcerted, I politely declined to disrobe, even though the others in the circle were gradually doing so. I barely smoked the dope being passed around, apart from a couple of quick draws. Marijuana made me feel paranoid, not uplifted. I was not hippy enough, nor liberated enough, as Richard might have said in the old days, cutting me to the core. However, in that warm, non-judgemental house, no one seemed to mind.

It was 1979, I was divorced, I had broken up with Ron as well. I was simply being myself, or, rather, finding myself, corny as that might sound, with new people, in new places. Along with another male friend whom I met regularly at the club, I chose to enjoy privately stripping, making love on the carpet, consuming nips of Tequila. It's all about context, personal choices, and the company.

Many of my male colleagues at that overly-friendly club, or around the campus, were married, looking for the proverbial bit on the side. Especially in the early evening, the atmosphere was often charged with lust, accompanied by very little caution, as the drinks flowed and the night wore on.

Feeling that I had the right to be as sexually free as any man, I would enjoy a chat, a drink, a flirt, hoping a real spark might be ignited. However, after several fleeting encounters with married men, I feared that at least one of them might end up at my front door, suitcase in hand. I decided to avoid disaster and hurt on all sides, and hop off that slippery 'other woman' slope, thereby reigniting my feminism, which, regrettably, lapsed at certain times when lust came calling.

Cousin Jan and I enjoyed the company of a robust group of philosophers, usually the affable Ian Hinckfuss (Hinck), who later became her partner, along with Gary Malinas, Robert Elliot, Dean Wells and others. No one who drank at that bar after dark seemed to care much about driving 'under the influence'. I used to comfort myself that another horrific accident could never happen to me, ever again. What were the odds?

Even so, I moved away from Wild-Drinking-Peter James and his antics, to a calmer man, Ian Harley, with whom I became involved. While I had seen attractive, soft-spoken Ian around the Club, I met him officially at a party thrown by elegant Ingrid Moses, with whom I was doing the multi-pronged research project on women returning to study.

At Ingrid's party, Ian and I spent a long time chatting. I discovered that his wife had recently left him for someone else, and he was caring for their four children, post-separation. At least he ticked the box for being (sort of) single. As our post-party affair blossomed and grew more intense over the ensuing months, I tried hard to be super-cautious, to hold my emotions back, to not fall in love with him.

Nevertheless, I found that what had started as fine, mellow sexual attraction did blossom into love. Practically at that precise, revelatory moment, his wife abandoned her lover and returned to Brisbane, back into the bosom of the family. While she agreed that he could still see me, things spiralled out of control. Ian and I had to split up.

On the one hand, I was devastated, while on the other, I grudgingly admired her for insisting that he owed her the time and money to return to study for her personal pursuit of a higher degree. As with many an academic marriage then, the male partner's career and further study was usually valued, unquestionably, over that of the female partner.

From a feminist perspective, ironically, I had been researching this very topic. Even so, I couldn't really think of her, objectively, as a subject for my research. Instead, I suffered lovelorn after-effects, and for a while I ignored Jill's wise caution when, like a pining schoolgirl, I would wait for his call after work. When he did ring, more often than not, I would catch up with him for a drink at that fickle comfort-zone, the University Staff Club.

By then, the situation had become quite humiliating, as I had morphed from being his lover into his social worker, his marriage guidance counsellor, whatever. When he finally did break up with his wife several years later, Ian left Brisbane for a prestigious job in London, where I visited him several times. While we tried to reignite the relationship, too much time had passed, and both of us were half-hearted at best.

Brisbane was quite a party-city in the eighties and nineties. With my sociable buddies and fellow researchers, Diana and Ellie, I went to several parties, in sequence, just about every Saturday night. We used to sit down on Friday evenings, carefully working out the order in which we would attend those particular events the following evening. Timing was all. Certain parties might peak too soon, or not at all. Savannah Susan vividly remembers our first meeting at a party in the depths of the staid suburb of Ashgrove, back in late 1979.

I arrived at the party with Pierre. Susan came with her partner, Cossack Peter, whom I'd met at an earlier party, sitting at the top of a long set of very steep stairs, high on a hill in Hamilton. Most of that night, Cossack and I ignored the others, companionably pondering the meaning of life, gazing out over the dark river and the iconic Breakfast Creek pub. We met up happily again, at an equally so-so party, probably run by the same network of vaguely mutual acquaintances. A few posers dominated the dance floor, progressively stripping down, practically screwing on the spot.

We four bystanders laughed a lot, and at the end of the evening, I invited Savannah Susan and the Cossack, my new favourite people, to a party Pierre and I happened to be throwing the following Saturday. And thus began a beautiful friendship. Savannah Susan and I agree that we were wit personified that fateful night, although neither of us can recall any of those dazzling one-liners.

From time to time, Pierre and I would throw parties, starting a fine tradition of memorable events at my house in Rainworth, in the tradition of parties-of-old in Annerley, decades earlier. My thirties wooden house would shake perilously on its foundations. As the night wore on, I was relieved that, as people drank more alcohol, they were not always moving in synch to the music. Pure, rhythmically attuned dancing could be highly dangerous to the stability of a wooden house on stilts.

I avidly recorded a number of playlists over the years, or party tapes as they were called then. Carefully designing the order of the songs for maximum dramatic effect, I started with a Beatles' classics, such as *I Saw Her Standing There*, and Manfred Mann's *Do Wah Diddy Diddy*. The chatter warmed up, the drinks flowed, people relaxed. Suddenly, at high volume, *Gloria*, the version by the band, Them, began to play. It worked every time.

Galvanised into action, the guests would swarm into the lounge/dining room, dancing their hearts out. In carefully chosen order, other great favourites followed, ensuring the party spirit would continue unabated: *Satisfaction* by the Stones, *I Will Survive* by Gloria Gaynor, and the Martha and the Muffins' classic, *Echo Beach* would tumble out of the hifi player.

Everyone on the floor had a favourite disco routine for *I Will Survive* and my friend Jenny Wren and I had created our own expressive choreography for *Echo Beach*. Another hit, *You've Lost that Loving*

Feeling, by the Righteous Brothers, inspired everyone to act out and sing along, soulfully, to those melodramatic lyrics. Then everyone would clear the floor, with Janetta and Pierre raising the temperature, performing their own dazzling routine to Bob Dylan's *Hurricane*.

Pierre and I had our own special song. We would jump around crazily to Plastic Bertrand's *Ca Plane Pour Moi*, re-living one outrageous night together at a Parisian nightclub, prior to our New Year's Eve debacle. Our guests also loved *Moscow, Moscow* by Dschinghis Khan, especially when Cossack Peter would perform a lively Russian dance rendition of that particular song, often bringing the house down – metaphorically speaking.

After Pierre moved to Sydney, he would travel back to Brisbane whenever he could for the school holidays. A Rainworth party was usually timed to coincide with his visit. I recall that these parties became increasingly lively, even steamy, triggering several people's marriages to fall apart, virtually in front of our eyes.

Mystery lovers were sometimes sprung in my rather strange, but handy, third bedroom, situated in the middle of the house, with two doors, a skylight, and no windows. Lust abounded, with very little caution. Spouses were shamed, tears were shed, one yelling, furious partner often charging home after a discovery skirmish.

Other guests, irresistibly attracted to each other, might disappear down the little dead-end street, to pash in the nearby park. Rumour had it that one couple, both of whom were married to someone else, made love while dangling on a particular swing in the children's playground. I suppose this could be termed a variation on swinging, minus the car keys.

One rather brutal morning after one of these events, while helping us with the massive clean-up, Janetta happened upon a mysterious pair of men's underpants in the freezer. Then it all came rushing back to me. At one point in the party, a rather large, loud guy, Kaftan Dick complained about how hot it was in the overcrowded kitchen.

Reaching beneath his colourful, flowing kaftan, without blinking an eye, he whipped off his underpants, popping them into the freezer, to cool them down. He must have forgotten to retrieve them later, or else his balls had cooled sufficiently as the evening breezes swept through the house. We gingerly placed this crumpled, unspeakable garment into the mounting rubbish.

Ever a beggar for punishment, on the final New Year's Eve of the eighties, I staged a grand party to see in the new decade. I was involved with someone at the time, but he was thousands of kilometres away. Ralph reported to me, with a chuckle, that he had overheard some old leftie mates working out which parties they might go to that particular New Year's Eve. They all agreed that they would make sure to 'rock up to Helen's place by midnight. That'll be the best one'. I did not mind having that kind of a reputation in 1989.

Speaking of lefties, during the eighties and into the nineties, I was a proud member of the KGB – that is, the Kelvin Grove Branch of the Australian Labor Party. Along with Pretty Pam, Savannah Susan, Cossack Peter, Ann Baillie, Robert Elliot, Helen Abrahams, Peter O'Brien and others, we would passionately discuss the latest political issues, often writing pointed letters of complaint to the ALP management, beginning: 'We of the KGB *deplore* the following policy decision…'

We heard on an ALP grapevine that Bob Hawke was becoming very frustrated with our habit of needling him so often from the left. He said, 'That's the last thing the Labor Party needs – a branch called the KGB!' We were not at all cautious in our robust questioning, which I found stimulating. It's called democracy in action. And I have loved the word 'deplore' ever since.

***

Helen and Ralph, my 50th

Liz and Andrea, party, 90s

Christine, Emma and Anne in Cuba, 2004

Cuban Film School, 2004

Clarissa's Birthday Party, Scotland, 1997

Helen and Jafar Panahi, BIFF, 2004

Helen and George Miller, BIFF, 2000

Mike Witt, West End Film Festival

Helen, Gough and Susan, Noel Pearson Mabo Oration, 2005

With graduating film students Will, Lucy & Tom, 2005

Film Noir Gang - Deb, Sean, Jason, Phoebe & Chris, 2017

Phoebe Hart and Susan McGillicuddy, 2015

Lilli and Lisa, 2014

The 57 Swann Road trio - Susie, Jan and Jeanne

Cousin Jan

Cinema-Joe Hardwick, Piano-Michael Allport, Brisbane, 2005

Deb and Helen at GOMA, 2016

Helen and Chris, BIFF opening night, 2012

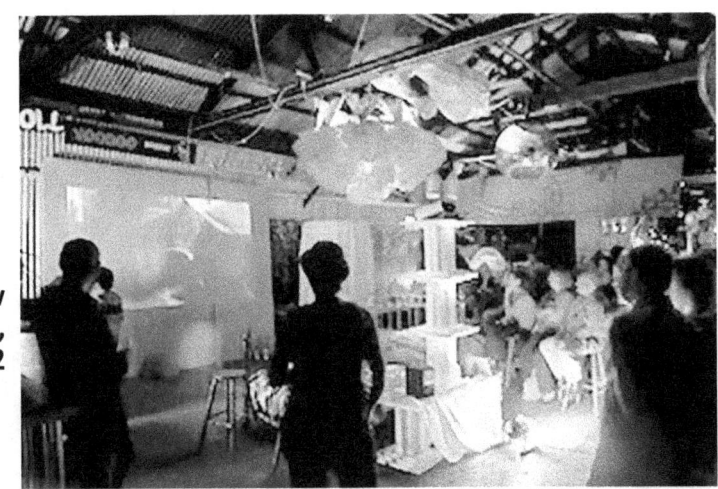

Do Look Now Exhibition, 2012

Stalking Isabelle, with Katrina Channells, White Rabbit Gallery, 2013

Helen and Lord David Puttnam, 2016

ATOM Award, 2017

Germaine Greer and Phillip Adams, 2018

Ann, Helen and Jenny, 2017

Margie, Jocelyn and James at my 75th birthday

With Matt, Anne, Stephen, and Mairi at my 75th birthday

With Susan & Gerry at my 75th birthday

Christine, Janetta and Stephen at my 75th birthday

The Wiffwaffers - Helen, Susan, Deb & Bronwyn, 2018

David and Catherine at my 75th birthday

Lilli and Ruby, my place, 2019

Bronwyn, Jenny and Peter, dancing at my 70th birthday

Dimity, Kings Cross Sydney, 2000

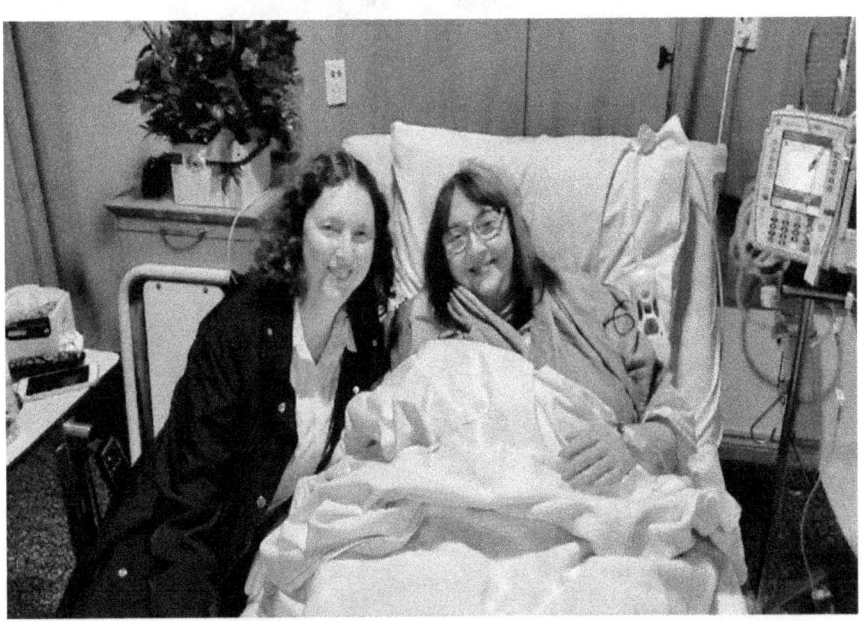
With Margaret Kay after my breast cancer operation, Wesley Hospital, 2016

New York Lisa Schubert in Central Park with King Ellis, 2015

Helen and Margaret Montgomerie, Greenwich Village New York, 2015

9.
ANOTHER ROUND

About the time I met Savannah Susan and Cossack Peter, I experienced a career moment with a difference, as an English teacher at BGGS, the inner-city all girls' school I attended back in the late fifties and early sixties. I realised that a slippery, uncertain tutoring contract at the University of Queensland was not going to give me viable future security. And Richard and I had spent much of the spare money from the accident fund.

The highlights of teaching at BGGS in 1981 and 1982 included inventing a Year Eleven student radio station called Radio Pawpaw, broadcast live across the school every second Friday lunchtime. Two of those keen participants, Janet and Vanessa, later worked as successful television producers. I also enjoyed working close to an old mate, Ian Stuart, Roger's brother, who taught science there at the time.

I designed an intensive elective unit called *My Brilliant Career*, where we engaged in a comparative, critical analysis of the Australian film, directed by Gillian Armstrong, alongside the original book by Miles Franklin. The Year Eleven students were keen, and this film/literature unit went down very well, or so I thought.

An angry father rampaged up to the school, demanding that the principal dismiss '*Ms* Yeates' forthwith, for teaching his daughter about feminism, telling her she could choose any career she liked. He exploded: 'That teacher said my daughter's future was her choice, and hers alone. Not in my house it isn't!'

Fortunately, the principal, Mrs Hancock, gave this spluttering man very short shrift, informing him that the school's main aim was to encourage all girls to be independent thinkers and doers, and the future belonged to them, or words to that effect. Even so, doubtless he felt entitled to throw his considerable weight around, as he was quite a powerful business person with a certain influence over the Bjelke-Petersen government at the time.

I was very relieved that I wasn't frogmarched out the door. Yet, from that moment on, I felt a certain unease. My friends and I had semi-joked for years that the Special Branch of the rightwing government held secret files on us all. I was concerned that I may have just earned a file, or if I already had one, my latest transgression was earmarked for it.

A few other parents were less incensed by my title Ms and my philosophy, although they questioned any innovation I brought to the classroom, saying, rather plaintively, 'What you asked her to do in that assignment just wasn't done in our day'. Well, no.

One mother was particularly exasperated that her daughter had not received a higher mark than a credit for her essay assignment. After talking to this mother for a while, I realised she was taking this assessment grade far too personally. Naturally, I couldn't prove that she had a leading hand in this essay writing project, but I was very suspicious.

After all this happened, and more, my workmate Janet Greenwood and I cooked up an escape plan. We would scamper away most Friday afternoons, a timeslot when we had some flexibility, to enjoy lunch in a French restaurant by the river, communing with her bon vivant husband/barrister Bob along with his best mates from the legal fraternity.

An hour or so later, we slipped by cab back to Gregory Terrace, to stand in front of our respective classes at the end of the day, looking happy, slightly disengaged, not at all guilty, and perhaps a little tipsy. Such a mildly subversive venture pales into insignificance when juxtaposed with the teachers' drinking antics in the Oscar-winning Danish film, *Another Round*. It would have been impossible to behave similarly at a school such as ours.

The famous final scene in *Another Round* is uplifting, largely because the riveting Mads Mikkelson unexpectedly reveals his awesome talent as a gymnast and dancer, while the students and staff wildly celebrate the end of the school year. When school finished for me in 1982, I performed my own liberating dance, although certainly not as memorably as the one by Mads, also releasing himself from a difficult year. His character was possibly staying on, while there was no ambivalence regarding my choice.

In my next career move, I gained a position as a Secondary Liaison Officer for the Department of Education Production Services and The Australian Broadcasting Corporation, advising producers, running teacher workshops, and helping secondary school teachers everywhere with their resource needs. It was great that I could return to being called just 'Helen' again in my workplace. When I was at UQ, the graduate students all called us by our first names. At BGGS, I was called Ms Yeates, a stark reminder that, even though I was divorced from Richard, I still legally bore his surname.

When we were married in 1967, no bride chose to keep her own name. By the late seventies, the pressure was on within some feminist circles for me to return to my birthname or perhaps even my mother's or a grandmother's birthname, thereby diluting, although not discarding certain patriarchal claims on me.[12] By 1981, I had been Helen Yeates for thirteen years, for most of my adult life, and had also published in the name. I let that pressure pass me by. I had had enough of altering legal documents.

Turning up at work on the first day in my new job, already knowing my male bosses, Rod Gilbert and Ray Land quite well, I was introduced to my immediate work colleague. I was dressed in the clothes I had worn to work at Grammar – quite conservative, modest, very straight, not too showy. Jenny Wright looked at me rather quizzically, but, even so, she welcomed me warmly.

Her long black hair flowing, wearing a breathtaking little concoction that looked as if she had sewn a few exotic tea towels together (she had), Jenny possessed the most beautifully sculptured cheek bones I had ever seen. She and her then partner, a filmmaker, both drove matching converted ambulances.

They lived with their blended family in an old Queenslander in Paradise Street, West End. A fresh media career world was opening up for me, with creative people to hang out with at work and at play. This became a new form of paradise for me.

'Jenny Wren' and I hit it off straight away, and we cherish our friendship to this day. We did work hard, but of course we appreciated the flexibility afforded by our position. And we loved travelling to places throughout Queensland, often with the Primary Liaison Officers,

---

12. Some people I know changed their surnames to 'What' and 'Who' to delete the patriarchal line altogether. I am refusing here to use that dated, loaded expression 'maiden name', for all that implies. I am also stunned that young women are still changing their birthnames on marriage, after some less conservative decades when they proudly would not do so. I did hear recently that a young man changed his name to his wife's family name. I found that refreshing. After all, the future is female.

running workshops for teachers. Within Brisbane, ever tactical, Jenny and I would strive to be working at the ABC building in Toowong around lunchtime on a Friday, ready to go with our colleagues in the ABC to the Coronation Motel for a cool drink, a prawn sandwich or a Spaghetti Marinara – the best in town. Or else we would spend the afternoon at the ABC, hopping over to the Royal Exchange Hotel across the road, for a few drinks before heading home.

Not having mobile phones back in the early eighties was a bonus, unimaginable now. Jenny and I could legitimately be in her large, rocky ambulance, driving between work places – from Everton Park, to Ashgrove (where the production studios were), or to Toowong, or back again, with a few diversions along the way, such as picking up her kids, Polly and Nova, from school.

An alternative popular hangout for us on a Friday afternoon, was with the Educational Production crowd and sundry ring-ins at the Paddo Tavern lounge bar, in Given Terrace, Paddington, conveniently situated half way between work and home. It seemed that our own version of *Another Round* was always within reach.

For decades in my film-going life, I enjoyed many a Woody Allen film, my early favourites being such love-letters to New York as *Annie Hall*, *Manhattan*, and *Hannah and her Sisters*. While I am not a devotee anymore, I fondly recall rolling up to view each film on the first screening release night, a special cinematic treat for me and my friends.

People used to tell me I had a Diane Keaton/ Annie Hall aura. Such a 'look' was out there in the fashionista zeitgeist in the late seventies/ early eighties. Flattered by this supposed star-like resemblance, I confess that I did cultivate her look, for a while, wearing the full stylish effect of those androgynous items – the black hats, ties, waistcoats, the white baggy shirts and the beige/khaki pants. Keaton was an influencer, well before Instagram.

This Diane Keaton lookalike narrative was brought to a head after a night at the Paddo Tavern when I was working at Production Services. The next day, the swaggering guy I had come home with, who, funnily enough, worked in the film industry, proclaimed: 'Being with you is like being in a Woody Allen movie!' I'm sure he meant this as a criticism of the way I looked, and the mouthy way I spoke.

Unperturbed, I deliberately misread his comment, embracing it as a compliment, sparring with even more Woodyesque one-liners.

However, when he later revealed he was an a supporter of the far-right Queensland Premier at the time, Dr Sir Johannes Bjelke-Petersen, I realised, to my horror, that this had gone too far.

A Woody critic *and* a Joh voter: sex and politics never mix, especially when combined with the obvious gulf in film tastes. That swaggering filmmaker had to be shown the door, despite the sex, surprisingly, having been top drawer.

In my second year at Production Services, Christine Whitelaw arrived in Brisbane from Melbourne, to work as a producer. She and her art conservationist partner, John Hook, seemed to be very Melbourne-cool. Not certain I was at all Brisbane-cool, whatever that meant, we still bonded.

Christine and I recently chilled out at our friend Bronwyn's place, enjoying our usual takeaway meal from Chop Chop Chang, building up to clearing the table, pushing it aside, and dancing our hearts out to one of Miss B's epic playlists. Traditionally we would finish on a high note, with Yothu Yindi's *Treaty*.

Quite often, we began with a Bruce Springsteen classic, such as *Dancing in the Dark*, played especially for the two Boss fans in the room, sweet Ann Baillie and me. The rest, Cossack Peter, Savannah Susan, Tom, Steve, Christine, whoever was there, faked a little sigh, smiled indulgently, and went with the flow. Daisy the dog was ecstatic to dance along to anything.

Between sets, I asked Christine what she remembered most about me when we first met, at least forty years before. It was my seventy-sixth birthday, and I had just experienced a sudden brain blast, realising, rather belatedly, that this could be a useful question to ask people as I tried to write my memoir.

After a little while, Christine then said, 'I remember us sitting together in the Paddo Hotel bar after work, very early in the piece, probably 1983, and you said, "I think I'll have to move to Melbourne. I've fucked everyone I want to fuck here in Brissie, and there's no one decent left".' She liked me from then on, which was a great relief. We had another drink and a dance to celebrate.

Back in the early eighties, I threw caution to the wind once more in the treacherous personal commitment stakes. This represented 'another round', on a different level. I started a loving relationship with Dennis, whom I met at a party given by our mutual friend, Jo, the woman who had suffered in the seventies from those infamous key parties.

Accompanying me back to my place that night, Dennis climbed into my bed, and stayed for a couple of years.

I was building up to turning forty, and he was about six years younger. Another positive was that he was definitely not an academic, not then, at least. This was refreshing, as I badly needed a change of script on that front. We seemed to be a good match sexually, given that most women reach their sexual peak the more they age, and I needed a younger man to keep up with me in bed. At least, this was my spontaneous rationale, at first.

One major downside surfaced pretty quickly. Dennis tolerated very few of my friends. He loved Savannah Susan, Cossack Peter, Pretty-Pam and her then current beau, Leon. Luckily, they enjoyed his company too. Dennis also took a shine to Gerry Kay, my wild, funny nephew-in-law, then engaged to my Medical Goddess niece, Margaret Hawes. He did like Pierre, when he visited, or when we visited him in Sydney. And that was all.

As time passed, he protested more and more about going to any social events or places where I was catching up with friends outside that tight inner circle. Both then and now, I had a rich social life, which I had no intention of sacrificing. He also struggled with tiresome father issues, and would barely speak to his dad after he remarried. I was very weary of any more father-son clashes.

Everything came to a head after a couple of years. We were on a collision course, and he had to move out. At one stage, early in the relationship, I fantasised that I might have a child with him, as my increasingly urgent body clock was nudging me in that department. As he was both good looking and healthy, at least his genes fitted the bill. That reckless fantasy promptly fell off the agenda when I discovered that he profoundly disliked children. He went on to do a doctorate in philosophy, on a topic that I think may have involved, strangely enough, Jean-Paul Sartre's writings. What goes around, comes around, in that particular existential stratosphere.

In late 1986, Pierre tragically died from complications arising from HIV Aids, barely eight years after our French adventures. By then, we had spent some time together in New York as well, along with our good friends, Janetta, NYCLisa and Straddie Sue. Together, we celebrated New Years' Eve 1980/81, at a club on the Lower East Side of Manhattan.

I recall that Pierre was mugged later that freezing night in the famous gay enclave around Christopher Street, in the West Village. [13] A few years earlier, he had suffered a similar mugging on a shadowy waterfront in Nice. Gay beats were, and still can be, dangerous spaces, with vicious homophobes waging war against men seeking same-sex company.

Pierre often recounted graphic tales of the vibrant gay scene in Sydney, where Oxford Street nightclubs such as Patchs and the Exchange were buzzy venues for hanging out and meeting people. Pierre's girlfriends, such as myself, liked frequenting such nightclubs where we could enjoy drinking, chatting and dancing, without being harassed or hassled. In those smoky, dimly lit spaces, the men only had eyes for each other. Sometimes heterosexual blokes might drop by, hoping to snag an abandoned 'fag hag'. Sex and sexualities were becoming more open, more fluid.

I suppose I was an occasional fag hag, with Pierre as my handbag when we frequented such places – or, conversely, I was his handbag. I'm not sure of the right terminology any more. Gay saunas became very popular spaces in the early eighties, where sexual practices could be wildly imaginative. Quite possibly, Pierre caught the virus in one of those exclusively male saunas.

In certain parks and other hang-outs in Sydney at dusk, gay men would cruise for sex. Some men would pick Pierre up, and afterwards go home to their wives and children. When he became HIV positive, I remember his saying that, as a matter of responsibility, he had to convey the bad news to various contacts, including two of those married, ostensibly heterosexual men.

Pierre returned to his family home in Brisbane during his final year of life. Eventually, he was admitted to the Wattlebrae Infectious Diseases Ward at the Royal Brisbane Hospital, for palliative care. At the same time as Pierre was dying, the girl I have called Angie suffered a massive stroke and was herself hanging on to life by a thread. This double tragedy was hard to bear. Both were young, vibrant, talented, with much to give, and much to live for.

At that time, I had moved out of the Secondary Liaison role, and was running a work group in Queensland Education called Media Inservice, managing one technical assistant, and four male teachers.

---

13. Christopher Street, a gay hub in West Greenwich Village, was immortalised by the Stonewall Inn, and the Stonewall movement for gay rights. The iconic gay writer Christopher Isherwood also wrote a book called 'Christopher Street'.

The latter travelled around the state, presenting practical workshops in schools on video production techniques. Brought in to manage and expand the section's offerings, I aimed to give more intellectual clout and more rigorous practical outcomes to this teacher-centred work unit.

I had also started studying part-time for the Graduate Diploma in Media, offered by the Australian Film, Television and Radio School in Sydney. I could take subjects at participating universities, including Griffith and QUT, and also go to intensive weekend workshops, run locally. Such an innovative program was heaven on wheels for me and many other media educators, such as my friends Ann Baillie, Anne Hickling-Hudson, Emma Felton and Pretty-Pam Ashby. Pam was the first Queensland graduate from this course.

After some huffing and puffing from the more established blokes in my team who preferred to operate 'free range', so to speak, and certainly not with a female manager, our upgraded media education brief began to take hold. Largely this happened thanks to my working with stalwart Greg from my team, along with the supportive, eccentric colleagues across the corridor in Visual Arts, Lance, Peter and Sukie. Joining forces with Jenny Wren, my workmate/soul sister from the previous two years, we held successful film/media/visual arts workshops throughout Queensland.

During the weeks that Pierre was in palliative care, I would slip out of work in the city for an hour or so, in order to spend some quiet, quality time with him. Heading downstairs in the building where I worked, I would inform the rather gruff, self-important guys on 'vehicle duty', that I had a meeting to go to, or a seminar to give, which was often quite true.

Not feeling any guilt, I was pleased that I could quite often stretch both time and logistics. With that convenient work car, I was able to park quite easily in the hospital grounds, on my way to or from a work gig, real or imaginary.

Blanche, his loving mother, would often be visiting at the same time. We had become good mates, and I admired her devotion to her darling son. His straight, younger brother Denis was also very loving and accepting. Dressed in our protective gear, Blanche and I tried to cheer Pierre up as best we could, although the tears often flowed.

Sometimes I harboured crazy, dark thoughts of going to Fortitude Valley, seeking out a cooperative drug dealer, and obtaining an overdose of pure heroin in order to relieve his suffering. Thankfully, I never carried out this promise of assisted dying, which he and I would talk about quite openly. At least now, in 2022, euthanasia has finally been made legal in Queensland, although too late for many who have wished to die with dignity from a diabolical terminal illness.

One of the few positive aspects of this whole calamity was the specialist in charge of that historic ward, a place which had seen better days. Dr Richard Kemp was a champion for the often cruelly stigmatised and shunned AIDS sufferers, his patients. Harmful homophobic myths, misinformation and hideous conspiracy theories were circulating, worldwide.

In the face of such vile prejudice, Dr Kemp and his dedicated staff demonstrated best practice, based on empathy, tireless advocacy, and the latest, most progressive medical knowledge. Pierre said that this remarkable doctor, regularly on duty both day and night, would sometimes lie in bed with his dying patients, hugging them, especially when they were at their worst, desperately needing comfort. Regrettably, this ground-breaking medical carer and researcher did succumb, accidentally, to this highly contagious illness himself.[14]

And the Band Played On was an award-winning US film, made for television. A medical thriller, this film concerned an intrepid, real-life American doctor, Don Francis, attempting for years to track the source of the AIDS epidemic amidst homophobia, bias, obstruction and criminal unhelpfulness, from within the medical fraternity, the politicians, and the media. Dr Kemp was another such medical hero. A long overdue film could well be made as a tribute to him and his magnificent, empathetic work.

To people outside Pierre's inner circle, including some of his workplace colleagues at that posh Sydney private school, the official story was that he was suffering from cancer. As HIV-AIDS did often bring on some form of cancer, it wasn't stretching the truth too much, and many people chose to do this, as a self-protective measure.

I found it difficult to tell my mother that Pierre was HIV positive. My father had died the year before, and she herself was very ill with

---

14. According to Tony Allworth, in 'The Australian Dictionary of Biography', Vol 19, 2021, Richard Kemp, AM, (1945- 1995) was a brilliant physician and infectious diseases specialist, a highly respected leader in the field of HIV-AIDS policy and research. He died a few years after accidentally piercing his skin with an infected needle. He then proceeded to use himself as a research subject, for as long as he could.

Parkinson's disease, exceptionally frail at the time, living on her own. Moreover, her generation had never really experienced, understood or condoned gay culture. Finally, even though she guessed that my dear friend had AIDS, we just couldn't talk about it.

I do regret this personal lapse of openness, of failed nerve. I thought I was trying to protect her, but probably I was only protecting myself. Just a few months after Pierre died, she had a fatal stroke on the very day I started teaching film studies in my new job at The Brisbane College of Advanced Education, an institution which later became part of the Queensland University of Technology.

When Pierre passed away, in late 1986, our mutual friends Janetta and Ian, and Susie and Simon, had given birth earlier that year to their first babies – Jack and Oliver, respectively, each of them a gorgeous gift of future promise, hope and joy. Janetta and Ian came from their property in Roma, while Susie and Simon arrived from Sydney for Pierre's funeral, babies in tow. There was quite a juggling act organising the babies to be cared for elsewhere, during the funeral itself.

As soon as the service at the Brisbane crematorium was over, Susie and I sought refuge in my car, which was parked around the back of the building. We cried, holding on to each other, trying to calm down, before we went to Straddie-Sue's place for the wake.

Suddenly, without warning, dark smoke spiralled out of the crematorium chimney directly behind us. The car windows were open to let out the Brisbane heat, and when we turned around, the reality of Pierre's death, literally hit us in the face.

Recalling this once buried, painful moment, I don't think I want to be cremated when I die, even though I have requested that procedure in my current will. Yet another issue to deal with down the track. Life, death, the whole damned thing, can be such a bugger.

On 31 May 2021, Pierre would have been celebrating his sixty-fifth birthday. It is hard not to try to imagine what that would mean, if only he had survived. He died at the age of thirty, while dear Angie followed him a few years' later, after several strokes and much suffering, aged just thirty-three.

***

10.
ALMOST FAMOUS

At various times over many decades, by chance, or through work, I have encountered people who could be called celebrities. At Christmas time in 1981, together with my brother Peter and his wife, Stephanie, I was spending a snowy Xmas and Boxing Day staying with their close friends, Derek and Mary. Another couple of friends were also present. The food, hospitality, the company were superb. We ate, drank, talked, played cards and other games for several blissful days and nights.

At one stage, another guest, Robin Douet, generously offered me a production assistant job for a film he was going to be working on as production manager, the following April in Scotland. That film was entitled *Local Hero*, to be produced by David Puttnam, and directed by Bill Forsyth. Moreover, Burt Lancaster, of Hollywood mega-fame, might be playing a key role in the film.

Naturally, this offer excited me, as I sensed that this might fulfil my long-held fantasy of being launched, somehow, somewhere, into a role in the film industry. Such a vision had been spinning around my brain for quite a while.

Of course, in the sobering light of day, this dream offer morphed into a mess of geographical impossibility, post-divorce financial risk, as well as much uncertainty and familial duty on the personal front, all of which bound me to Australia. Stephanie, whom I always loved as a sister, also made a valid, conscience-rattling point. I would be taking a job that a local aspiring filmmaker might very happily, and probably more deservedly, fill.

Local Hero has remained one of my favourite films, not only because I was, for a very short while, on the cusp of being part of the production crew, but also because it was 'love at first sight'. In the recent past, the celebrated Lord David Puttnam visited Brisbane several times for various conferences and film events, thanks to the Griffith University

Film School and the Asia Pacific Screen Association. While in Brisbane, he was very generous with his time.

One day, grabbing a private opportunity, I mentioned to him that I had almost worked on that early film of his, adding that *Local Hero* was my favourite of all his films. With a sparkle in his eye, he replied that it was also his personal favourite. I walked away, choking a little, speculating on what imaginary *Sliding Doors* alternative narrative might have driven my life path in another direction, had I made it onto that Scottish film set, that cold April, back in 1982.

Hollywood beckoned me, somewhat differently, in May 1985. I travelled to Los Angeles for a challenging fortnight, a whirlwind seemingly *Mission: Impossible*, to seek out a famous director to make him or her an offer they hopefully could not refuse. At the top of my list was Steven Spielberg, who politely declined my invitation to be keynote speaker in the film strand of the National Youth and the Arts conference in Brisbane, that coming December.

Thanks to my loyal workmate, Lance Courtenay, who had contacts everywhere, I was able to offer the film director a $10,000 package, courtesy of the Queensland Film Corporation. I wished that an esteemed female film director could have been at the top of my list, but, in 1985, such creative women were in very short supply, world-wide.

While in Los Angeles, I was very well set up. I had my own managerial office at the Pickford/Fairbanks studios along Santa Monica Boulevard, courtesy of my generous hosts, Polly's sister, Mary Perkins, and her then partner, Larry. They part-owned those historic studios.

Very quickly, I discovered that no one in the Hollywood movie industry ever answered telephone calls in the morning. I would leave a message on an answering machine or sometimes talk to an assistant, and one of the filmmaker's people would respond in the afternoon, if my message had been of any interest.

As I twiddled my thumbs in my executive office, waiting for famous film directors to return my morning calls, scenes from the film *Girls Just want to Have Fun* were being shot in one of the studios close by my office. Inspired by Cindy Lauper's hit song, this average comedy/musical starred Sarah Jessica Parker and Helen Hunt. I witnessed singers and dancers having their smokos in the shared areas outside – not at all glamorous, but a rather amusing diversion.

Towards the end of my first week in Hollywood, my celebrity scouting appeared to be coming to fruition. I was very excited when the charming, down-to-earth actor/director Ron Howard accepted my invitation to the conference. He had directed *Splash* in 1984, and *Cocoon* was being released later in 1985.

The next day, however, my mood shifted dramatically. Ron Howard withdrew, apologising, as he had just realised that the dates meant that his wife, pregnant with twins, would be unable to travel with him in early December. I had to go back to the drawing board.

That weekend, I flew to New York, hopeful that I had lined up both Wim Wenders and Jim Jarmusch as possible contenders. Their helpful agents wanted to meet me in person, with Jim's agent saying that he would be in attendance at our meeting in New York.

Jim Jarmusch had recently released his wonderfully off-beat first film, *Stranger Than Paradise*, while the more established German filmmaker, Wim Wenders, his friend and mentor, had also just directed his achingly beautiful film, made in America, *Paris, Texas*. Both these films caused a sensational critical buzz that year.

My red-eye trip across country did, sadly, turn out to be wasted. However, of course, my love of New York and hanging out with NewYork City Lisa again, lessened the pain. Having double-checked their schedules, these two directors found they would actually be together in Berlin that December, for the release of Jim's film, *Stranger Than Paradise*.

The date for that significant event had been finalised while I was jetting across America. I wished them both well, holding back my tears – not of anger, but of disappointment. Back in Los Angeles again, the clock was ticking. I felt a flutter of real concern that a colleague's dark pronouncement before I left Australia, might regrettably come true. He had said, through gritted teeth, 'You know, Helen, your career will be finished if you don't succeed in LA'.

His words were reminiscent of that daunting old film industry cliché: 'You'll never work in this town again'. Shaking myself free of his negative prophecy, I determinedly went back to that shaky drawing board, yet again. Within a few days, I broke the curse, landing two distinguished candidates, Gil Cates and Dan Petrie, both keen to come to Brisbane that December. Gil was then President of the Directors Guild of America, and director of such films as *The Last Married Couple in America*.

Daniel Petrie Senior had already made many acclaimed films, including *Sybil, Fort Apache the Bronx,* and his most recent film at that time, *The Bay Boy*. A gracious gentleman, Dan, organised for us to meet in person at a café in Santa Monica, where he introduced me to his film and television producer wife, Dorothea. We sealed the deal.

Gil would have been a fine choice as well, but fate landed Dan into my orbit, just a few hours before Gil contacted me. This was what happens in Hollywood, I felt, although I'm sure it could happen anywhere.

Dan enthusiastically offered a special Brisbane screening of his latest film, *The Bay Boy*, starring the sublime Swedish actress, Liv Ullman, along with young Kiefer Sutherland, in his first film role. This was to be the Australian premiere of his semi-autobiographical film, set in Canada, where Dan was born.

I promised him that the screening would be a very special, gala celebration linked to the conference. This did happen, with as much glamour and glitter as we could muster, one festive evening at the Schonell Theatre, on the University of Queensland's St Lucia campus.

Young filmmakers clung to his every word at the conference. Post-conference, Dan and I flew to Sydney to dine with some film people, including the critic David Stratton, Carl Schultz, director of *Careful He Might Hear You*, and Kay Morphett from the Australian Film Institute. As it was late in the year, many people in the film industry were out of town. Dan and I stayed friends and warm letter-writers over many years.

My Los Angeles trip and Daniel Petrie's trip in 1985 were generously funded by the Queensland Film Corporation. My workmate Lance Courtenay and I convinced Brian Williams, the CEO, that this event would be a great move, creating Hollywood links for future Queensland filmmakers. Brian was very pleased with the outcome. Unfortunately for him, he lost his job in the years that followed, when the QFC was shut down.[15]

---

15. I later wrote a history of that corporation which had dissolved after several major scandals, none, thankfully, involving either Lance or me. The director of the corporation, Allan Callaghan and his wife Judith were both jailed for the misappropriation of QFC funds, in 1987 and 1986, respectively. My chapter appeared in the book, *Queensland Images in Film and Television* edited for UQP by Jonathan Dawson, and my then boss, Professor Bruce Molloy.

For that same conference, I organised several top Australian speakers as well, such as Phillip Adams, always charming and irreverent. The young Richard Lowenstein discussed his experiences in the industry, and we screened his latest film, *Strikebound,* based on his mother Wendy's novel *Dead Men Don't Dig Coal.*

Sitting beside Richard during the screening, my heart went out to him. He was trembling, twitching, at each twist and turn in his film. Highly sensitive, he tuned into the audience's reactions and, most probably, to his own visceral memories of giving birth to each scene. Seeing one's precious creative work on public display often does this to filmmakers, as I have found since then, although this was my first tangible realisation of the scale of such an impact. Many filmmakers prefer to leave the cinema during a screening, returning for the Q and A afterwards.

Much later, in the nineties, brother Peter and I met up in New York. He was there to sort out the publication of one of his books, a biography of the actor, Jack Nicholson. Along with NewFarm Lisa, who was living and working there at the time, we headed to the Carlyle Hotel one Monday night, to hear Woody Allen playing clarinet in his band.

Woody was very serious, barely acknowledging the audience, until the very end when he thanked us for coming, adding he was going home to watch 'the game'. Lisa, Peter and I did not mind. We were soaking up the history of that hotel, famous for many celebrity events, including the fateful encounter between Marilyn Monroe and President John Kennedy.

The following Sunday, with her glorious mane of red-hair flowing, Lisa, a performing artist, and I were sitting in a sidewalk café in Soho, happily watching the crowds go by. We noticed that many young gay men seemed to be dining out with their mothers. Gradually it dawned on us that this was Mother's Day.

Sitting close by, a man on his own was reading the New York Times Sunday magazine. Noticing our Australian accents, he leaned across, smiling, asking if we were a mother and daughter duo, on holiday from Australia. We laughed, agreeing we were definitely Australians, but, no, we were not related.

He introduced himself as the Australian painter, David Rankin, who lived in New York City with his novelist wife, Lily Brett. We chatted for a while, and he invited us to the opening of his art exhibition later that week. Unfortunately, I was heading home on the morrow, and Lisa was not free the day of his show. Nevertheless, this had been a special encounter for us. We remember this with fondness every Mother's Day, which I still celebrate with Lisa, and her beautiful filmmaker daughter Lilli Corrias-Smith, my imaginary grand-daughter.

During another visit, on the top floor of an old Lower East Side warehouse, I recall being with the other Lisa, NewYork Lisa, at an Off-Broadway hit play with mobile actors, sets and audience, graphically depicting the history of slavery. After I politely told two women who had just exited the lift, that the end of the queue was down the stairs, they paused, then happily complied. Suddenly, the organisers rushed out, pushing past us, quickly ushering them inside, shutting the entry door firmly behind them.

Poor Lisa was mortified, as was I, when I realised, belatedly, the identities of those VIP guests. I had just ordered writer Susan Sontag and photographer Annie Liebowitz to join the queue. Later, I managed to apologise, when, by chance, we ended up sitting close to them on that fluid set. They laughed, and were very gracious.

Several years later in Paris, on the bridge to Île Saint-Louis, I saw Annie walking towards me. Her partner, Susan, had died in 2004. Our eyes met, and I gave her a sympathetic look. I doubt that she remembered me, of course, although she did give me a small smile of acknowledgement.

In London, over many years, I have had similar, mini-brushes with fame. In 1992, I was staying in London with my old sweetheart, Ian, who was then a Professor in Photogrammetry and Surveying at University College, London. He took me to a witty talk given by Germaine Greer, about the Prime Minister of Australia, Paul Keating, scandalously breaking protocol, touching the Queen on her back. After Germaine finished speaking, we were invited to an exclusive little cocktail party.

Ian and I chatted with her for a while. She insisted that she had met me before. Somewhat bemused, I finally pointed out that she had signed a copy of her latest book for me at the Brisbane City Hall a while ago, but, as there were around eight hundred people at the launch, I doubted that she would remember me. She disagreed, saying, 'Yes! That was it!'

When I said I was an academic in film and television, she asked what my current research was about. Rather embarrassed, I told her that I was giving men centre-stage yet again, by exploring the media representation of masculinities, both sporting and ageing. To my relief, she said, 'No, no, that's great. You must keep going. We have to dig deep, to understand patriarchy in all its forms'. I felt I had just been given a little gold feminist star.

Another time in London, in the Tate Gallery foyer, the great actress, by then a politician, Glenda Jackson, signed the rather tatty cover of my London A-to-Z map book. I approached her, blurting out: 'Ms Jackson, I hate to be a pain in the butt, but I'm from Australia, and I would love to have your autograph, please'.

She smiled wryly, hesitating for a few moments. Then grabbing my A to Z, she signed her name with a flourish. I would have loved to talk to her about some of her films, especially *Women in Love*, and her riveting performance in *The House of Bernada Alba*, which I had seen back in 1988 at the Lyric Theatre in London's West End.

I was also interested in finding out more about her sterling work as a Labour Party member in the British Parliament. Nevertheless, I was under no illusion that Glenda Jackson would invite me to join her for high tea at the Ritz, or even for a cuppa at the Tate Gallery café on the Embankment. I heard later that she was usually very standoffish. At least, gormless Australian openness scored that day.

Later, Bob Geldof and Paula Yates sat next to me at the opening night of a play at the National Theatre. For some unknown reason, I had been ushered to the cordoned off VIP section. I guess Bob and Paula imagined that this woman beside them was also famous, although they couldn't quite place me.

We exchanged nods and polite smiles, none of us knowing what the future might hold. Later, she left him for Australian rock royalty. Talented Richard Lowenstein's dark film, *Mystify: Michael Hutchence*, gives powerful insights into the life of that rock god, and that tragic relationship saga.

On another trip to London, I had a different kind of encounter with a unique celebrity. Clarissa Dickson Wright rose to fame as one half of television's *Two Fat Ladies*. The previous year she had met Peter at the London home of Gloria, Lady Cottesloe, and identified our family as her long-lost Australian cousins. A striking, dominant personality, Clarissa had an encyclopaedic knowledge of all things ancestral and historical – and she possessed a photographic memory.

Her Australian-born mother, Molly Bath, came from a wealthy Singapore family. Our supposed link was through the Irish ancestry of her father, Arthur Dickson Wright, who was born in Dublin. An esteemed surgeon serving the Queen Mother and other members of the Royal Family, he was, as Clarissa claimed, an abusive father given to drunken rages: 'I've fallen out with all my living relatives here', Clarissa roared heartily. 'I'm thrilled to find some new cousins I actually like'. We were also pleased, if a little mystified.

At my first encounter, I enjoyed her hospitality in her little cottage in South London, along with Peter and other friends, tucking into a prime beef dinner with all the trimmings. After that, I made several forays to Books for Cooks, the shop she managed in Blenheim Crescent next to the Portobello Road Market in Notting Hill. This tiny store teemed from floor to ceiling with world cookery books, both rare and mainstream, along with a higgedly-piggedly treasure trove of kitchen implements.

From time to time, she prepared lunch in the tiny kitchen at the back. Tempting aromas wafted through this foodie paradise, out onto the street. Whenever she was the chef-of-the-day, word would circulate in the market. All the marketeers and regular customers knew that, if you timed your visit well, sitting cramped up inside on chairs around a few rickety tables, you could enjoy a feast cooked by Clarissa herself.

It was hard not to be swept away by her charm, and become convinced by her authoritative way of speaking. None of her mental faculties appeared to have been dampened too much by her years of heavy drinking, after having once been, as she claimed, the youngest, brightest barrister in London.

Taking to alcohol in the mid-seventies because of multiple family traumas, she proceeded to waste a hefty inherited fortune, mainly by partying very hard. She would, for instance, fly friends to the French Riviera for wild parties held over many days, endlessly entertaining her burgeoning entourage, until everything fell apart.

In less than ten years, she was disbarred from practising as a barrister, and lost other jobs through her excessive drinking. Looking back on all this, Clarissa said: 'My main health problem at the end of it all was really the quinine. That's what ruined, poisoned my body, made me ill, made me fat.' I replied, 'Quinine? Not the alcohol?' Clarissa, shaking her head vigorously: 'No, all that quinine in the bloody tonic. I consumed more of that in my G & Ts than the actual gin. Gallons and gallons of it'.

During her darkest times in the eighties, she was homeless in London, ultimately being rescued by old friends. 'Homelessness is a choice', she once informed me, in her definitive way. Doing a double take, I replied: 'No, Clarissa, I believe it's systemic. The poor don't choose to be poor. Inequality is rampant in the UK'.

Finding some of her views hard to digest, I also could not condone her public support of shooting and hunting, and her loyalty to the British Conservative Party. But, somehow, we rose above our differences of opinion, and our bond appeared to strengthen.

In early August, 1997, I accepted her invitation to stay with her in a village outside Edinburgh, for as long as I liked. With another famous foodie and cook, Jennifer Paterson, Clarissa had, by that time, became a celebrity in the *Two Fat Ladies*, riding around the UK on a motor bike with a side-car, cooking up a storm for particular groups of people, such as other bikers. At its peak, this series had seventy million followers across many countries.

When I arrived in Edinburgh, Clarissa was engaged, full-throttle, in the making of this series. Earlier that year, she and Jennifer had embarked on a successful world tour, landing in Brisbane with ample merchandise such as cookery books and tea-towels, along with good will and many funny stories.

We met up in person, along with my sister Jocelyn Hawes, our cousins, Patty Purves and Nancy Tow, and some of my foodie friends, Savannah Susan, Cossack Peter, Andrea Mitchell, and others. The Sheraton Hotel could have sold out that celebrity lunch several times over, as the cooking ladies were immensely popular.

I also discovered the (now well-known fact) that there was not, after all, a close friendship between her and Jennifer, the driver of the bike – their onscreen and offscreen relationship was quite different from popular perceptions. Clarissa explained: 'Jennifer drank after the shoot each day with the *Two Fat Ladies* crew. She drank them all under the table. I tried to stay in different hotels from Jennifer and the others.'

Having moved away from London for good, Clarissa occupied a little gatehouse in the grounds of a friend's manor. The annual Edinburgh Festival had just started by the time I settled in. I lapped up her company and her home-cooked meals, the ingredients being sourced fresh from local farmers.

Taking me to some of her favourite haunts around Edinburgh, at any delicatessen, restaurant, and butcher's shop, she was welcomed with open arms. Suddenly, however, our time together was cut short, as she was called away on an unexpected production rescheduling, somehow linked to the English weather.

Living on my own for the next two weeks, I was not lost for company and events to enjoy. I became friendly with Sophie, Clarissa's close neighbour, who was working for the Edinburgh Film Festival. We would often go to the venue together. That year I was honoured to be representing the Brisbane International Film Festival, as an invited guest in Edinburgh. I saw many great films, including my first viewing of *The Ice Storm*, presented by the esteemed filmmaker himself, Ang Lee.

During that time, I also caught up with several friends from Brisbane. Talented actors and musicians, they were performing their original creations at the Edinburgh Fringe Festival, in ancient church halls and other small, rather crusty venues dotted around the city. The Writers' Festival was also buzzing, with Doris Lessing as one of the keynotes. The time passed very amiably for this particular festival junkie.

Towards the end of my time in Scotland, Clarissa returned for her deliberately delayed fiftieth birthday party. A day or so before the party, I met up with Jennifer again at a special luncheon for close family and friends, in Clarissa's small double-storied cottage. To my surprise, Jennifer treated me as an inferior colonial cousin.

'Thinner, thinner!' she screeched imperiously. Having been tasked with slicing the cucumber 'super thinly' for a particular salad, this gormless kitchen hand from Down Under feared cutting off several finger tips in the process. I failed dismally, at least in Jennifer's eyes.

Over those last days in the cottage, and then at the party, I found that several of Clarissa's friends were upper-class snobs, still holding outdated colonial modes of thinking, and indulging in quite rude, patronising behaviour. This went with that entitled territory, I guess. I strove to be less sensitive, seeing them as rather comical, which they were.

As expected, Clarissa's party was very grand. Set in the grounds of the palatial Lennoxlove House in East Lothian, a huge marquee had been erected for music, dancing and eating. Angus, the 15th Duke of Hamilton, warmly wished his old friend, Clarissa, a happy birthday, welcoming her guests to his family's ancestral home.

People from abroad and from all over the United Kingdom thronged there that night to celebrate with her. Earlier that day, Peter arrived from London. We enjoyed the evening under the stars, listening to the excellent West Indian band transported to Scotland for the event, all the way from the Portobello Road. Members of this steel band were great friends of the irrepressible Clarissa, harking back to her humbler days in that iconic cookery bookshop.

The delicious, to-die-for food was served inside the grand house. For months, Clarissa had been meticulously designing the menu style, its substance and presentation. The caterers followed her masterpiece culinary and service instructions to the letter. One person whispered: 'Some of this food is usually only served for Royalty', pointing reverentially to the princely sturgeon, along with an exclusive Scottish wild smoked salmon.

At this 'open mouth/open house' night, guests were invited to wander through the majestic rooms, including a hallowed bedroom where Queen Mary had once slept. In that room, guests could admire her tiny four-poster bed, her beautiful sapphire ring, and an historic silver casket laced with gold, from the 1670s.[16]

I liked the larger-than-life Clarissa I knew. The close research into our Irish ancestors carried out over many years, firstly by my mother, decades earlier, then later by my sister Jocelyn and other relatives, never confirmed this intra-family link that Clarissa claimed so convincingly. As we moved into the new millennium, she faded from our lives.

Clarissa Theresa Philomena Aileen Mary Josephine Agnes Elsie Trilby Louise Esmerelda Dickson Wright died in 2014 in Scotland, aged sixty-six. Placed on Clarissa's coffin was a Viking helmet and a wreath made of chillies, artichokes, broccoli and sage. Clarissa, renowned for

---

16. It is said that this casket once held the 'notorious letters that allegedly incriminated Mary, Queen of Scots in the murder of her second husband, Lord Darnley.' https://sites.scran.ac.uk/vhp/treasures11.html Accessed 18 September, 2021

her eccentric flair, always liked to make a statement, just as her parents certainly did, with her multi-pronged name.

Whether this had all been true or fantastical did not really matter to me. With Clarissa at her ivy-covered cottage in that perfect little village, I felt I had been transported into a kind of alternative reality, frozen in time, a brief, luminous side-step, a different kind of being *Almost Famous.* Close at hand, I was witnessing and recording how some of the famous actually operate, as writer/director Cameron Crowe tells it in that semi-autobiographical film about rock stars.

My experience was also not dissimilar to that of the spellbound characters entering the mythical Scottish world of the fifties film, *Brigadoon.* In the spirit of that film, Clarissa's enchanting olde worlde ways shone, and then, mysteriously, faded into the mist.

In a different way, the singer Bob Dylan has also enchanted me, gifting me one of the key soundtracks of my life. I have attended many, if not all of his live concerts since the sixties, whenever he found his way to Australia on his Never-Ending Tour.

One early evening in May 2015, while celebrating my seventieth birthday in New York, I was on my way to the Greenwich Village Apothecary searching for a mysterious over-the-counter American drug, to help cure a drippy nose. Suddenly, I bumped into Bob in person.

Earlier, I thought had seen him walking past me. I said to myself, 'That person in that dapper coat and hat just has be Bob Dylan', but I wasn't entirely sure. After my apothecary visit, I encountered him again, this time walking directly towards me. Carrying some groceries in a string bag, he frowned a little, seeing that I knew who he was. He signalled to me to restrain myself.

Trying to be very New York-cool, despite my excitement and that infernal leaky nose, I smiled, nodded in his direction, and kept on walking. There was no photograph, no selfie, no chat, no visible, concrete souvenir for me. This grumpy old icon walked on home with his pasta, while people drove by in cars, yelling 'Hey Bob!'

Two days before, in a parallel street in the Village, I caught a glimpse of Patti Smith and Leonard Cohen, engaged in deep conversation, brushing past me and my friend Cossack Peter, while we were window-shopping at *The Big Lebowski* souvenir shop. I felt at home in Greenwich Village. And I wasn't hallucinating regarding any of these celebrity glimpses.

As Dylan sings in *My Back Pages*, 'I was so much older then, I'm younger than that now'. Pre-Covid, I often travelled to Sydney for special cultural events, with a group of friends from Brisbane. Being with them wherever we were going, was a kind of anti-ageing tonic, as I felt younger day by day, even though I always seemed, technically, to be the oldest person in the room.

On one of those Sydney jaunts, we were there specifically to see the stars Isabelle Huppert, Cate Blanchett, and Elizabeth Debicki in the Sydney Theatre Company production of *The Maids*. We loved Cate and Isabelle, and would practically crawl over hot coals to see them live on stage, together. That same year, 2013, Elizabeth was just starting her own, soon-to-be illustrious career.

I was staying in Sydney with friends, my former student Katrina Channells and her parents, Coralie and Jim, heroes of the socialist left. They had spent a few years in Venezuela, supporting the early days of the revolution under Hugo Chavez, while Katrina, another New Farm girl, studied film at QUT.

One afternoon, Katrina and I encountered Isabelle Huppert and her cool companion, relaxing pre-show, at the White Rabbit Gallery in inner Sydney. Using the pitch that I particularly admired Isabelle's work, and that I had taught French cinema at University, Katrina asked if she could please take a photo of Isabelle with me, side by side. Isabelle refused.

Downstairs, we drowned our sorrows in aromatic herbal tea. Isabelle then showed up once more, sitting down near us in that little gallery café, her smile communicating, wordlessly, 'No hard feelings'.

Later that afternoon, we encountered Isabelle again, by chance, walking towards us in a back street near where we were staying. She looked as startled as we were. We nodded and smiled, awkwardly, turning down a side street, suppressing our embarrassed, nervous giggles.

To this day, Katrina, recalls our manoeuvring around the back streets to be in closer proximity to Isabelle, after sussing her from a distance. My own, possibly convenient memory loss denies our indulging in such overt stalking. The truth surrounding that celebrity street encounter has remained, ever since, in the lap of the fickle memory gods.

In the theatre the following evening, my French filmstar/stalker drama began to unravel. The film buffs in our group, particularly Joe Hardwick and myself, had booked perfect seats for this adaptation of Jean Genet's play: three rows back, centre stage.

At the last minute, I swapped seats with our friend Deb Polson, heading towards the back of the theatre, out of Isabelle's direct line of sight. I was anxious that she might stumble over her lines at a crucial moment, if and when she spotted her creepy woman stalker, too close for comfort.

It would seem that this memoir also holds, deep within it, a multiplier effect. Friends recall and/or interpret different versions of my life, including these celebrity chronicles. For instance, one Sydney friend, Simon, has pronounced that, in all probability, Isabelle was stalking me in Sydney, that she herself engineered our brief encounters, firstly at the gallery, then in the café, and finally in the street near where I was staying.

Still on my case, two years later, Simon elaborated further, claiming that a similar, inverted stalking scenario related to my brush with Bob Dylan in Greenwich Village, evidenced by the fact that 'he timed his return from the grocery store so he could meet you face-to-face'. Case closed. Simon's interpretations significantly improved my mood, both then and now. After all, the aura of celebrity itself is in the eye of the beholder.

As for Isabelle Huppert, my friends and I eagerly await her return to Australia for an opening night launch of a future Alliance Française French Film Festival, in Brisbane. No doubt, she is also keenly anticipating such a prospect.

***

11.
MY BRILLIANT CAREER

In my first degree, back in the mid-sixties, I discovered Nordic noir, although of course it wasn't called that back then. My early obsession, which, in one form or another, has haunted me all my life, involved a passionate immersion in the spirited texts of Old Norse and Old Icelandic literature. I conquered the sagas in the original in my English honours class, with that goddess lecturer, Felicity Currie. She always seemed, eerily, to be from another mythical time and space.

Felicity had helped repair the wounds of my battered brain and restore my shaky life, giving me the grit and the confidence to move forward in my studies. Later, as a teacher myself, I would try to be as inspirational and as daring as she was. And nearly two decades after she taught me, I engaged, along with a team of passionate media teachers, in our own 'Brisbane noir' saga. We would gird our loins and march into alien committee rooms.

Along with earlier battle champions of media education, such as Mirva Harrison and Michael How, we somehow convinced the extremely conservative National Party government that media education was a worthy pursuit. Of course, these were trigger words. Joh and his ministers feared and hated the media. When we introduced critical media studies, fortunately they jumped to the reductive conclusion that this endeavour would be instructing kids on the dangerous effects of the media.

In their minds, they were endorsing the so-called inoculation approach to media education: inoculate/vaccinate/destroy the media virus, along with critical thinking, as a bonus. They also did not pay much attention to the considerable weight given to creative, original production in our proposed courses.

Luckily, for us, they weren't very bright.

By 1985, I had become President of the Queensland branch of the Australian Teachers of Media, ATOM, a large National organisation comprising dedicated member/teachers, mostly who specialised in teaching film and media education as separate subjects, or within English. As media education warriors, we regularly crossed swords with colleagues in the more established arts, particularly music. From the very beginning, the music people resented this new, shiny arts subject, flying in on a seemingly indestructible dragon, luring students away from the traditional pathways. It was like *Game of Thrones*, played out on a volatile curriculum-based canvas, fighting for power over students' artistic choices.

Somehow, despite the odds, we emerged, battered but triumphant, both locally and nationally. In many ways, we forged ahead of the other states, much to their astonishment, and ultimately, their grudging praise. By and large, we had always been patronised by media educators in the southern states. According to them, we were doomed to be languishing in the backward 'Deep North', in an education system run by a bunch of hicks and rednecks.

Those of us who didn't move south in despair and disgust, remained and re-energised our education battles strategically, day by day, on the barricades, confronting the hicks and rednecks. In the long run, the resolute ATOM warrior team managed to achieve the impossible. Amidst all the blood, sweat and tears, we crafted the most innovative media education curriculum in Australia at the time.

This was especially so, given that we devised a film and television subject that counted for tertiary entrance, and not just a sideline elective, as happened elsewhere, even in the UK. And we also ran exciting conferences.

In the cut and thrust of this media education saga, another highlight was the founding of the Queensland New Filmmakers' Awards, originally called the Young Filmmakers' Awards. I managed these annual events successfully through the Australian Teachers of Media (Queensland) with much government, industry and creative filmmaker involvement over twenty-five years.

Like a pack of invading barbarians, the Liberal/National Party Newman government tore these awards down around 2013, in their crude attempt to destroy or at least maim many of the creative industries, including film. In so doing, they obliterated a significant legacy, a prestigious Awards culture which had championed emerging filmmakers over many years in Queensland. And, of course, the year before, they had already sacrificed all arts credibility by axeing the Premier's Literary Awards immediately on being elected in 2012. It has been noted that the latter cut saved them less than 0.04 percent of the state budget. Their short-sighted, supposedly cost-saving, ideological mantra was 'Let the market decide'.

Overlapping with many of these events, from 1987 onwards, I was employed as an academic at the Brisbane College of Advanced Education, which later amalgamated with Queensland Institute of Technology, becoming the Queensland University of Technology in the early nineties. When the amalgamation happened, I moved from training film and television teachers, into teaching filmmakers about film.

One happy memory flash shows me hanging out in Peel Street where the old film studios used to be, taking refuge from departmental politics across the river at Gardens Point. Before the new creative industries faculty was formed, along with moving to the Kelvin Grove Campus, I would occasionally work in West End, comfortably chatting to my film production colleagues.

I also encountered the occasional dishevelled students, bleary-eyed from twenty-four hours in an edit suite, crafting their latest creations, forming relationships, breaking up once the film ended. Alternatively, the students were hyped up, building sets, shooting their original film productions in that musty, productive studio, for days on end. It was very satisfying to immerse myself at the pointy creative end of the film course I was managing at the time.

Over the years, I thrived on the subjects I taught, with the *Feminist Media Studies* unit being the most treasured one, until the curriculum heavyweights decided that any so-called 'boutique' units would have to be ditched for more mainstream, larger units. Follow the money, follow the ideology. Even so, I made sure that feminist films, issues and discussions remained a strong thread in my subjects.

I loved the students, eloquent, bright-eyed, both in my film classes and in my honours and postgraduate research methodology classes. As her supervisor, I was thrilled and proud to see Phoebe Hart's doctoral film, *Orchids: My Intersex Adventure*, finally shown on the big screen at the Palace Cinema, in all its non-binary glory.

However, I also had to put in the hours, running a massive compulsory unit called *Media and Society* for many years, catering to hundreds of cross-disciplinary students across the faculty each semester. Often the class spilled over into another lecture room next door, simultaneously being fed the lecture live. It was all rather clunky, technically speaking, back then. Overall, feedback from the students was mostly positive regarding their experience of this mass subject.

In this class, I would receive multiple requests for extensions of student assignments. One major excuse was that a grandmother had died. Initially, I was, naturally, very sympathetic. Gradually I started to ask to see documented proof of this, which seemed cold and unfeeling to the legitimate applicants. My colleagues and I felt that, sadly, too many students were using this excuse, probably repetitively, semester by semester.

I recall another late assignment excuse which was quite original, and not simply 'a dog ate my homework'. A wide-eyed acting student told me a very dramatic story of how he had been trapped for days in West End, unable to attend university and bring in his assignment, because a mad dog had bailed him up in his house. I granted him the extension.

In my *Australian Film* subject, I taught films that were, to my mind, great examples of the craft of filmmaking in the industry many of them would one day would gain work. Such stand-out films were often controversial, in story, theme and style, sparking interesting debates both in the academic literature, and in class. Such films included *Shame, Man of Flowers. The Boys,* and *Head On*, amongst many others over the years.

I thought the very original, arthouse film, *Man of Flowers* would be enjoyable, even mind-expanding, for students over eighteen. Sexually, it was quite advanced and mature, and the director, Paul Cox, pushed other boundaries in this, his first major film. One semester, mid-screening, a girl ran out of the class, in tears. I tried to calm her, fearing she was ill.

However, it turned out that she was reacting to a mild lesbian love scene in *Man of Flowers*, declaring, 'I became a born-again Christian three weeks ago, and I'm now forbidden to watch such stuff in films'. I replied that she was entitled to her views, which I respected. However, I wished that she could continue to watch the whole film, so that she could contribute to the tutorial discussion, where her views would provide a welcome perspective. She never returned.

Shame and the later film, *The Boys,* both dealt with issues of male violence and rape in different ways, although these films were not offered in the course at the same time. While I did warn the students about the confronting content, some students with family members or friends who had experienced such horror, became quite distressed.

One girl found *The Boys* upsetting, personally, on witnessing the powerfully executed abusive relationship between the David Wenham character and his girlfriend, played by Toni Colette. This student saw close parallels to her relationship with her then partner being starkly played out on screen. She became quite traumatised. At least this experience did trigger her to end the relationship, ultimately a positive outcome.

Others had to confront their own overt or covert homophobia while dealing with the film, *Head On*. There were stirrings of racist resistance when we studied Indigenous films, such as *One Night the Moon, Night Cries: A Rural Tragedy* and *Samson and Delilah*. Teaching Film Studies was a challenging, educative ride, for all involved. One of my goals was that this experience would be liberating, leading the students to critically examine where they stood in the world and, for the budding filmmakers, within their creative craft.

Today, lecturers are bound to give 'trigger warnings' regarding textual content. I gather that sometimes these warnings themselves may trigger adverse reactions. I'm glad I am still not trying to manoeuvre the teaching of significant, carefully chosen films. If pallid, whitebread romcoms are all that is left, that would be a major trigger for me, in a different way.

For years, the film and television discipline in creative industries developed a very successful procedure in relation to the annual student entrance interviews via portfolio. Staff would select the most creative, most promising students to be admitted into the highly competitive Film and TV Fine Arts Degree. As course coordinator at the time, I was dedicated to this process, as were my colleagues.

The aspiring short-listed students would arrive, bursting with ideas, showing us their poetry, video productions, scripts, art work, whatever, in order to help their selection prospects. A parent often tagged along, helping to carry awkwardly large paintings and other proof of their progeny's exceptional creativity.

This was also a great way of forging a relationship with many of the students before they even started, giving us insights and joy, both professionally and personally, with reciprocal rewards for the successful students. However, the people in the upper echelons decided one year to take all that away, pronouncing that this long-drawn-out process was an expensive waste of staff time and money.

To them, more students, and hence more money, could pour into the faculty through the popular film course, once entry was based on graded, tertiary entrance scores, given the very high demand. Nobody really cared much about staff morale, the burden of larger classes, heavier workloads, or about the sparkling creative talents we might miss. Funnily enough, the portfolio method still remained for fashion and acting students, a source of some tension within the Creative Industries ranks.

Darker memories have slithered now into my brain, cascading randomly, further revealing more of the underbelly of life in that institution, with which I had a love/hate relationship over many years. In many ways, I was fiercely loyal, but I was employed there a long time over many changes, for better and for worse.

One day, I was stunned at a refusal to attend a feminist conference in Arizona, USA, because the 'faculty did not support feminism, in any form'. Another time, I was shocked and distressed when a student made a false complaint against me. This was not well handled by those in administration. One frantic day, I rushed to a different student's aid on receiving a suicide note, just in time.

A close colleague had recurring nightmares after a shocking time at work, caused by bullies. Someone in another discipline jumped to his death from the fifth floor, just down the corridor from my room, in between tutorials. Nothing could be done. It was personal, apparently. At one time, I'm shouted at, hassled relentlessly; at another time, I sought tepid counselling help. Management cried, 'There's nothing to see here', or, alternatively, they 'would fix everything'. Mostly they did not, continuing to apply small bandaids on gaping wounds. It could be a wild roller-coaster ride.

On the plus side, I was rewarded for my research efforts by travelling extensively to national and international conferences, and even to feminism conferences, once I was no longer working in that old retro faculty. Nevertheless, I shall always remember the look of undisguised, masculinist triumph and power on that particular manager's face, back in the day.

The work/ travel highlights were many and precious. For instance, a buzzy masculinities conference in Seville, with friends and colleagues David and Alfredo; Console-ing Passions feminist conferences in Los Angeles, Montreal, Bristol, Sydney, Adelaide, with my special international mate. I presented at conferences in Cuba, Nice, Beijing, Paris, Hong Kong, Sydney, New Orleans, Melbourne.

I attended media education conferences in Toulouse, London, and in most Australian capital cities, along with my Australian Teachers of Media tribe. Aiming at a different kind of conference, Donna Lee Brien and I gave papers at a Law, Literature and Society conference in country Victoria, staying in the renovated Aradale Mental Hospital, under the auspices of the Melbourne Polytechnic. The stone walls of each of our tiny bedrooms were the original walls of some poor patient's cell. My dreams were very dark over those few nights.

Amidst all this teaching and conferencing, my next 'romance' turned out to be very much a long distance one, linked, in a way, with the conference circuit. In 1988, along with a great ATOM team, I organised a major national media education conference in Brisbane, which was a terrific success, and Graham was a top keynote speaker from England. He was charming and very intelligent, and we hit it off very well. Once I found out he was living with a partner, any thought of a closer liaison went up in smoke.

After the conference, back home in England, he started writing letters which became increasingly intimate and loving, assuring me that his partner had moved south to London and that he was single again. When he declared his deep love for me, I was carried away, gradually becoming equally committed. Long distance phone calls and many letters followed. We tried to work out when we could catch up again in person. There was talk of meeting half way, in India.

When he came to Australia for a few visits, both work and geographical obstacles to our relationship seemed irresolvable over the following few years. At one stage, we thought of moving to the United States and starting afresh there, when he was certain he would be appointed as a professor at one particular university.

The love letters still flowed between us, although more erratically. My close friends were horrified that I might move to another country without an actual job to go to, as everything about this latest scenario concerned his career, not mine. However, sadly for him, and possibly for us, he did not achieve that coveted professorial position.

Finally, we committed to having a holiday together, to sort everything out between us. This involved time in London, then in the Lake District at my ex-sister-in-law Stephanie's award-winning bed and breakfast place, finishing in romantic Paris. Afterwards, I was committed to present at an international media education conference in Toulouse, France, hopefully after a happy resolution.

On our second night in London, I discovered that Graham's former girlfriend had returned to live at his place, north of London. Assuring me that she was only there temporarily, he pleaded that he felt sorry for her as she had nowhere else to go after she had finished her dancing degree. She rang him, and, according to Graham, she threatened to burn his house down and kill the dog, if he stayed with me. Whatever was really happening, he had to hurry back by train overnight, to calm things down with the Spanish dancer.

Meanwhile, I felt the love draining away, along with his credibility, minute by minute. We broke up at Euston Station in less than a week. When he insisted on handing over his share of the expenses in cash, I nearly threw those wretched pound notes down onto the trainline.

A few days later, in Paris, old friend Roger and I were mugged in the Marais metro station. The mugger reached into my half-open handbag, grabbing my purse with that sizeable amount of English money in it. Brave Roger, trying to intervene, was headbutted, his nose broken. I was unhurt, but very shaken. After some emergency help at a nearby pharmacy, we went to a police station not far from there. However, that Paris copshop turned out to be solely for people who had been robbed, but not hurt.

Roger was working at the OECD, living in Paris with his family, and they had kindly offered me their guest bedroom. Fortunately, he could speak French fluently. As I discovered that afternoon, French bureaucracy can be quite a minefield, although I think Roger already knew that. We were instructed to go across town to a station that dealt with both robbery *and* assault.

Even the police at the far-flung station were perplexed, as I had been robbed, but my companion was the one who had sustained an injury. We didn't fit into any neat reportage category for them. They fussed around, shaking their heads, changing the forms where they were trying to type all the details.

I described the robber as 'tall, black, wearing a black leather jacket', who had opportunistically 'leapt over the railings and grabbed my purse' at the Marais metro station. I doubt they ever found this person, who must have enjoyed a great time on that accursed cash windfall.

Six months on, I received a parcel from the Australian Embassy in Paris. This mystery parcel contained my old purse, with my long-renewed ID cards such as my licence, minus the cash and credit cards, of course. A worthy French citizen had salvaged the purse from a wastebin, and handed it over to the Embassy. That faded empty purse threw into stark relief those stolen, wasted years of yet another doomed affair. It took a while to throw the effects of that relationship into the bin of my own personal history.

I found out later that another Australian female academic had experienced a similar devastating affair with him, years before. Hearing this, my foggy head miraculously cleared. I had been depressed, blaming myself for the whole catastrophe, for not reading the signs. I was thankful to her for being so open with me, for her empathetic generosity of spirit.

Exhausted, I was very cautious as to where I might go next on my seemingly jinxed love trail. I began to wish I could be as determined as the heroine, Sybylla, in the film *My Brilliant Career*, dedicating my life to my career, forsaking all romance.

In any case, no one in my circle knew that mythical nice bloke, who 'wasn't married, or gay, or both', as the saying goes. People I worked with tended to occupy a 'no go' zone, even though my former university job had proven to be quite prolific in the 'love/lust' stakes. I became very cautious, burying myself in work. I wasn't as daring as Sybylla, but I did turn my back on the pitfalls of romance, for a time.

On the other hand, I cannot ignore Bob Leach from that supposed no-go zone. With my workmate Bob, I shared some great times, the warmest conversations. And he kindly gave me a shoulder to cry on through the whole miserable Graham saga. We became close, very discreetly. This arrangement suited us both.

Bob would regularly go on holidays to Cuba, helping the socialist cause by picking oranges. I had to tell him that fruit picking in the Cuban fields wasn't really my thing. He also wanted me to accompany him on a fact-finding mission to the Middle East, starting in Egypt, 'just to see for ourselves, Helen, what is really going on over there'.

When he retired early from QUT, at fifty-five, he was busy planning a fresh, new political party on the left, inspiring many like-minded people with his passionate rallying cry for change. Sadly, Bob died from a massive heart attack, aged fifty-seven, when he was on his way to Cuba for the last time. I still miss him, a great, warm comrade, an esteemed history and politics lecturer.

While I did not go fact-finding to the Middle East, or fruitpicking in Cuba, I ventured forth on extended study leave to some of the more standard places, from the early nineties onwards, with a few diversions: L.A, New York, Tucson, Paris, London and Northern Ireland.

In 1992, for instance, I was invited to visit with feminism and film Professor Ann Kaplan, whose theoretical work I had drawn on for my Masters degree. I was also lined up to give a lecture at the State University of New York, Albany, about my becoming the controversial object of glaring media attention when I dared to criticise toxic Australian masculinity in Rugby League football, both on and off the field. Immediately before this New York visit, I had an unexpected setback, slipping and breaking my wrist in a rather poorly designed Los Angeles' hotel bathroom.

The recommended delegates' hotel in South Central Los Angeles was situated close to the University of Southern California campus, where a feminist conference was wrapping up. That day, after much dithering by the twitchy hotel management, overly concerned that I might sue them, I was finally taken to a local clinic.

While charging a small fortune, the clinic administered a rapid diagnosis and treatment. As I was rushed back to the hotel, everyone was on edge. Riots were imminent in that neighbourhood, triggered by the earlier savage beating of Rodney King by police officers who eventually were acquitted, despite the grim visual proof.

The community was expecting more trouble, as the verdict was about to be handed down. Thanks to the rush job on my injured wrist, I had to have it broken and reset again in the SUNY University hospital in New York. My woes faded into insignificance, however, when seen up against the injuries meted out to Rodney King. Black lives certainly did matter then, and still do.

After New York, I flew to England for some time, meeting up with colleagues at several London tertiary institutions. The young surgeon who mended my wrist in New York referred me to his mentor in Harley Street, London. This posh English orthopaedic surgeon took me on, although he was, as it turned out, a top sports medicine person, usually catering solely for top English soccer players. I figured that I was probably a diversion.

On April 10, 1992, the evening before I left England for Northern Ireland, IRA bombers blew up buildings close to the centre of the City of London, causing three deaths, many injuries, and much destruction to property. The security at Heathrow airport the very next day was, of course, extremely thorough regarding the movements, backgrounds, intentions, baggage of all passengers taking off from London to Belfast. Finally arriving in Belfast, exhausted, I found their security was similarly on extra high alert.

One pleasant duty organised by my hosts at the University of Belfast, was that I deliver a talk on 'Women in Australian film' to a diverse, receptive group in Derry. On the journey between Belfast and that IRA hotspot, my Irish colleague Sarah Sharp and I were checked and double-checked by the grim occupying British soldiers, loaded guns obscenely at the ready.

Towards the end of my time in Ireland, I felt decidedly edgy as I drove back to Belfast airport. I had spent a long weekend in Dublin with colleagues on study leave from Melbourne, also visiting some family connections, on my mother's side, around Kilkenny. A military helicopter, flying quite low, appeared to be tracking me all the way from the Irish border to the airport in Belfast.

It was difficult not to be paranoid, imagining that the helicopter occupants were checking up on me, personally, in quite a threatening way. Not only had I arrived from London the morning after a terrorist bombing attack, I had also given a talk within 'enemy' territory, in Derry. And I was heading back from the south, after another incident several days earlier at the border.

Innocently enough, or more probably, stupidly, I had stopped to buy some wine to take to the south, as I had been warned that the prices in Dublin were highly inflated. Parking in a restricted fifteen-minute zone, I became concerned when the bottleshop person took at least eighteen minutes to serve me. Any abandoned parked car was considered a huge security risk in that volatile, troubled place.

By the time I returned to the parking spot, several soldiers were already circling my nifty red sports car, at the ready. Within a few more minutes, the car and all my belongings would have been blown to smithereens. No one messed with the British military. Mystery helicopter and all. I was relieved to be back in London in one piece, even though the deadly bombings were still of great concern there, with sandbags stacked up everywhere in inner London.

A different career highlight, very close to my heart, happened on two separate occasions in Paris, quite early in the new millennium. I was privileged to deliver lectures to Professor Waddick Doyle's bright students at the American University. My first topic was about female popular cultural icons such as Madonna. A few years later, I talked about my new feminist research on masculinities in the media, concentrating on the television series, *The Sopranos* and *NYPD Blue*.

After my second enjoyable stint there, for about half an hour in a Parisian bar, I wondered if all my Paris dreams might actually come true. The amiable Waddick, who was originally from Brisbane, revealed that, unexpectedly, he had to appoint another lecturer in his area, almost immediately. Excitement very soon fizzled into disappointment, when I discovered that an EU passport was a fundamental requirement.

In the end, Cuba was the dream standout, the winning conference of them all. In 2004, dear friend and colleague, Anne Hickling-Hudson was the international president of the World Council of Comparative Education Societies, holding a hugely significant conference in Havana.

Spurred on by fond memories of my friend Bob Leach's passion for the place, I was very excited to be going to see where Che Guevara and the revolutionary heroes had bravely fought against the monstrous corruption and exploitation by the Spanish colonisers and the American mafia. However, Fidel Castro was definitely not one of my heroes.

Already being overseas on holiday, I travelled from Spain to Mexico City, meeting up with friends Emma Felton, Christine Whitelaw and Mark Newman, before we excitedly flew to Havana to be with Anne, to support her, partake in the conference, and experience our first time on the island of Cuba, where the beautiful Caribbean Sea meets the Gulf of Mexico and the Atlantic Ocean.

A Spanish speaker stood beside me while I gave my paper presentation. Every now and again, I paused while he translated what I had been saying. There is a first time for everything. People flocked to this prestigious conference from around the world, although very few came from the USA, given their problematic relationship with Cuba over too many years.

We relished the beautiful architecture of Old Havana, the cars, the harbour, the clubs, the hotels, the ongoing renovations, often sponsored by a town in Spain, all under the World Heritage listing by UNESCO. We savoured fabulous Mojitos and other cocktails in interesting bars. And we stuck mostly to fish, beans and rice, at various eating places around town. Nevertheless, a 'funny tummy', left over from a dose of food poisoning in Mexico City, hampered my enjoyment a little.

One day we Australians visited the famous Cuban Film School outside Havana, an event I had pre-arranged. It was uplifting to make this special connection in the field of film education. The mix of live-in students there from Cuba, other South American countries, and also from Canada was unexpected. I felt for all involved, as resources were sparse compared to our developed world abundance at QUT. They had also recently suffered considerable damage to their premises from a hurricane.

Later that week, I arranged a meeting with Charles, a former Cuban diplomat. I had brought him a gift from Australia, a DVD copy of a film he featured in, the documentary called *Fond Memories of Cuba*, by Australian filmmaker, David Bradbury. I cannot now recall the way I connected with Charles in the first place, but I'm glad I was able to bring him this special film gift, in person.

Threaded through the many years I worked at QUT, there was another definite high, that lasted for years. I responded without hesitation to the rallying cry to perform 'academic service' work with the Brisbane International Film Festival, practically from its inception in the nineties. This was an integral part of my duties, but also a great honour and pleasure, working with the dedicated artistic director, Anne Démy-Geroe and her team.

I reviewed and recommended films for consideration, sent by filmmakers from all over the world. For years, I spent many a weekend and evening in dark, cloistered viewing rooms with other serious film people, such as Archie Moore, Scott Knight, Mairi Cameron, enjoying our lively discussions on the pros and cons of the films on offer. We worked closely with great BIFF staff such as Anne, Mat Kesting, Kristy Matheson, Gary Ellis, Hussain Currimbhoy, Coreen Haddad, Andrew Rose, Kiki Fung and many others over those years.

During festival time, I was privileged to conduct some post-screening Q and A sessions with world filmmakers, and to attend the occasional private dinner with the guests. As well, I attempted to nurture a generation of festival film lovers, largely through our students in International Cinema, organising the teaching program so that they could freely attend, and at the same time, earn credit in this subject.

Around 2004, I spent one memorable day and evening in Brisbane with the Iranian auteur, Jafar Panahi. Unexpectedly, I found myself lending him a considerable amount of money, in order to help his son, Panah, come to Australia to study film at QUT. As a return gift for Panah's being accepted, Jafar promised that he would run directing workshops for our film staff and students. This would have been a great coup for us, gaining world-wide publicity, if everything had worked out. Panah Panahi was definitely eligible to come and a quick holding deposit had to be made to QUT.

While unpredictability reigned for a while, I didn't really care. It was a risk worth taking. In the end, Panah Panahi did gain entry to a film course of his choosing in Tehran, and of course I was repaid the $3000 deposit by his famous father. At the time, I was teaching one of his brilliant, award-winning films, *The Circle*, in the International Cinema class, as well as specialising in other Iranian filmmakers' works. During the Festival, Jafar gave a talk that my students and I eagerly attended.

Afterwards, he told me that the Iranian government would fund certain young people on special overseas university scholarships, who were obliged to report back on what any Iranian might be saying and doing in such public arenas. A couple of these spies appeared to be present at that talk, firing some quite aggressive questions at him, busily jotting down his replies.

I caught an unnerving firsthand glimpse into the life of a courageous radical filmmaker, under duress. All of his films since his first one, *The White Balloon*, had been banned from publicly screening in Iran, despite widespread international critical acclaim. Several years later, in 2010, Jafar Panahi was placed under arrest by government forces who judged his films as attacking the State of Iran.

Because of an intense worldwide backlash, he was imprisoned only for a short time. Then he was promptly placed under house arrest, on a criminal charge of propagandising against the regime. He was strictly forbidden from making any films for at least 20 years. I'm pleased to say that he has admirably defied such a ban, in spectacular ways. [17]

Playing a part, over many years, in helping to deliver a triumphant film festival brought me great professional and personal satisfaction over those years teaching at QUT. Politics, powerplay and machinations are in the very air we breathe, the very festivals we love. Since Anne stood down, puzzlingly, unceremoniously, the quality of the BIFF experience has never again been of the same high calibre, regrettably.

As a counterpoint, I loved working with my dear mate, Mike Witt, on the West End Film Festival, post-BIFF, for a few short years. With great flair and a big heart, he directed this small scale, community-based event, transformative for many local filmmakers, career-wise. For instance, Joe Brumm, who later created the hit children's series *Bluey*, won an award one year, for Best Animation.

In 2006, I was privileged to be sent overseas to South America, this time on a marketing exercise to enrol students from Chile and Brazil. Already experienced in dealing with amazing students all the way from Scandinavia to Botswana, I was briefed to represent the whole university, along with the more savvy, unflappable Jess from the English Language College.

One non-course related question many Brazilian parents asked, apart from the cost of living, concerned safety issues for their offspring in Australia. Many had already checked the relative death by violence

---

17. In defiance of this ban, Jafar Panahi made *This is Not a Film*, smuggling it out the following year on a USB stick inside a cake, to be presented at Cannes. I admire his ever-renewing creativity, his daring. He has since managed, secretly, to make other films, including Berlin Golden Lion winner *Taxi*, in 2015. He can now move around Iran, but is still blocked from travelling further. Jafar has also continued to support other persecuted Iranian filmmakers and human rights activists. Being a creative, free-thinking soul in Iran can be very difficult indeed.

and mugging statistics in Australian cities. Brisbane showed up pretty well, comparatively.

I heard some very confronting stories about muggings, thefts and murders in Brazil, especially in the capital, Sao Paulo. From the dubious safety of a taxi, I had personally witnessed police chasing and shooting at men fleeing on motorbikes along a busy street. I could see why parents wanted a safe study environment for their kids. I did my best, even becoming quite an expert on QUT's offerings in engineering.

Another academic highlight at QUT for me was teaching about research to many post-graduates, working with shining lights such as Cheryl Stock, Daniel Mafe and Brad Haseman. One-on-one, I also enjoyed supervising those who came to university straight from a considerable time in the film and television industries, such as Phoebe Hart, Ivo Burum and Wendy Rogers. Rosalind Nugent was another delight, from a legal and drama background. Working with them was a creative learning experience for both myself and, I trust, for these talented students. We explored another way of looking at research, through a creative practice lens.

Around 2007, I gained a special film industry award for 'dedicated service to the unearthing of new film talent in Queensland', largely through my founding and longstanding management of the Queensland New Filmmakers Awards. Later I won the Dean's Award for Excellence in Post-Graduate Supervision, and I was a nominee for a University Vice-Chancellor's Award for Excellence. I had also gained a QUT prize for my work in fostering equity. While these accolades were very uplifting, by the end of 2009, I was definitely in countdown mode.

My stoical friend, Professor Sue Carson, is still hanging in there, doing remarkable work. We fondly remember our time working together with postgraduate and honours students, along with the occasional ethical clearance issues concerning several cutting-edge projects.

For instance, I was the associate supervisor of a bright international student, Renee Tamayo, whose principal supervisor was Victoria Garnons-Williams, an old friend from Visual Arts. Renee had her own body x-rayed in Mexico for her stunning visual arts/film installation on the tragedy of multiple breast cancer surgery deaths in Mexico. An ethical clearance would be needed for someone else's body, but when it was the student's own body, the rules became challenging, but not insurmountable. Renee gained her Masters with flying colours.

Another innovative student, Hugo Presser, had to be restrained from working with a Brisbane man who was on the brink of death. The latter had cheerfully agreed to donate his own severed hand, post mortem, all in the cause of that particular student's experimental photographic work on death and dying. Hugo received first class honours, minus the severed hand prop.

Despite the highs that such students brought, the downside for me was that academia itself had become an increasingly demoralising space within which to work. As a dedicated feminist and unionist, I had always tried to stand up for my rights, and for the rights of others, during my long tenure there.

However, the ground was always shifting. Knowing where many of the bodies were buried, I mourned the fates of good people who had been pushed aside and overlooked, their bright ideas dismissed, or sneakily reworked in another form. All that hurt and pain, the toxic politics, those subterranean secrets and lies, weighed heavily on me, year after year.

Looking back over much of my career, I can say with some conviction that during my time in and out of secondary education, as well as within tertiary education, certain people bestowed on me the badge of the token feminist in the room, a stereotypical role with unwanted baggage. Constant jibes can be wearing, and it is hard to sustain equanimity, grace and humour.

Moreover, tokenism can turn into something uglier and more perverse. Until the end of the Bjelke-Petersen era in Queensland in 1989, many Queensland 'radicals' in all walks of life suffered forms of discrimination, persecution and harassment. Standing up to be counted was a political act, with possible dire repercussions.

I was very fortunate to be able to hold my head high for as long as I did, despite opposition and even mockery from some powerful quarters. One colleague called me a 'seventies feminist', meaning that my work was out of date, and no longer relevant. Yes, the feminist foundations had been set in the sixties and seventies, and even earlier. I took the slur as a badge of honour, at the same time realising that this person had not bothered to keep up with my well-documented, topical work on masculinities.

As with many female academics, I found myself close to the bottom of the pecking order, one way or another, even when I had titles like Deputy Head of School, or Course Co-ordinator. In the final analysis, such honours meant that I had more administrative work on my plate, something that men often liked to pass on to women, while they could advance their own careers through research.

Academia is still a male-dominated culture, despite some significant inroads made by women at the top. Often however, women in power behave conservatively, modelling themselves on their male mentors, propping up familiar, often divisive ways of doing things. Power changes people.

Finally, in March 2010, I turned sixty-five. Despite all those travel opportunities, working with creative industries students and the best of my workmates, I was looking forward to hanging up my ID card, my DVDs, my antique VHS's, my well-thumbed academic books, my voluminous, untidy files, and other work paraphernalia, when the time was right.

In the midst of all this, Christopher Strewe came more and more into my private life from the early 2000's onwards. In a nutshell, he was one of the most blatant *Lust, Caution* 'characters' thus far in my life, at least since Richard. I met him across many decades, through mutual friends, through the film industry where he worked, firstly as a cinematographer, then as a locations manager. Over and over, around the ridges, he kept popping up, smiling his open, seductive smile, always flirting, sometimes alone, other times with different women in tow. He was definitely a player.

It is hard to write about 'the good, the bad and the ugly' of any relationship, its inevitable swings and roundabouts. The material is highly personal, intimate, risky, hurtful to myself and to others. All I can say is that this is my truth. Any people featured in this memoir are welcome to write their own versions of what happened. Part of me is past caring.

Back in the seventies, I knew Christopher's father Odo, just a little. He was close to my friends Jeanne, Nicholas and Janetta. A special gardener, a poet, a left-wing activist who escaped Nazi Germany, a lover of freedom and of many women, Odo built a house by hand in a Sunshine Coast hinterland rainforest, tending that haven until he died. Chris inherited his father's spirit, and his passion for that forest, crafting his own special cabin there.

While I found Chris attractive, he also radiated danger, which was part of the appeal, I suppose. I made mistakes, taking the challenge, even though the cautionary signals were all there. Some of my close friends were concerned for my well-being. He was well known for playing the field. When he first asked me out, I wanted to resist, but I was also very drawn to him. He was like a lighthouse – throwing light and full attention on me, then twisting and turning, leaving me in the dark. We saw each other, on and off, over many years.

When Chris's marriage broke down, he told me he loved me and asked could he come and stay with me. Knowing he wasn't serious about the latter, I did, however, become hooked on that word 'love'. To me, no one whispers those words into another person's ear, unless he or she is totally sincere. There have to be consequences. A wise friend proclaimed, when I was feeling upset one day at work, 'I bet he whispered exactly the same sweet nothings in several women's ears around that time, to cover all bases'. He knew the type.

For a time, I held on to my romantic illusions. Chris quite often stayed at my place. His full-on physical presence was hard to ignore. It was a bumpy ride of mixed messages, of happy times, of deep hurt. Once he was presenting himself to the world as supposedly single again, he was, as his father before him, living the bohemian dream from earlier decades. The focus was always on his freedom, his desires, his multiple partners. He was a walking ambivalence machine. Jealousy was forbidden. What was I even thinking?

Over the past decade or so, Chris has endured several serious accidents and life-threatening injuries, including damage to his brain. The latter injury has brought us closer again. It is a wonder he is still alive. We lightly keep in touch, after more than forty years of knowing each other, having on/ off times, in synch, out of synch, being friends, lovers, enemies, friends again.

As longtime Labor party supporters, Chris and I endured the horror of the 2019 Federal election night together, along with other friends, Janetta, Ian, Savannah Susan and Cossack Peter. No one could even speak after that devastating result. The 2022 Australian Federal election is looking rather promising as I write, although the dominant Murdoch media is appallingly biased. People seem to be ridiculously, wantonly ignorant of all the lies, corruption, misogyny, racism, homophobia, transphobia, the refugee cruelty, the anti-intellectualism, the hawkishness, the climate change denialism, the poor support of the arts, etc. of the current Government under Morrison. The 24-hour news cycle has a lot to answer for, as do poorly trained, unethical journalists.

I'm not sure how my friends and I will survive another defeat. One solution might be to surround myself with more of the following, if at all possible: films, books, art, satire, dancing, writing, pingpong/wiffwaff, the ABC (if it still exists), and, of course, good-hearted, likeminded people, caring for the arts, the poor, the dispossessed and the environment. Where is Filthy Phil (the early version) when you need him? And, every day, I miss discussing all the issues, the politics, the state of the world, with my learned, peace-loving friend, dear Ralph Summy, sadly now deceased.

***

12.

COCOON

Looking further back once again, after forty-two years of being in the workforce full time, I retired at the end of my sixty-fifth year, in 2010. On retiring, people of my vintage are primarily concerned about how much is in their superannuation retirement accounts, what the old-age pension and health cards involve, how they might be able to live day-to-day, and for how long. All these are appropriate, existential questions with which to wrestle.

Many workers in my generation suffer from not having had a properly regulated system for providing for our future, until we were around forty years old, when the Keating Labor Government brought in the current superannuation scheme in 1992. Warmest thanks, Paul Keating, for your practical, inclusive, humanitarian vision.

Around 2008, some much more fiscally responsible friends pressured me to start thinking about 'my retirement plan'. Filled with dread, I dutifully visited a financial adviser. Hunched over my financial details, frowning, sweating in his ill-fitting brown suit, the adviser proceeded to patronise and shame me, saying that he simply could not understand how I was over-spending my income every fortnight.

According to his calculations, I should have been able to invest more into my superannuation fund, and/or into my limp savings account. He was also very surprised that I had never bought a second property as an investment/ tax dodge, or at least a healthy portfolio of stocks and shares.

Trying to explain my philosophy, my lifestyle, I said, rather too quickly and breathlessly: 'Well, I go out a lot, to films, theatre, concerts. Oh, and I eat in restaurants with my friends. I often buy clothes, and jewellery. And I travel overseas pretty regularly'. The more I spoke, the more lavish and irresponsible my life sounded. As far as he was concerned, nothing seemed to stack up. It dawned on me that he might even suspect that I had a secret drug habit.

According to his calculations regarding my sizeable debts and my errant lifestyle, I would probably not be able to retire until I was about ninety years old. Rubbing it in even further, he spelled out something that actually did ring true: 'You should pay off your mortgage and clear any debts before you can retire comfortably'. Feeling a fiscal failure, I slinked, red-faced, out of his office. Hesitating for a moment, I shook myself, then headed up to the Myer Centre, to indulge in some much-needed retail therapy after that weighty encounter.

During the final part of the 2010 academic year, I took some long overdue long-service leave, for which, strangely enough, I had to fight very hard. It appeared that such workplace entitlements were suddenly no longer being granted, under a tricky new regime shift.

The university was becoming more fiscally edgy, or, to put it another way, much more reluctant to spend money, especially on those employees who were not very high up in the hierarchy. Nevertheless, I had been around long enough to know there should be real money available, in reserve, to cover my duties in my absence. At the eleventh hour, I was grudgingly granted the leave.

An early retirement deal, which I had been hoping for during the previous couple of years, did not roll out until late that year. This was bad timing, for me at least. Under the rules, I could still partake, although colleagues under sixty-five received a more generous payout. Even so, my jovial accountant Wayne Lyons (a visual artist at heart) cried, 'Take it!'.

At the time of the offer, I was in London, enjoying that hard-earned leave. For the first time in my life, I had made it to the annual British Film Institute London Film Festival, a personal and professional highlight. By going there, I suppose I was actually working, even though, technically, I was on personal leave. However, this minor detail had often been the case over the previous twenty or so years. Whenever a film festival or film event of any kind appeared on the horizon, full-on engagement for me was never a burden, no matter when it might occur.

This particular festival feast served up an abundance of quality films and events. One of the most thrilling was a director's workshop (really a live on-stage, illustrated interview) featuring the Mexican auteur, Alejandro González Iñárritu. Towards the end of the festival, a surprise extra event was added: the world premiere of the music documentary *The Promise: The Making of Darkness on the Edge of Town*, to be introduced by Bruce Springsteen himself, in person. In my mind, such treasured filmic experiences were completing my career on a high note.

Flowing from all this, the good retirement news for both me and that disgruntled financial adviser-from-hell, was that I would be able to pay off my mortgage, and even have a reasonably comfortable life, well before I turned ninety.

I have kept in touch with Jillian and Chris, workmates who took that package with me back in 2010, along with others who have left or retired from QUT since then, such as Cheryl, Barbara, Emma, Jeanette, Vivienne. From far away in a beautiful French village in the mountains, visual artist Dan keeps in touch by Instagram.

It is important to have supportive friends who let you spill it all out, at any time, without judgement. Recently retired from the University of Queensland, Liz Ferrier, whom I was very lucky to meet and bond with when we worked together long ago at QUT, is one such person. Laughing is good therapy, as is venting.

Geoff Portmann, who used to run Comedy at the ABC, and then Film, Television and Animation at QUT, tragically died not long into his own retirement. No *Cocoon* reprive for him, sadly. Along with other close colleagues, I'm still waiting for QUT management to honour him by respectfully holding a memorial service on campus.

On the plus side, post-retirement, I have been honoured to have been an Adjunct Associate Professor in Film, TV, Animation at QUT, although at the end of 2021, my ten-year-long contract was terminated.

Regarding the close-knit group of tutors who worked directly with me, back in the day, in particular in Australian Film, International Cinema, and Film Language, Margaret currently soars as an academic in film at Griffith University, Tess is doing wonders in entertainment studies at QUT, while Tim continues to conquer new heights in emerging communication technologies.

Another former colleague, Michael is an admirable film professor overseas, while glowingly talented Natalie Bailey is a successful film and television director. The remarkable Susie Mac is roving the world, from Shanghai to Los Angeles, writing dazzling scripts and graphic novels, as far as I'm aware.

When she first laid eyes on me, Susie Mac thought I was Marianne Faithfull, or perhaps even a proud biker's moll, with my leather jacket.

I lost her somewhere in the mountains of Nepal, taking refuge from Covid 19. I still miss her formidable talent, her originality, her personal warmth, her sense of humour.

Susie Mac was yet another special industry talent, gobbled up and not properly appreciated within that Behemoth called academia. The rhetoric and the reality in creative industries did not always synchronise. Not every 'real world' person could fit into a particular cookie-cutter academic type. This lack was often seen as a blight, a curse, but I think it may well have been a blessing.

My brilliant friend, Deb, has also left Brisbane. Amongst many delights, both professionally and personally, she once organised on campus a welcome five-minute disco session for all comers, every Friday at 11.55 am, when she occupied a room just along the corridor from me. With strobe lights whirling, we jumped around, yelling the words, dancing to old disco favourites, letting off steam.

Often this gig went on longer than the allotted five minutes. I miss her close, warm presence in my life, and I miss her dazzling design innovation. She is now a Professor in Digital Design. Lucky RMIT. Yet again, QUT, you blew it, big time.

Before Deb moved to Auckland and then to Melbourne, she, Savannah Susan, Miss B/Bronwyn, and I would enjoy playing table tennis regularly. We called ourselves the Wiffwaffers, and after a great night playing, we would head out to dinner, knowing that whatever we said would never go beyond the group's cone of silence.

We also loved going dancing with mutual friends, hiring places such as an old Greek hall in West End, and later, when that hall was demolished, an upstairs function room at a hotel in South Brisbane, near the old Boggo Road Prison. Susan, Bronwyn and I try to keep up the table tennis as a three-way match, not always successfully. We still dance, although Covid has recently intervened, thwarting many such pursuits.

Along with many retirees, I have been involved with a thriving bookclub, although writing this book has become all-consuming, and I have had to forsake reading many books. Up until the end of 2020, I also helped host a monthly Salon, where various passionate people could meet, share and discuss books, films, podcasts, cultural events, whatever took their fancy.

Pre-Covid, back in 2011, during my first year as an Adjunct Associate Professor, I was awarded the title of Culture Champion by the Queensland State Government. This surprise was made all the better because my friend, Ann Baillie, gained the same recognition and award at the same time, for her work in museums over many years.

Spurred on by other creative, shining lights around me, in 2012 I produced a video montage called *Do Look Now*, working with two great young editors, former students Chris Cosgrove and Steph Dower. Following in the hallowed footsteps of Australian photographer/filmmaker, Tracey Moffatt, my video montage comprised the best sex scenes from around twenty-four of my favourite films, selected in an intuitive, evocative sequence, mirroring my personal sex life along with my love of film.[18]

For the Queensland Photography Festival in 2012, shiny Catherine Gomersall and I cooked up a collaborative moving image/photography project, joining forces with other female talents across QUT and Griffith University, Victoria, Hillary, Jay. We created a multi-installation event called *One Night Stand*, in an old props warehouse in Brisbane's West End.

Thanks to some talented film students, we shot a short documentary on the night. Even though I was retired by then, I had no desire to stop pushing boundaries in new and different ways within my two main fields, feminism and film.

Later that year, my film, *Do Look Now*, was chosen to screen, for free, at the Brisbane International Film Festival, as part of a controversial section on erotica. There was a robust question and answer session afterwards, and I enjoyed being the target of the questions, for once, at this festival. Liberated by my own creativity, I was feeling great.

Then, in September 2012, while preparing to fly to Vienna to present a research paper on my video montage *Do Look Now*, I was literally stopped in my tracks. The morning of the flight, out of breath, I simply could not climb up the forty-eight steps to my top floor Art Deco unit. Rushed into Emergency, I ended up in intensive cardiac care. I whispered 'I have to be on a plane to Vienna at eight o'clock tonight'.

---

18. I published a short academic piece on this venture. See https://eprints.qut.edu.au/67365/.. The chosen films are also listed at the end of this book.

Finally, one of the nurses retorted, 'If you get on that plane, you will die'. After that, I kept very quiet.

He was right. I was suffering from severe bronchitis, along with a new heart-related complaint, atrial fibrillation. I did miss that plane. Sadly, I also missed catching up, post-Vienna, with my dear friends, Viktoria in Berlin, and Margaret and Anne in Budapest. I had also planned to pitch the installation project to a funky art gallery in Berlin, with Viktoria's help.

In the whole scheme of things, that was a sobering time for me. At Margaret Montgomerie's kind urging, I did, however, manage to send my film *Do Look Now* to screen at the International Console-ing Passions Feminist Conference she was running, early the following year in England, even though I could not be present in person.

Under the care of Dr Sean Mulhearn, a top cardiologist, I was able to rally in autumn, 2013 to attend a wedding in Italy. Jenny Wren and I had been invited by our old workmate, Lance and his wife Marie, to the wedding of their second daughter Sarah, to be held in a castle overlooking stunning Portofino on the Italian west coast.

Tragically Marie passed away a few months before the wedding. She had atrial fibrillation also, but had been administered the wrong drugs in hospital, a shocking blow to all who loved her. This further inspired Jenny and me to sort out our funds and fly to Italy, as supportive long-term friends during such a difficult time.

In some endearing ways, it was just like old times, travelling with Jenny, Lance, his son, James, and others by car from Milan to Portofino. After the splendid wedding, high above the town and the bay, Jenny and I went overland to stay in a villa owned by one of her cousins, deep in prized porcini mushroom country, not far from Rome.

Always inventive, Jenny worked on one little art project each day, drawing, painting, weaving, or building sculptures out of found objects, whatever she turned her heart and mind to. I relaxed, read a lot, enjoying Jenny's artistic creations, along with our treks to a simple village wine bar in the late afternoons, before coming home to a hearty meal, usually cooked by Jenny. I felt very spoiled.

Her creative energy knew no bounds. She also entertained me with beautiful songs as we explored the villages and countryside near the villa, and later when we drove to Milan via la bella Bologna, towards the end of our holiday. Practising for a choral festival to be held in Christchurch, New Zealand, immediately on her return from Europe, Jenny wanted to be in fine voice.

At times, she surprised me by breaking into song, no matter where we were. For instance, while we were waiting at Dubai airport, before boarding our flight to Milan, she began singing a Jewish lullaby, in the original Hebrew, totally unself-consciously.

At the end, one young man, in tears, came over and warmly thanked Jenny, saying his grandmother had sung a similar melody to him as a child. I feared for a moment that an Arabic official might view us as provocateurs in some way. But we were not stopped and searched, boarding that Emirates plane for Italy without further incident.

A while later, in March, 2015, I was feeling quite well again. Turning seventy, I celebrated in New Farm at the Merthyr Bowls Club, situated on the Brisbane River. We danced the night away. Never one to enjoy only one event for any decade birthday, I flew to New York a few months later.

On my first two nights there, I fulfilled a long-held dream by staying in the famous Algonquin Hotel, in the heart of Manhattan. I wanted to hang out where famous writers, such as Dorothy Parker, from *The New Yorker* and other magazines, had met each day for lunch at the Round Table, roughly from 1919 to 1929. That hotel still resonates with their witty, writerly legacy.

After that art deco treat, I stayed in a small apartment in trendy Chelsea, in a building that included both a bed and breakfast section as well as self-contained apartments. Struggling with my keys on the first night I was there, I simply couldn't open the door. It was after 10.30 pm, the building did not have a concierge, the owner/manager and his partner lived off-site. To my great relief, I suddenly heard happy voices wafting up from downstairs.

The wife of the building's owner was a strong peace advocate and educator. She had organised some eminent Japanese survivors of the Hiroshima bombings to come and stay at their bed and breakfast accommodation, as honoured guests giving talks over several days to groups of school children in New York. Those frail survivors were leaving the next day, and, luckily for me, there was a little surprise farewell party going on.

For the whole three weeks I stayed in that apartment, I never locked my door again when I went out, taking my chances, even though I had purchased some beautiful art deco antique jewellery in a very tempting shop close to the Algonquin Hotel. Having struggled once with a similarly grim, mystifying door-lock situation in Paris, I reached the same solution. At least I could safely secure such pesky doors, from the inside.

Ever since I first came to New York in 1980 with Janetta, my first solo tourist destination was always the Frick Museum, that small, delectable, brownstone building on the Upper East Side. After time well spent there amidst some ethereal art, I felt calm, knowing I was now 'wearing' my New York skin.

Old friends, Savannah Susan and Cossack Peter, from Brisbane, Margaret and Anne from England, and Carol, a former film colleague, from Sydney, all arrived in the city a few days later, to help me celebrate in that beloved city. We were quite a diverse group. Susan and Peter were both lawyers, Margaret was a retired English academic in my field, her German partner Anne was a linguist, while Carol had lectured in scriptwriting at QUT, before she retired and returned to Sydney to live. She had once worked as a scriptwriter on the British police procedural series, *The Bill*, one of my all-time favourites.

Miss B/Bronwyn had given me a great birthday gift, which was membership to the Museum of Modern Art. This card allowed me to have certain special discounts and privileges. I loved simply being at MoMA, hanging out in the sculpture garden, meeting up with people, eating, drinking at the restaurants, shopping, and of course viewing the exhibitions there.

Over ten days, we savoured many different galleries, bars, restaurants, comedy clubs, theatres, covering considerable territory. It was also intriguing to familiarise ourselves with the distinctive districts in which each of us stayed.

Peter and Susan were in Hell's Kitchen, Margaret and Anne hung out in Washington Square, while Carol was in a rather strange little hotel run by nuns, conveniently close to me in Chelsea. We all enjoyed the new green walkway, the High Line, in central Manhattan. My 'birthday' feast at the Gramercy Tavern in the Flatiron district was very special. Yet again I celebrated my new septuagenarian status, in fine style.

For one big day out, Peter, Susan and I headed by train to Poughkeepsie, to the fascinating historic property of Eleanor and FDR, where we paid tribute to them, while learning a considerable amount about their fascinating public and private lives. We also enjoyed getting our tongues around the word Poughkeepsie, and the name of another train station on the way, Peekskill.

Savannah Susan and I were planning to visit film star Susan Sarandon's first ping pong club SPiN in Manhattan, renowned at the time for private Naked Ping Pong parties. However, we didn't quite make it there, which was disappointing. Playing our beloved table tennis game, nude, in New York, could well have been life-changing on so many levels.

Once she was free from other commitments, I caught up with my old friend, NewYork Lisa, enjoying special cultural events, such as a modern ballet performance, a concert by the New York Symphony Orchestra which she organised at her workplace, the beautiful Cathedral of St John the Divine (complete with peacocks in the garden), and a glamorous evening fundraising event for a charity promoting peace. At the latter event, during the meal, the speeches and the awards, Lisa had to leave for a while, as there was an emergency at the Cathedral concerning one of the ageing peacocks who had gone missing.

As a director of cultural events, it seemed that Lisa had even wider responsibilities, including the welfare of the Cathedral garden peacocks. Later that night, we reunited in a bar high above Columbus Circle, looking out over Central Park. The lights along the Avenues were so beautifully evocative, it seemed as though we were back in the good old days, in one of my favourite Woody Allen films, *Manhattan*.

Confirming that the peacocks were safely bedded down, I asked her about the showy, overly-lit Trump Tower. Little did we know then, in May, 2015, what horrors would arise from Donald Trump's being elected President, two years later. He was just the sleazy host of *The Apprentice* at that stage, and a real estate wheeler and dealer.

In Chelsea, many people displayed signs in their windows or out the front of their buildings, supporting Hillary Clinton to be the Democrat candidate for the Presidency. Like them, I was feeling optimistic that there might be a first woman president, at long last.

However, the following year, my rapt attention to the build-up to the next American election was diverted into another sphere of concern altogether. I was brought back to earth by a sudden diagnosis of breast cancer.

Any films concerning characters suffering from cancer are usually very confronting, especially the more subtle, powerful ones, the best ones, without excessive sentimentality. I am still haunted by the Spanish film, *Raise Ravens*, and Bergman's *Cries and Whispers*. Both films concern a woman suffering dreadfully from cancer, operating on narrative, aesthetic and emotional levels, far above the usual fare. These films should, however, be viewed with a warning, 'proceed with caution'.

As John Lennon once said, 'Life is what happens to you while you're busy making other plans'. When a personal tsunami happens, everything changes, old certainties go out the window. Breast cancer was a most unwelcome health crisis, turning my life upside down, and shutting out creative ventures, along with many other pursuits, for a time. I simply had to focus on going with the riptide, surfacing awkwardly to gasp for breath, and, somehow, staying alive.

Very late on the day of the diagnosis in early September, 2016, at the Wesley Breast Clinic, after what was supposed to be a routine annual check-up, my ever-attentive niece Margie Kay and her husband Gerry Kay sprang immediately into action, picking me up, bringing me home, calming me down.

At that stage, Gerry had been working for years as a drama and history teacher at an exclusive girls' school. In more recent times, he has worked at a college for students with severe disabilities. Before this, whenever he could do so while on leave, he would go overseas, working in some of the most challenging schools in the world.

In depressed areas in England, in Soweto, South Africa, he was welcomed as a guest teacher, while in North Queensland he spent a semester on exchange at an Indigenous boarding school. I have always admired his talent and his grit. After his mother's death, as a very young boy, he had migrated with his working class father and sisters to Australia from the slums of Glasgow. Gerry became a champion soccer player, and later, a great educator.

Margaret, Jocelyn's eldest daughter, gained first class honours in medicine, along with, a much lauded doctorate on doctors' health from the University of Queensland, where she also worked for a while as an academic. A specialist in general practice, she was also a key doctor involved at a clinic for refugees at a local hospital. Amidst all this, including caring for their two boys, Thomas and Alexander, she and Gerry have been there for me, over many years. In early 2022, she was awarded the AM, for her services to medicine, medical education and migrant health.

Not long after that fateful night, I had two operations, two weeks apart, to remove the cancer. Being a breast care legend, my surgeon Professor Owen Ung used apt metaphors to describe my cancer ('a Rottweiler pup'), my lumpectomy surgeries ('scooping a brown spot out of an avocado'), and 'multiple airbag protections in a car', symbolising the post-operative radiation and hormone suppressant treatment. Luckily, I had no need for any 'chemotherapy airbags'.

Early one morning, after both surgeries and some recovery time, I was sitting in the waiting room near the radiation rooms, in the third week of a six-week intensive radiation therapy treatment at the Wesley Hospital. I was wrapped, uncomfortably, in a medical gown that was designed by a man for male patients, as one nurse had said to me a couple of weeks earlier, a wry smile on her face.

A feisty older woman patient walked past, then stopped. Looking directly at me, she announced: 'I'm not going to wish you a good day. It isn't a good day, and anyone who says so should just be told to fuck off.'

Returning her wry smile, I agreed with her, finding her attitude refreshing amidst all the polite, kind mumblings from other patients and staff I encountered there each day. A few days earlier, I had received a similarly frank text from my dear friend, Liz Ferrier, who had undergone breast cancer surgery and treatment that same year: 'If anyone tells you to be positive about all this, just tell them to fuck off. What we have is a horrible disease'.

Ms Feisty Older Woman elaborated even further, saying that she saw the radiation therapy treatment as a form of barbaric torture, not unlike the horrors that witches were subjected to in the Middle Ages. Furthermore, she had made her candid views well known to the staff at the clinic. I liked her spirit. We formed an instant bond; yet I never saw her again in that radiation dungeon.

When I first went into one of the theatres, benignly entitled the Rainforest, I wasn't too happy when I was placed in a tight position, lying flat on a slab with my arms stretched and clamped up behind my head. For the mapping procedure, I was tattooed and lined up with coordinates in preparation for the daily zapping treatment. Indeed, the sense that I was regularly in a torture chamber had already been going through my mind.

Prior to this zapping prep, I had met with the clinic's financial adviser, who put me through another form of torture, by outlining the massive charges I would be facing over the following six weeks. Apparently, I would ultimately receive much of this money back from Medicare, so there was some light on that horizon. However, my head was spinning at the end of our confusing discussion. The nurses and the clinic staff were kind. Mostly they didn't have the same grim reaper aura of the financial adviser, the type I seem to attract in my life, whenever money is involved.

Over those six weeks building up to Christmas, each weekend I was granted a reprieve from the relentless daily treatment routine. Several great friends and family members, such as Bronwyn, Ann, Jan, Christine, Jocelyn, Liz, came when they could to pick me up, cheer me up, take me to lunch, to the art gallery, wherever, if I felt well enough after the treatment.

Two very special helpers were pure gold. Jenny Wren/ Summers at the very beginning, before she had to return to her home in Toowoomba. Janetta Hargreaves, many times from then on, would also sit with me when I was seeing the various specialists, jotting down notes, asking questions on my behalf. Jenny and Janetta's calm, loving help was, naturally, much appreciated, as I found it difficult to absorb everything all at once in that alien, sterile universe, even though I had three expert specialists treating me.

My psychologist, Penny Gordon was a total rock throughout it all, and beyond. And my niece Margaret Kay was there, helping me at every stage. Another brilliant niece, her sister Diane Spearritt, a pathologist who lived away from Brisbane, was also on tap, kindly giving me her expert guidance and support along the way.

Susan and Peter were overseas in Paris, but they generously paid for my use of Uber transport during that crisis treatment time. My former film student, Stephen was also on standby, kindly driving me to my first operation. When I was back home, Chris would come and stay, sometimes bringing me flowers, and lush limes from his own orchard.

No one told me that, after Christmas, when the radiation treatment was finished, I would feel worse for a few months, and also that my immune system might be compromised at any time. Possibly I was told, but such information didn't always sink in. In February of the following year, I developed shingles, dangerously close to my right eye, which was quite a shock. I realised then, that this was a long haul. The good news is that, by September 2022, I anticipate that I will have been six years in recovery.

Immediately prior to this health saga, I had planned to move to a smaller unit in a building with a lift, a goal I finally achieved by mid-2018. I missed the best option for investing my post-sale money. Perhaps I should have waited until after August 2018 to sell and then buy, with any profit being able to be placed in my superannuation account, under a new 'downsizing' policy from the Government. It seems I jumped the gun, selling too quickly. It is hard to plan exactly when to take a retirement package, or when to sell and move house. I don't seem to have the knack for such timing.

During this process, I was inspired by Katrina to create an autobiographical documentary about the 'big D's' – downsizing and decluttering, prior to leaving my top-floor apartment. This was a life-changing move for me to document, and quite topical at the time, as retirees were busy considering a downsizing, free-range move. Ironically, the themes merged, in a way: the decluttering of my home paralleled the decluttering of my breast. I abandoned the film project, although there could yet be a documentary film emerging out of this mess, like a phoenix rising from the ashes. For a time, I even became a sort of decluttering whisperer.

Finally, I have managed to throw out my precious Shakespeare teaching notes, stored across many decades, just in case I ever had to go back to teaching secondary school English. While I'm sure this won't happen now, I still have disturbing, recurring dreams that I am back in front of a wriggling Grade Nine classroom, without a clue regarding what text I'm supposed to be teaching, or even where the staff toilet might be.

At least having cancer did not deter me from keeping up with my blog, *Seeing Me Out*. Ever since early in my retirement, I had written online film and television reviews, short pieces on topics-of-the-day, as well as past reminiscences. In this blog, I was also striving to debunk some of the myths about ageing and retirement.

For instance, I recoiled from people's comments when I bought a new car soon after I retired: 'Oh great, Helen. That will see you out'. I reacted quite strongly, as I wasn't at all ready to be 'seen out', especially by some consumer product, off into the sunset. I still wanted to grow old, as gracefully, and/or disgracefully as possible.

Now I still engage in endless conversations with my peers relating to their projects, finances, along with our medical problems. I have been through several ups and downs, healthwise. My latest mini-dramas have concerned cataract removal from both eyes, and pain-relief injections in my shoulder because of bursitis. To my surprise, just about every second person I know on the retirement spectrum, not only has sympathised with me, but also has recounted, in quite graphic detail, their own cataract and/or bursitis experiences.

In late 2021, I was rushed to hospital, this time caused by my irregular heartbeat, atrial fibrillation, once again. It is said that this latter illness is in' pandemic' mode across the world, amongst middle-class ageing people in developed nations. Pandemics seem to be happening at every turn. Regrettably, no alien presence is about to spring forth, to take away mounting health cares and scares, granting immortal youth to me and my friends, as in that delightful, classic 'retirement' film, *Cocoon*.

Post-cancer, in late 2017, a special career surprise happened, a gift, finishing off that year very happily. For my long-time services to film and media education in Queensland and Australia since the early eighties, the Australian Teachers of Media organisation presented me with a beautifully designed trophy, in special recognition of my decades of work and leadership in media education.

The Queensland ATOM Committee have also set up an annual award called the *Helen Yeates Award for Excellence in Media Education*, with certificates and trophies to be presented each year to an outstanding primary or secondary teacher in the field. I was very moved, honoured and humbled by this unexpected tribute.[19]

---

19. More details may be found here: https://www.atomqld.org.au/2017/11/celebrating-our-champion-our-pioneer-our-inspiration-helen-yeates/ This also gives a link to the short bio documentary made about me and my work, produced and directed by Dr Phoebe Hart.

I still bump into former students locally, and even across the world. Some I can barely place, while many of them I remember clearly. I feel embarrassed at times when I draw a blank, although they don't seem to mind: 'Helen, Helen, your Australian Film subject/ your Feminist Media subject changed my life!' I smile and nod, say how pleased I am to hear this, thanking them, wishing them all the best. Mostly I do recall people when they tell me their names.

One young man, Robert, who was in my English class at St Peter's College way back in 1969, hurried across the Brisbane City Mall to speak to me, about ten years ago, exclaiming, 'You were right, Mrs Yeates! I didn't agree with you on the Vietnam War then, but I do now'. I was pleased that enlightened discussion finally had had an impact.

Occasionally, a female graduate from a QUT class might pop up, telling me that, in her student days, she could take or leave my feminist philosophy. However, having experienced sexism and misogyny in her working life, post-university, she understood what I had been teaching, and was now passionate about feminism. That's another tick.

In late 2021, at an ATOM Queensland event, a film teacher thanked me for saving his life back in the early nineties. In his eyes, I was professional enough and flexible enough to allow him some time-out to work on a film in another city, earning money for himself, his partner and their unborn child: 'We would have literally starved otherwise. You saved our lives', he exclaimed, sincerely, his voice breaking. I was very moved by his declaration. It seemed to make it all worthwhile.

***

13.

THE LAST PICTURE SHOW

I love the beautiful State Theatre picture palace in Sydney, despite some seating and viewing arrangements being quite uncomfortable. Somehow, aesthetics reigns over comfort there. At least this architectural treasure will most probably be preserved for posterity. I have often enjoyed attending the Sydney Film Festival tat the State Theatre over many years, with my film buff friends such as Simon Taaffe, Susie Scott, Ann Baillie, Stephen Stockwell, Jeanne Scott, as well as dear formerfilm students such as Lucy Gaffy, David Dutton and Sally Brown.

By contrast, the last working picture palace in Brisbane, the Regent, built in the late 1920's, has been functionally destroyed by commercial developers, despite being heritage-listed. After seeing a film at the Regent, I used to love walking down the majestic staircase, beneath the glamorous chandeliers. There is nothing like some sparkling glitter and glamour to get a film lover's heart pumping. [20]

For many years, the Regent was the throbbing hub of the Brisbane International Film Festivals. From the Festival's inception in the early nineties, up until 2012, I would hang out in the buzzy, stylish foyer, enjoying a drink or a coffee between sessions, chatting about films just seen, comparing notes on the program offerings, sharing with enthusiasts, colleagues, students, amicable strangers.

All spruced up, I would arrive at the grand Opening Nights at the Regent, ready for a special celebration of the art of film, and hopefully dancing with a film star at the after party. My dear friends Savannah Susan, Cossack Peter, Cinema Joe, Music Michael still talk about one especially memorable opening night. Legendary Gerry, my 'plus one' that year, elated after a win at the races that day, insisted on buying us

---

20. Images of that precious cinema can be found on this link
http://cinematreasures.org/theaters/1593/photos

expensive drinks at the theatre bar throughout the night, even though the food and drinks were actually included in the ticket price.

Brushing this aside with a flourish, he bonded with the bar attendant who was only too happy to charge him for all our drinks. Along with some random ring-ins, we imbibed Gerry's classy offerings instead, mingling, dancing and getting up to more and more mischief as the night wore on. I forget what the festival opening film was that night, as well as the year this actually happened, but we all remember Gerry's boundless largesse that night.

Thanks to an inner-city re-development travesty in 2010, the Regent foyer now operates as the Brisbane Visitors' Centre, purely for tourists to pop in, acquire brochures and public transport timetables, and move on. The trusty Aromas café remained for just a few years after the closure of the cinema.

I would go to the café occasionally to experience a nostalgia hit, fantasising that the cinema was still functioning. While some bare bones of the original picture palace décor still remain inside, the heart and soul of this iconic space has been systematically destroyed over many decades, and any hint of the original now is purely tokenistic.

Echoes of those other long departed picture theatres of my childhood still live on within me. Before the Boomerang shut down in 1995, I would occasionally go back there, when alternative, even controversial films would sometimes hit the screens. To this day, I regret my enthusiasm for the Australian film, *Bad Boy Bubby*, at least on a personal level. Always ready to promote an exciting new Australian film, I wholeheartedly recommended this latest one to various friends, including Sandy Susan and Beachy Barry.

They travelled across town from Toowong to the Boomerang in Annerley, dutifully supporting the Australian film industry by attending a cutting edge, independent film – at least, that is how I pitched it to them. To their horror, these avid cat-lovers found the opening scenes increasingly unbearable. They had to walk out after the first twenty minutes or so, when the poor cat was wrapped in plastic gladwrap by Bubby.

It took another thirty years before they dared ask for my film advice again. This momentous event occurred during Covid lockdown in 2020. Calling this my 'Netflix Redemption', I was relieved to hear they enjoyed my first recommendation, the New Zealand film, *Boy*.

These reflections on picture show spaces trigger memories of lecturing in film at the Queensland University of Technology. I set up pre-lecture viewings for my students in rather uninspiring, impersonal lecture halls, none of them really fit-for-purpose. Making the best of it, my colleagues and I believed in everyone viewing a film together on an appropriately-sized screen, as close as possible to the screen dimensions for which the production was originally created.

When the end credits started to roll, I attempted to discourage students from jumping up immediately and racing out of the darkened lecture theatre, unless they had another class, back-to-back. In my opinion, this practice was followed by too many people in most cinemas, all apparently experiencing faulty bladders, extreme hunger, or an urgent family crisis. Rather, members of my audiences-in-training were asked to 'please sit still and watch until the final credits finish rolling', and to leave, 'only when the lights are switched on again'.

With such rigour, I was trying to instil respect for the culture of filmmaking itself, for the cohort of talented craftspeople and artists involved, the carefully chosen songs, musicians and musical pieces on the soundtrack, the locations used, and the gratitude expressed to all who helped make this film possible.

While this rule did not make me too popular, many budding filmmakers understood the value of what I was trying to achieve. These days, in this full-on digital age, I gather that the special screening slot for communal viewing and sharing is, unfortunately, no longer timetabled into most crowded university film courses. The computer has finally said 'no' to that timeslot luxury.

I used to teach my film students the production history, the multi-layered meanings and cultural impact of Australian films, including the Peter Weir classic, *Gallipoli*. When I first started teaching at the Kelvin Grove College of Advanced Education, in the late eighties, I would try to screen the celluloid 'pure' version of the films. Each film arrived on reels within large, suitably numbered containers from the State Film Library or the National Film Library in Canberra.

We used a rather wobbly projector in a cloistered projection room, situated at the back of certain lecture theatres. Once, on completion of this particular film, I became distracted, probably yet again affected by

Archy's pointless death. Without warning, the film totally unravelled, even though I leapt up and tried to stop this disaster from happening.

Much of *Gallipoli* ended up swirling off the spools, landing on the floor. Feeling ashamed at such a technical failure, I fortunately knew the friendly audio-visual guy pretty well. He helped me fix it up, without making me feel I was completely inept, as some of his colleagues most probably would have done. Audio-visual 'help' people in universities are a very particular breed. From then on, as often as possible, I embraced video copies, and later, DVDs.

Cinemas screening less mainstream, more arthouse films started to pop up or be rebranded around Brisbane. Among these were the Elite, Toowong, the Crystal, Windsor, the Classic, East Brisbane, the Astor/Village Twin, New Farm, and the Schonell in St. Lucia. As the years pass, I also love seeking out picture palaces and alternative cinemas in other cities around the world.

One year, in the nineties, on holiday in Sydney, I headed to the Valhalla, an art-house cinema in Glebe, sadly now closed. They were running a mini-festival of best films from different eras, some of which I had not seen, all to be especially shown for film buffs via the projector. Until then, I had avoided Marty Scorcese's eighties film *Raging Bull*, thinking it was 'just another film about boxing'.

However, this time I was willing to watch it with a more open mind. I was captivated by this masterpiece, and I still cherish that revelation, that smashing of ill-informed expectations, slowly becoming more wide-eyed, mesmerised, soaking up the cinematic magic of what is certainly one of the greatest films in any decade.

Another special, elusive film screening at this same little gem of a festival, was the 1954 Japanese film, *Seven Samurai*, directed by the master, Akira Kurosawa. This film about epic battles for survival, about heroes-for-hire attempting to save a village from invading marauders was released in America in 1956, although Google tells me that, mysteriously, it was not released until 1993 in Australia. It seems that my friend Simon and I were honoured to be present at one of the first screenings here, savouring this fifties masterpiece on the big screen where it belonged.

For many years, the Brisbane International Film Festival screenings were carefully handled via projectors, making comforting vision and sound, giving a special, purist kind of filmic authenticity for the audience sitting in the dark. One year, a foreign language film screened at BIFF in the wrong reel order – 1, 4, 3, 2, I think. Not realising this sequencing misadventure, the audience tried hard to piece it all together, clutching for a form of artistic coherence, trying to make sense of the narrative.

Feeling a bit spaced-out, I sipped my wine, concluding that I was witnessing an arthouse filmmaker's probable masterstroke in mysterious, jarring time-shifts, deliberately flashing forward, then flashing back again, leaving us hanging, cryptically, in the middle of the storyline. I have no memory of the name of that film, nor did I go to the apology repeat screening later in the program, this time with the reels in the correct order. Instead, I rather liked the memory of the topsy-turvy, nonlinear world that captivated and mystified me.

Most films are, of course, now shown digitally. No one sits in that little room at the back of the dark cinema, carefully, or not so carefully, monitoring it all. A Brisbane projector enthusiast, Michael, used to hold special nights for film lovers at the Old Museum, organising food and drink for the appropriately dressed-up audience, as well as screening classic thirties and forties films. Many a Bette Davis, Katherine Hepburn or Humphrey Bogart look-a-like turned up on the night. Cine-Retro still happens occasionally at the Museum, although I gather people do not dress up anymore.

Special newly restored, remastered films are sometimes exhibited at the Gallery of Modern Art cinema, treating us to sumptuous screenings via the trusty, humming projector. For instance, pre-Covid, friends and I were able to worship at the altar of a beautifully restored version of *The Leopard*, directed by Luchino Visconti.

A few years earlier, over another glistening week at GOMA, we attended a retrospective of the films of the hallowed Russian master, Andrei Tarkovsky. Of all the 'big screen' filmmaker retrospectives for many years, Tarkovsky's was the one I had been waiting for all my life, or so it seemed. Going to sublime celluloid retrospectives is yet another integral part of my personal film story, my own *Cinema Paradiso*.

In early March, 2020, I celebrated My Last Big Bash, my seventy-fifth birthday, with around seventy-four close friends and family members at the riverside Gallery of Modern Art restaurant, right on the cusp of the Corona virus epidemic. In my birthday speech, I talked about my favourite films of all time. In no particular order, I mentioned *Double Indemnity, The Leopard, In the Mood for Love, Amores Perros, La Haine, All About My Mother, Solaris, The Boys, Days of Heaven, Raging Bull*. If anyone asks me again in a year or so, this movable film feast may well be tweaked, at least a little.

Another special film 'list' comprises my comfort films, kept in a special emotional and mental health zone, to be watched during those days when I'm not feeling on top of things. These include the exquisite Jane Austen 1995 film adaptation of *Persuasion*, starring Amanda Root and Ciaran Hinds; Billy Wilder's perfect screwball comedy, *Some Like it Hot*; Marty Scorsese's rock concert tribute film *The Last Waltz*, farewelling The Band, with Bob Dylan. And, of course, Bill Forsyth's poignant, funny little gem, *Local Hero*.

Post the first Covid 19 lockdown, late in 2020, the people of Brisbane were allowed back into the cinemas again. Christine and I rushed to see a grim, beautifully shot Icelandic film *A White, White Day,* stirring us up, capturing a sense of being 'home' again. We found ourselves in a familiar, local, highly air-conditioned multiplex, where functionalism and new technologies have triumphed over aesthetics and nostalgia.

I gingerly lowered myself into one of the standard seats, shivering, fumbling through my stuff, adding an extra layer of clothing. Wine glass in hand, seated in little separate clusters, Covid masks on, Christine and I realised it was impossible to sip wine and remain masked. Whatever was going on, we were just grateful to be back in the cinema.

At other times, my companions and I find ourselves practically reclining within the semi-luxurious comfort of boutique golden screening spaces, sinking into soft, roomy lounge chairs with complicated, adjustable head and foot rests. We nearly knock our glasses off the side of such chairs, while staff appear to crawl around in the dark, attempting to serve us. The film continues screening, almost as a wallpapery afterthought, a ghostly sideline to the main action.

Such cinematic experiences represent an historic transformation, far from my sensuous, action-packed childhood 'picture show' days in those beloved, long-gone theatres, with their half-torn canvas seats, clattering wooden floors, the sounds of kids yelling, laughing in delight. The old Brisbane trams that took us there are silent.

As depicted in that American film mourning a lost era, *The Last Picture Show* remnants have been destroyed, or converted into new dream spaces, with velvet and faux-leather semi-recliners. In retirement, it is still quite an event to head to the cinema, often with friends followed by a meal and a lively discussion afterwards.

For instance, we might head off to the latest Isabelle Huppert film, or films made by stand-out filmmakers such as Michael Haneke, Claire Denis, Christian Petzoid. Many of the films we like are screened during international film festivals – French, Italian, German, Scandinavian. Sometimes we take a punt on a film that has received mixed reviews, or one we know nothing about, hoping for a cinephile surprise.

Some people in the audience chatter too loudly, including those who can't seem to help but give a running commentary to their companion, imagining they are still at home in their own private loungerooms. There are also the loud rustlers, chomping on obscenely huge servings of popcorn or chips, seemingly for the duration of the film.

Recently I saw *Happening* by yet another brilliant, emerging French woman filmmaker. In my mind, this may well be one of the best films of 2022. A pesky elderly male talker was sitting beside his wife in front of Susan and me, reacting in inappropriate, voyeuristic ways to the delicate, non-gratuitous female nudity on screen. I had to 'shush' this old bloke quite forcefully. The schoolteacher inside me is still very much alive and well.

Alternatively, I love watching films quietly, at my own pace, on smaller, more intimate screens, curled up in my loungeroom. Sometimes I am with a friend, other times alone, high on the 13th floor, with views of the river on all sides hugging the peninsula, patterned by the rainbow lights of the Story Bridge.

The best films contain unforeseen, fresh angles, inviting further re-viewing and re-thinking. These include the German films *Transit, The Wings of Desire,* the French films *Frantz, In the House, Beau Travail, Stranger by the Lake,* the Mexican film *Roma,* the Polish film *Ida,* the Japanese films *Drive My Car, Departures,* the Korean film *Burning,* the Icelandic film *Woman at War,* the Turkish film *Once Upon a Time in Anatolia,* the British film *The Souvenir.* I await with bated breath for the sequel, *The Souvenir Part II.*

Having already enjoyed many of these and other gems on the big screen, I embrace them, like old friends, on a smaller screen, at the same time, making new discoveries. I remain flexible and open-hearted in my evolving *Cinema Paradiso* world.

In the sixties modernist apartment building where I now live, a few scary moments have a way of intruding into my personal film dreaming. The fire alarm sounds and everyone has to head downstairs into the back garden. However, some neighbours and I on the 13th floor are reluctant to use the precipitous, slippery stairwell to escape. One person did fall in that cavernous space, fracturing several ribs.

Given our unwillingness to use the stairs, the elderly inhabitants on the 13th floor have now been told to wait in our apartments for the fire people to come and escort us/carry us down. Since I have been living here, the alarms have been false ones, triggered once at 3 am by a would-be burglar. Other times, the culprits have been storms and lightning raging into the building from across the river, at a certain ferocious angle.

Most recently, the alarm was set off on a boiling hot afternoon. The building was simultaneously inflamed and wilting in the excessive heat and humidity, along with all the occupants. Momentarily, I became a little excited at the thought of the muscly 'firies' who might come upstairs to rescue us.

However, they decided the culprit was simply the scorching temperature. No heroic Steve McQueen-lookalike scaled up the building to carry us down, as in the disaster film, *The Towering Inferno*. Climate change will sadly give the spirited occupants on the 13th floor increasing opportunities for a dramatic rescue. In some ways, I would rather just stay up here in my little cocoon, immersed in a great film, no matter what drama is happening out there in the real world.

****

14.
STORIES WE TELL

As a regular attendee at film festivals, I am often asked, immediately after a screening, 'What did you think of *that* film, Helen?' While I enjoy the person's enthusiasm, I find it rather difficult at times to come up with an instant, coherent response. I need to reflect, emotionally, intellectually, to let the film wash over me.

Over the years, the power of certain films has literally left me speechless. For instance, in 2000, in the musty Dendy Cinema in George Street, I was frozen in my seat for at least twenty minutes after a preview screening of *Amores Perros (Love's a Bitch)*, directed by the Mexican auteur, Alejandro González Iñárritu. Amidst other palpable reactions, visceral, emotional, intellectual, I was stressed that, at around three hours long, the confronting, amazing *Amores Perros* would not fit into the two-hour slot set aside for our university screenings.

Catching my breath, I left the cinema in quite a state, determined that, come what may, this film had to be included in the international film program. My colleagues Margaret, Tim and I found a workable way to deal with teaching this long film in that special unit we ran. Not many films have overpowered me in quite the same way, although the following are certainly up in that same gold class: *In the Mood for Love, La Haine (Hate), The Circle, Three Colours: Red, Cache (Hidden), Samson and Delilah, All about My Mother*, and another recent masterpiece, *Drive My Car*.

On a darker side, film festival or reviewer screenings can also deliver some total duds, or at least, films that are very difficult to watch. Janetta and I rue the day we saw the unspeakable Spanish film *Madrid, 1987*, which hopefully has disappeared without trace. It concerned a lecherous elderly journalist trying to seduce a beautiful young journalism student, while locked naked together in his bathroom.

This abomination has become the useful litmus test for all other films we see together. We laughingly ask, 'Could it possibly be better than *Madrid, 1987,* or worse?' Luckily, most films we see far surpass *Madrid, 1987,* although that one set a very low bar. Lately we saw the Spanish film, *Parallel Mothers,* which was a delight.

Similarly, Ann Baillie, Steve Stockwell and I have found our own communal, bottom-line test. Over many years, we have experienced memorable films together at the Sydney Film Festival, the Gold Coast Film Festival and BIFF. In terms of sheer distress beyond endurance, the film that reached a special kind of rock bottom for us was the unrelenting documentary set in the mountains of Myanmar, *Jade Miners.* In October 2021, we had to laugh, ruefully, when we encountered yet another festival film which might well replace *Jade Miners* at the bottom-feeder rung. The jury is still out on this one.

Earlier that fateful day, we enjoyed the glowing, mysterious German film, *Undine.* After a short break, we hoped for another glorious gem. Instead, we encountered the noisy, unrelentingly grim Venetian documentary film, *Atlantide,* showing the shocking obsessions of drifting, out-of-control teenage males, in the backwaters of Venice.

While the film was scheduled to run for eight-five minutes, it lasted at least fifteen excruciating, self-indulgent minutes longer. From the timing point of view, this was not good programming from BIFF 2021, although, at least the programmers had correctly placed this film in their *Adrenalin* strand.

Festival managers should know that film buffs plan their schedules down to the last vital minute. We were late for a quick dinner planned across the road at The Continental Café, between *Atlantide* and the next film, the more elegant, mysterious *Bergman Island.* Thanks to the lovely restaurant owners, we somehow managed to head back to the cinema, missing only the first ten minutes or so.

As far as *Atlantide* was concerned, Steve had just published a wonderful book, telling his own stories through poetry. In one of the longer poems, he celebrated Venice imaginatively, with poets Allen Ginsberg and Ezra Pound meeting up with Peggy Guggenheim at her beautiful art museum. Hoping, through this documentary film, to catch views of as much of his beloved Venice as possible, he hung in there to the grim end.

Even though the final helter-skelter images in *Atlantide* are presented on a desperate tilt, taken from a speedy, lurching boat, Steve did catch a sideways glimpse of one of his favourite little churches. We were grateful for that, at least.

Bergman Island was certainly worth a second viewing, in full. Fortunately, I achieved this a week later, with my dear film friend, Margaret. The elusiveness of the storyline, along with the female French director's fresh voice, appealed to us both. We especially loved the setting on Fårö Island where Ingmar Bergman made many of his great films, including *Scenes from a Marriage*. Margaret visited this iconic Swedish island herself several years ago, a pilgrimage undertaken by many a Bergman enthusiast, as this film reveals, rather tongue-in-cheek.

Close to that exact place, Margaret had once bought me a special pair of earrings, giving another dimension of personal connectivity to *Bergman Island* and its grappling with issues of female creativity, showing a woman's attempt at finding her own voice amidst overpowering male voices. The filmmaker, Mia Hansen-Love, captures what many creative women confront every day. Interestingly, the French film industry, in particular, has many such talented women directors currently making quality films, such as this one, telling their personal/political stories. They give me some hope for the future of both filmmaking and feminism, my two lifelong passions.

Digging further into my film festival memory bank, I respect my dear friend Dimity Torbett's stance on the Sydney Film Festival. Until there is a film offering that beats the power of Tarkovsky's sublime *Solaris* from the seventies, she is reluctant to attend anymore. I guess we are all living in hope, searching for another Tarkovsky-esque masterpiece. I settle for special chats with her about the old Sydney days, the beginnings of the film event, Tropfest, in the Tropicana café near where she lives, her work as a journalist, her being part of the 'Push', that radical intellectual subculture, along with Germaine Greer and many others. And I love hearing her stories about her dear departed sister, Sandy.

Regarding the SFF, I am pleased that my former film students David and Sally are happy to take a chance on whichever contemporary film I choose. The last one we saw together at the 2019 Sydney Film Festival was the award-winning Franco-Israeli film *Synonyms*. Always a sign of a non-mainstream film worth experiencing, this particular one left us struggling for words to describe our rather stunned, quite possibly slightly stoned reactions.

The slow process of finding my own creative memoir voice, assembling memory fragments, frame by frame, is reminiscent of my trying to mount errant film stock onto those cranky old projector spools, in an earlier era. However, a more fitting 'memoir-writing-metaphor' probably relates to the parallel craft of documentary film-making itself: choosing the content to 'shoot', what to leave in or leave out, wrestling with how to manipulate time/place shifts, with how to craft narrative arcs, and when to time the unleashing of various 'reveals'.

Throughout this writing venture, I have interwoven a grand parade of world filmmakers, whose works have helped sustain my sense of self, my humanity and my own story-telling. My friend and former film student Stephen Lance's first feature film, *My Mistress*, was, in part, autobiographical, in the sense that, as with many first-time filmmakers and novelists, he was drawing deeply, creatively on his personal coming-of-age memories and experiences. The fine lines between fiction and non-fiction can be telling, often blurred, bubbling up from the risky subconscious.

I have also gained inspiration from Agnès Varda's touching memoir film, *The Beaches of Agnès,* made when she was eighty. Her final film, *Faces Places* produced with the enigmatic JR, is another memoir of sorts, documenting the timelessness of creativity. Such highly personal films by this great French female auteur sustain me by their boundless beauty and authenticity.

In that other grand memoir film, *Stories We Tell*, by Canadian actor and director, Sarah Polley, her father/narrator Michael quotes Pablo Neruda: 'Love is so short, forgetting so long'. Her luminous film shows that her most significant gift lies in remembering and truth-telling, no matter how twisted, complicated and revealing the stories are, for herself and for those close to her.

I have attempted to create my own memoir 'gift', researching my memory and other, more tangible archives, holding up faded sequences to imperfect light, choosing some, discarding others, at the same time confronting pain, embracing pleasure. Inevitably, in the midst of this mind-juggling act, I have drawn blanks, perhaps because I once suffered brain damage and amnesia, perhaps not. The process of ageing itself may have caused the loss of memories, or clouded and distorted them. Time may also bring others rushing back, fully focused, glaringly lit, with nowhere to hide.

Scene by scene, I trust that the finished whole somehow stays safely threaded on those creaky old reels inside my brain. Some memoir material naturally ends up on that cold, uncompromising cutting-room floor. No fatherly voiceover creates an ironic sense of objective distance for me. All that remains in this documented offering is a jagged montage of remembrances, of films, filmmakers, feminism, family, friends, lovers, politics, travel and work, stitched together by my invariably faulty, subjective voiceover, spoken from the heart.

***

FILM REFERENCES

A White, White Day	(Hlynur Palmason, 2019)
A Woman's Face	(George Cukor, 1941)
All About My Mother	(Pedro Almodóvar, 1999)
Amores Perros (Love's a Bitch)	(Alejandro González Iñárritu, 2000)
An Affair to Remember	(Leo McCarey, 1957)
An Unmarried Woman	(Paul Mazursky, 1978)
Annie Get Your Gun	(George Sidney, Busby Berkeley, 1950)
Annie Hall	(Woody Allen, 1977)
Another Round	(Thomas Vinterberg, 2020)
Atlantide	(Yuri Ancarini, 2021)
Bad Boy Bubby	(Rolf de Heer, 1993)
Beau Travail	(Claire Denis, 1999)
Bergman Island	(Mia Hansen-Love, 2021)
Bob & Carol & Ted & Alice	(Paul Mazursky, 1969)
Boy	(Taika Waititi, 2010)
Brigadoon	(Vincente Minnelli, 1954)
Broken Arrow	(Delmer Daves, 1950)
Bull Durham	(Ron Shelton, 1988)
Burning	(Lee Chang-Dong, 2018)
Cache (Hidden)	(Michael Haneke, 2005)
Calamity Jane	(David Butler, 1953)
Careful He Might Hear You	(Carl Schultz, 1983)
Citizen Kane	(Orson Welles, 1941)
Clueless	(Amy Heckerling, 1995)
Cries and Whispers	(Ingmar Bergman, 1972)
Cocoon	(Ron Howard, 1985)
Custody	(Xavier Legrand, 2018)
Days of Heaven	(Terrence Malick, 1978)
Departures	(Yogiro Takita, 2008)

Do Look Now	(Helen Yeates, 2012)
Double Indemnity	(Billy Wilder, 1944)
Drive My Car	*(Ryusuke Hamaguchi, 2021)*
Faces Places	(Agnes Varda, JR)
Flirting	(John Duigan, 1991)
Fond Memories of Cuba	(David Bradbury, 2002)
Fool for Love	(Robert Altman, 1985)
Fort Apache, the Bronx	(Dan Petrie, 1980)
Frantz	(Francois Ozon, 2016)
Gallipoli	(Peter Weir, 1981)
Gaslight	(George Cukor, 1942)
Girls Just Want to Have Fun	(Alan Metter, 1985)
Hannah and Her Sisters	(Woody Allen, 1986)
Happening	(Audrey Diwan, 2022)
Head On	(Ana Kokkinos, 1998)
High Noon	(Fred Zinnemann, 1952)
Ida	(Pawel Pawlikowski, 2013)
If	(Lindsay Anderson, 1968)
In the House	(Francois Ozon, 2012)
In the Mood for Love	(Wong Kar-Wai, 2000)
Jade Miners	(Midi Z, 2015)
Jedda	(Charles and Elsa Chauvel, 1955)
Jules et Jim	(Francois Truffault, 1962)
La Haine (Hate)	(Mathieu Kassovitz, 1995)
Labyrinth of Passion	(Pedro Almodóvar, 1982)
Local Hero	(Bill Forsyth, 1983)
Mad Max	(George Miller, 1979)
Madrid, 1987	(David Trueba, 2011)
Man of Flowers	(Paul Cox, 1983)
My Mistress	(Stephen Lance, 2015)
Mystify: Michael Hutchence	(Richard Lowenstein, 2019)
Newsfront	(Phillip Noyce, 1978)
Night Cries: A Rural Tragedy	(Tracey Moffatt, 1989)
Oklahoma	(Fred Zinnemann, 1957)
Once Upon a Time in Anatolia	(Nuri Bilge Ceylan, 2011)
One Night the Moon	(Rachel Perkins, 2001)
Orchids: My Intersex Adventure	(Phoebe Hart, 2010)

Parallel Mothers	(Pedro Almodóvar, 2021)
Paris, Texas	(Wim Wenders, 1984)
Persuasion	(Roger Michell, 1995)
Picnic at Hanging Rock	(Peter Weir, 1975)
Pillow Talk	(Michael Gordon, 1959)
Raise Ravens	(Carlos Saura, 1976)
Reach for the Sky	(Lewis Gilbert, 1956)
Roma	(Alfonso Cuarón, 2018)
Samson and Delilah	(Warwick Thornton, 2009)
Scarface	(Brian De Palma, 1983)
Seven Brides for Seven Brothers	(Stanley Donen, 1954)
Seven Samurai	(Akira Kurasowa, 1954)
Shame	(Steve Jodrell, 1988)
Shane	(George Stevens, 1953)
Sliding Doors	(Peter Howitt, 1998)
Solaris	(Andrei Tarkovsky, 1972)
Some Like it Hot	(Billy Wilder, 1959)
Stranger by the Lake	(Alain Guiraudie, 2013)
Stranger Than Paradise	(Jim Jarmusch, 1985)
Strikebound	(Richard Lowenstein, 1984)
Sunday Too far Away	(Ken Hannam, 1975)
Sybil	(Dan Petrie, 1976)
Tammy and the Bachelor.	(Joseph Pevney, 1957)
Taxi	(Jafar Panahi, 2015)
The Admirable Crichton	(Lewis Gilbert, 1957)
The Belles of St Trinian's	(Frank Launder, 1954).
The Bay Boy	(Dan Petrie, 1984)
The Beaches of Agnes	(Agnès Varda, 2008)
The Big Lebowski	(Joel and Ethan Coen, 1998)
The Boys	(Rowan Woods, 1998)
The Bridge on the River Kwai	(David Lean, 1957)
The Cars That Ate Paris	(Peter Weir, 1974)
The Circle	(Jafar Panahi, 2000)
The Dambusters	(Michael Anderson, 1956)
The Desert Fox	(Henry Hathaway, 1951
The Desert Rats	(Robert Wise, 1953)
The Good, the Bad and the Ugly	(Sergio Leone, 1966)

The Guns of Navarone	(J. Lee Thompson, 1961)
The Heartbreak Kid	(Michael Jenkins, 1993)
The King and I	(Walter Lang, 1956)
The Last Married Couple in America	(Gil Cates, 1980)
The Last Picture Show	(Peter Bogdanovtch, 1971)
The Last Waltz	(Martin Scorcese, 1978)
The Leopard	(Luchino Visconti, 1963)
The Night Porter	(Liliana Cavani, 1974)
The Party	(Blake Edwards, 1968)
The Prime of Miss Jean Brodie	(Ronald Neame, 1969)
The Promise: The Making of Darkness on the Edge of Town	(Tom Zimny, 2010)
The Servant	(Joseph Losey, 1963)
The Seventh Seal	(Ingmar Bergman, 1957)
The Shiralee	(Leslie Norman, 1957)
The Souvenir	(Joanna Hogg, 2019)
The Souvenir Part II	(Joanna Hogg, 2021)
The Story of the Kelly Gang	(Charles Tait et al, 1906)
The Towering Inferno	(John Guillermin, 1974)
The White Ribbon	(Michael Haneke, 2009)
The Wings of Desire	(Wim Wenders, 1987)
This is Not a Film	(Jafar Panahi, 2011)
Three Colours: Blue	(Krzysztof Kieślowski, 1994)
Three Colours: Red	(Krzysztof Kieślowski, 1994)
To Hell and Back	(Jesse Gibbs, 1955)
Transit	(Christian Petzold, 2018)
Undine	(Christian Petzold, 2020)
White Feather	(Robert D. Webb, 1955)
Woman at War	(Benedikt Erlingsson, 2018)
Women in Love	(Ken Russell, 1969)
Women on the Verge of a Nervous Breakdown	(Pedro Almodóvar, 1988)
Y tu mama también (And Your Mother Too)	(Alfonso Cuarón, 2001)
Z	(Costa-Gavras, 1969)

Do Look Now (Helen Yeates, 2012)

The 'Sex Scene' excerpts woven into this video montage come from the following films:

Betty Blue	(Jean-Jacques Beineix, 1987)
Body Heat	(Lawrence Kasdan, 1981)
Brokeback Mountain	(Ang Lee, 2005)
Bull Durham	(Ron Shelton, 1988)
Desert Hearts	(Donna Deitch, 1986)
Don't Look Now	(Nicolas Roeg, 1973)
Female Perversions	(Susan Streitfeed, 1996)
Five Easy Pieces	(Bob Rafelson, 1970)
In the Cut	(Jane Campion, 2003)
Japanese Story	(Sue Brooks, 2003)
Klute	(Alan J. Pakula, 1971)
Lust, Caution	(Ang Lee, 2007)
My Own Private Idaho	(Gus Van Sant, 1992)
Secretary	(Steven Shainberg, 2003)
Stone	(Sandy Harbutt, 1974)
The Big Chill	(Lawrence Kasdan, 1983)
The Big Easy	(Jim McBride, 1986)
The Conformist	(Bernardo Bertolucci, 1970)
The Graduate	(Mike Nichols, 1967)
The Ice Storm	(Ang Lee, 1997)
The Piano	(Jane Campion, 1993)
Thelma and Louise	(Ridley Scott, 1991)
Wild at Heart	(David Lynch, 1990)
Y tu mamá también (And your mother too)	(Alfonso Cuarón, 2001)

Television Series referenced

Bluey
Game of Thrones
The Apprentice
The Bill
Two Fat Ladies

Authors mentioned

Adams, Phillip
Albee, Edward
Blyton, Enid
Bogarde, Dirk
Camus, Albert
Comfort, Alex
De Beauvoir, Simone
Franklin, Miles
Grant Bruce, Mary
Greer, Germaine
Hawes, Jocelyn
Hemingway, Ernest
Isherwood, Christopher
Lowenstein, Wendy
Lunn, Hugh
Macklin, Robert
Parker, Dorothy
Rees-Jones, Tony
Rice Burroughs, Edgar
Sartre, Jean-Paul
Sontag, Susan
Stockwell, Stephen
Summers, Anne
Thompson, Peter
Turner, Ethel
Yeats, W. B. and Marx, Karl

CREDITS

Before the 'lights' come back on, a list of credits completes this book.

Warmest thanks to all who have been supportive in many special ways, including those who have given incisive welcome feedback on parts of this book. And to those who have just been there for me, loving, patient, non-judgmental. I'm not going to say, 'You know who you are', and leave it at that. Sorry if I've missed anyone…

Peter Thompson, brother, for your supportive love and feedback.
Jocelyn Hawes, sister, matriarch. Thanks for letting me read my first chapter to dear **Lawrie** when he was so ill. He was one of my heroes.
Jan Hodsdon/Massey, for all the years, a shining cousin princess.
Margaret Kay, the high goddess of love and medicine, my darling niece.
Gerry Kay, a man for all seasons, for love and great times.
Elizabeth Kable, Diane Spearritt, Jennifer Hawes, my beloved, talented nieces.
Pauline Yeates/Smith, my other sister, for hanging in there, supporting me against the odds, for Spain and all the lunches.
Janetta Hargreaves, my rock, my delight, for **Jack, Lucy, Harry**, and **Ian**, my beloved 'outlaw' family, for the soirees at 57 Swann Road.
Susan Booth, Deb Polson, Miss B/Bronwyn Fadden, for wiffwaffing, dancing, keeping the faith. **Savannah-Susan** – for the KGB.
Peter Bridgman, fabulous masterchef, for **Cossack** dancing, for the KGB.
Joe Hardwick, cinema-king extraordinaire, for French films, for Isabelle.
Peter/Pierre Gall for languages, love, and for Paris, for dearest 'Angie'. RIP.
Susie Scott, Simon Taaffe for long-time joy, the soirees at 57 Swann Road, impeccable Sydney Film Festival timetabling delights, for **Marge**.
Jenny Wren/Wright/Summers, for vibrancy, creativity, boundless love, for Italy.
Ann Baillie, Steve Stockwell, for loving support, film-going, dancing, publishing - for the KGB.

Lisa Smith and Lilli Corrias-Smith, for shining Piscean delights, for turning me into an occasional mother/grandmother, for New York, New Farm.
Dimity Torbett, for Sydney-cool, for epic chats.
Liz Ferrier for love, for warmth, for wisdom.
Jeanne Scott and Nicholas Pounder, for friendship and inspiration, for the soirees at 57 Swann Road, for the hot pink pantsuit.
Christine Whitelaw, John Hook, for love, for Melbourne-cool, for dancing. And for Cuba.
Anne Hickling-Hudson, Brian Hudson, for loving friendship, for the fireworks. And for Cuba.
Emma Felton, Kevin Hayes, for happy times, for trusting me with your home and Mojo. And for Cuba.
Kerry and Keith Adam, for love, for lunches, for always caring.
Kay Saunders, for warm inspiration, for love of context.
Margaret Montgomerie and **Anne Reck,** for feminism, for New York, for precious zooming from the Isle of Wight.
Viktoria Dzudzek for love, for London & Berlin.
Michael Allport, for good times, for piano-man extraordinaire.
Hugh and Helen Lunn, for inspirational story-telling, for memories, for Annerley.
Susan Carson, for warm support, cool professionalism, for all the stories.
Phoebe Hart, for creative highs, for West End-cool.
Catherine Gomersall, for bubbling creativity, for the blog, for *One Night Stand.*
Sean Maher, for warm shiny support, film noir-cool. For *Bladerunner* and *The Big Lebowski.*
Cheryl Stock, for warm creative intellectual inspiration and **Ross Searle** for art and West End-cool.
Lance Courtenay, for wildly working together. For Los Angeles, for Italy, for the special Cottontree writer's retreat, for James, for Sukli Finney and Peter Fenoglia.
Lisa Schubert, ever classy, New York-cool, for Sam Shepard plays.
Christopher Strewe, for staying alive, for the rainforest, for bingeing marathons.

Andrea Mitchell, for being a champion every day.
Prue Gibbs, for beautiful music, the soirees, the movies.
Diana Edwards, for those UQ days, for Dirk, for bella, for Alan and Cathy.
Pamela Ashby/ Pretty-Pam, for all the fun, for AFTRS, for the KGB.
Robyn Hargreaves, Sue Burns, for the dear sisterhood we share, for the elegant pantsuit.
Geoff and Coralie Porter, for remarkably saving my life on Coronation Drive so long ago.
Jillian Clare, for warmth, thoughtfulness and ever-shining light, for Reg.
Sean Maher, for sanity, for loyalty, for film noir.
Victoria Garnons-Williams, for caring, for everything visual.
Margaret McVeigh, for lyrical feedback, for happy working together, for film teaching.
Mike Witt, for Bruce Springsteen, for the hats, for West End Film Festival.
Ruari, Sean and Michael – for the wolfpack.
My beloved cousins: Jan Hodsdon, Nancy Tow, Kate Heiner, Jane Heiner, Michael Heiner, Tim Heiner, John Peak, Pam Dickins, Geoffrey Hodsdon, RIP: Patty Peak/Purves, June Brown/ Oldham, Keith, Graham and Cecile Mary Heiner, Philip and David Tow.
Hilary Summy, for peace, for dinners with Ralph.
Sue Horton/ Straddie-Sue, for being there.
Susan Francis and Barry Cotterell/ Sandy Susan, Beachy Barry, for forgiving my film choices.
Sue Wighton, for the songs, for printing tips.

Kris Olsson, fabulous memoir queen.
Sandra Hogan, editor-extraordinaire, simply the best.
Chris Cosgrove, for being brilliant, for the flash cover design, for the photograph assembly.
The Avid Reader Bookshop Memoir Group: Susan Currie, Sue Bond, Leah Cotterell, Narelle McCoy, Moira Von Keyserlingk, Scott Avery, Gina Baker, Trish Eats. Alison Lees, Nadine Littledale, Antoinette Bauer.
Avid Reader gurus, Fiona Stager, Krissy Kneen.
Benjamin Law, Melanie Myers, for warm encouragement.

Old Schoolmates, still in my heart, keeping it ticking:
Primary: Polly Perkins/Jordan, Jan Elliott/ Jenyns, Wendie Robinson/Hirsch, Janet Winship, Heather Woodrow/Parker, Helen Bickley (RIP much missed), Tim Robinson, George Symons, Rod Gibson, Noel Craig, Greg Jolley...
Secondary: Vivienne Harris, Helen E. Hunter, Margaret Aboud, Jennifer Goddard, Ade Casey, Janet Talbot-Stern, Cheryl Hughes, Sue Macqueen, Brenda Scotney, Susan Dixon, Sue Easy. RIP Mary Thomson, Johanne Halstead.

Book Club, for bright discussions, for tolerating the odd memoir chapter readings: Kathryn Kelly, Janetta Hargreaves, Helen Devane, Robin Francis, Jane Andersen, Jan Ford, Jenny Nayler.
LGBTIQA+ Book Club mates: Yianni Faros, Ingrid Tall, Damian Dewar, Tony.
The Salon, for stretching my mind, my love of all things cultural and creative: Anne, Joe, Susan, Janetta, Christine, Liz, Judy, Jill, Fabiola, with Margaret, Kiki, Ann, Shannon, Susie, Lynne, Chris and others passing through.
Angels on the 13th Floor: Judy, Jill, Jenny, Bill.
QUT mates, resigned or retired in style: Deb Polson, Susan McGillicuddy, Jillian Clare, Cheryl Stock, Barbara Adkins, Christine Comans, Emma Felton, Anne Hickling-Hudson, Brian Hudson, Daniel Mafe, Vivienne Muller, Carol Williams, Jeanette McGown, Christopher Cosgrove, Wayne Taylor, Colleen Brydges, Patsy McCarthy, Evan Jones, Michael Noonan, Stella Eastman, Anne Watson, Carine Chai, Donna Lee Brien, Bruce Molloy, Kerry Mallan, Jill Borthwick. RIP: Wayne Murphy, Geoff Portmann, Bob Leach.
QUT current staff, all gold: Sean Maher, Phoebe Hart, T'fer Newsome, John Willsteed, Ruari Elkington, Jason Tolsher, Joanne Kenny, Sam Taylor...
ATOM media education wondrous warriors, past and present: Moneth, Aimee, Michael, Colin, Sybil, Tracey, Alison, Jenny Wren, Laura, Kerry, Chris, Sally, Alison, Derek, Prue, Mirva, Michael...

My film students, still inspiring me: Katrina Channells, Stephen Lance, Mairi Cameron, Lucy Gaffy, David Dutton, Sally Brown, Phoebe Hart, Ruari Elkington, Patrick Kelly, Will Goodfellow, Tom Noakes,

Christopher Cosgrove, Tim Milfull, Tess Van Hemert, Jessie Gray, Lucas Miller, Nathan Mayfield, Scott Walmsley, Luke Pratt, Alecia Elkington, Colin Cosier, Steph Dower, Rosalind Nugent, Ivo Burum, Wendy Rogers, Tessa Saville, Aaron Catling, Hugo Presser, Renee Tamayo, Bruno Starrs, Meredith Irish, Peter Bagley, Martin Kenny, Robyn Evans, Polly Pierce, Rosie McGregor, Helen O'Loan, Ange Graf, Akemi Koh, Tim Marshall, John Paul Davies, Michael Kraft, Emilie Hollins, Melissa McLeary, Lydia Holt, Sean Gilligan, Angela Leonardo, Tanya Schneider, Bronwyn Kettels, Christine Spooner, Linton Vivian, Cheryl Potter, Rebecca Wolgast, Patrick Clair Peter Tkacz, Chris Allery, Goldie Soetianto, Riccy Felixberto, Boitshepo Balozwi, Camy Ling, Ethan Waghorn, Natalie Beak, Alan Nguyen, Siri Bergerud, Natalie Gee, Judi Lyn, Daniel Stevenson, Morten A. Mjones, Marty Moynihan, Felicity Rose, Liam Price, TS, Viktor Aquino, Nadire Ilana, Grace Julia, Kate Scantleton, Simon Gardiner, Greer Ambrose, JC, Jay K., Dylan Wiehahn, Quincy Letshwiti, David Wright …and many more.

BIFF and Asia Pacific Film: Anne Demy-Geroe, Matt Kesting, Kiki Fung, Kristy Matheson, Maxine Williamson, Hussain Currimbhoy, Gary Ellis, Andrew Rose, Coreen Haddad, Rhonda Clark, Amanda, Rosie Hays, Jimmy Malecki, Dean Pollock, Archie Moore, Mairi Cameron, Scott Knight, Geoffrey Vagg.

Feminist stars: for the best times at Console-ing Passions: Margaret Montgomerie, Phebe Chau, Roger, Jackie, and Mary Beth Haralovich, for Tucson hospitality, for the jewellery, for the Palm Springs Film Festival.

St Peter's students and colleagues: Leanne, Christine, Louise, Henny, Steven, Robert, Rod, Tony, Linda, Jane Fehlberg, Claire Tomlinson…
IGGS students and colleagues: Janetta Hargreaves, Susie Scott, Sally Hatton, Robyn Tank, Elspeth MacFarlane, Lilias Rush, Pauline Smith, Maria Stevenson…
My IGGS teachers: Dorothy Marsden, Alison Goleby, Veronica Stark, Thalia Kennedy, Lorraine Mansfield, Joan Benson, Deirdre Brown. Legends all.
BGGS colleagues, students: Janet Greenwood, Ian Stuart, Elizabeth Jameson, Vanessa Coates, Jane Lynagh…

Moira Duffy and Noddie, for the joy.
Roger Stuart, for Paris, for the broken nose.
John and Claire Tomlinson, for revolution.
Bronwen Levy, **Lesley Synge,** for kind encouragement.
Mary Perkins for warm generosity, for Los Angeles.
Lynne Gross inspirational colleague, impeccable host, for Los Angeles.
Waddick Doyle for stirring collegiality, for Paris.
Alfredo Martinez for Spanish film, for masculinities.
David Buchbinder for masculinities, for Seville, for Paris.
Jane Arkinstall, for kindness, for the piano.
Nadia and Beau, for the great Continental Café, New Farm.
Wayne Boyle, for best hairdressing, for gossip, for turning me silver
Penny Gordon, for being the best psychologist. Ever.

www.ingramcontent.com/pod-product-compliance
Lightning Source LLC
Chambersburg PA
CBHW051910160426
43198CB00012B/1831